Dear Sc

In memory of your
Lovely Mother!

Love Mike & Kathleen
Van Wingerden

The Book of Ruth Explained
in Twenty-Eight Homilies

The Book of Ruth Explained in Twenty-Eight Homilies

Ludwig Lavater

Translated and Edited by Michael Hunter
Introduced by Jonathan Gibson

REFORMATION HERITAGE BOOKS
Grand Rapids, Michigan

The Book of Ruth Explained in Twenty-Eight Homilies
© 2022 by Reformation Heritage Books

Reformation Heritage Books
3070 29th St. SE
Grand Rapids, MI 49512
616-977-0889
orders@heritagebooks.org
www.heritagebooks.org

Printed in the United States of America
22 23 24 25 26 27/10 9 8 7 6 5 4 3 2 1

Library of Congress Cataloging-in-Publication Data

Names: Lavater, Ludwig, 1527-1586, author. | Hunter, Michael (Theologian), translator. | Gibson, Jonathan, 1977- writer of introduction.
Title: The Book of Ruth explained in twenty-eight homilies / Ludwig Lavater ; translated and edited by Michael Hunter ; introduced by Jonathan Gibson.
Other titles: Liber Ruth. English
Description: Grand Rapids, Michigan : Reformation Heritage Books, [2022] | Translation of: Liber Ruth per Ludovicum Lavaterum Tigurinum, homilis XXVIII expositus (Zurich : Froschauer, 1578). | Includes bibliographical references and indexes.
Identifiers: LCCN 2022026230 (print) | LCCN 2022026231 (ebook) | ISBN 9781601789518 (hardcover) | ISBN 9781601789525 (epub)
Subjects: LCSH: Bible. Ruth—Commentaries—Early works to 1800. | Lavater, Ludwig, 1527-1586. | BISAC: RELIGION / Biblical Studies / Old Testament / Historical Books | RELIGION / Christian Ministry / Pastoral Resources
Classification: LCC BS1315 .L2813 2022 (print) | LCC BS1315 (ebook) | DDC 222/.3507—dc23/eng/20220802
LC record available at https://lccn.loc.gov/2022026230
LC ebook record available at https://lccn.loc.gov/2022026231

For additional Reformed literature, request a free book list from Reformation Heritage Books at the above regular or email address.

To my friends
Shane and Georgiana Anderson
Blake and Leah Blount
Jesse and Rachel Light
Tim and Donna Roof
Thomas and Heather Roof
Michael and Melissa Spangler
and Ben Woodring.

Men, may you be like Boaz, אִישׁ גִּבּוֹר חַיִל (Ruth 2:1).

Ladies, may you be like Ruth, אֵשֶׁת חַיִל (Ruth 3:11).

Table of Contents

Translator's Preface

This book is an English translation of Ludwig Lavater's (1527–1586) homilies on Ruth. The work, which the author also refers to as a "little commentary," was published in 1578 and includes material from sermons and exegetical lectures by Lavater, a Swiss Reformed pastor and theologian.[1] Generally, each section or homily begins with Lavater's version of the biblical text, followed by a description of the sense or scope of the passage; an exegetical discussion of the text, which frequently includes philological, cultural, and historical observations; and finally, practical application. Lavater describes the purpose of the book of Ruth, which he aims always to keep in view, as follows: "This whole book was written for this purpose, namely, that we would know the genealogy of David and, consequently, of Christ, who was specifically promised to him.... For the scope of the evangelists and the apostles is that Jesus is the Christ, that is, the King and High Priest of those who truly believe. And so they needed to show that He descended from those to whom He was promised." Aside from a 1586 translation of the book by Ephraim Pagitt, an eleven-year-old boy, which is generally poor, omits material, and is written in Elizabethan English, this is the only translation of Lavater's commentary published in English.[2]

---

1. Ludwig Lavater, *Liber Ruth per Ludovicum Lavaterum Tigurinum, homiliis XXVIII expositus* (Zürich: Froschauer, 1578).

2. Ludwig Lavater, *The book of Ruth expounded in twenty eight sermons, by Levves Lauaterus of Tygurine, and by hym published in Latine, and now translated into Englishe by Ephraim Pagitt, a childe of eleven yeares of age* (London: Robert Waldegrave, 1586).

My aim in translating this work is twofold. First, I hope the commentary will be useful to laypeople, scholars, and pastors as they study and apply the book of Ruth. Indeed, when Johann Heinrich Heidegger (1633–1698) in his *Enchiridion* lists recommended commentaries on each book of the Bible, he includes Lavater's commentary on Ruth.[3] Gisbertus Voetius does the same.[4] If Reformed churches found this commentary useful in the seventeenth century, perhaps Reformed churches will find it useful today.

Second, I believe this commentary will be useful to students of church history, especially those interested in the Reformed church's exegetical tradition. The Reformed theologians of the sixteenth and seventeenth centuries are generally known for their systematic theology, but a failure to recognize their contributions to biblical exegesis and the sophistication and practical adaptability of their interpretive methods is an unnecessary loss to the modern church. This translation helps to remedy that loss.

For the same reason, I have included, as an appendix, Konrad Pellikan's (1478–1556) *Exposition of the Book of Ruth*. Pellikan held the chair of Hebrew at the *Carolinum* in Zürich, influenced the exegesis (especially Old Testament exegesis) of other ministers in Zürich, including Theodor Bibliander, whom Lavater calls "my most honorable teacher," and Lavater himself. Pellikan was preceded in his position by Jakob Ceporin, the first professor of Greek and Hebrew at the *Carolinum*; he was succeeded by Peter Martyr Vermigli. The reader may be interested to compare and contrast Lavater's and Pellikan's commentaries on Ruth.

As for my approach to translating, I have sought to remain reasonably close to the vocabulary and syntax of the original text, though I have been more flexible wherever I believed that such changes would improve clarity or accuracy.

As far as reasonably possible, I have tried to conform the translation of Scripture citations to the King James Version, though, of course,

---

3. Johann Heinrich Heidegger, *Enchiridion Biblicum IEPOMNHMONIKON*, 2nd ed. (Amsterdam: Boom, 1688), 108.

4. Gisbertus Voetius, *Exercitia et bibliotheca, studiosi theologiae*, 3rd ed. (Frankfurt: Wohlfart, 1685), 176, 677.

I have not followed the KJV wherever Lavater's Latin text departs from it. Yet I have generally attempted to maintain the vocabulary and spelling conventions of the KJV in all translations of biblical texts. "LORD" is in small caps only when it appears in small caps in the KJV; if the corresponding passage in the KJV has "Lord," without small caps, or if the KJV has neither "Lord" nor "LORD" and yet the Latin has *Dominus*, the translation has "Lord."

Greek, Hebrew, and German terms appear throughout the commentary. I have translated the Greek and German wherever it appears in the original, but I have placed the Greek or German word or phrase in parentheses following the translation. If Lavater translates the Greek or German, then I have not placed the Greek or German text in parentheses. If Lavater provides an explanation that does not function as a translation, I have translated the word or phrase and placed the original word or phrase in parentheses. Wherever the original text contains Hebrew, Lavater translates it. He also frequently includes transliterations of Hebrew terms, as well as some Greek terms, which I have placed in parentheses after the Hebrew or Greek word or phrase. Transliterations appear exactly as they appear in the original text. Occasionally, Lavater will only include a transliteration, in which case I have provided the lexical form of the Greek or Hebrew word followed by Lavater's transliteration in parentheses. I have not included vowel points in the reproduction of the Hebrew in the translation, since the Hebrew text of the original does not contain vowel points. Occasionally, I have placed the original Latin text in brackets beside the translation of a Latin word or phrase if Lavater is making some point that depends on the morphology of the Latin words themselves (e.g., establishing a word's etymology). I have italicized quotations from Ruth, in any version, provided that the quote is from the portion of Ruth that is being discussed in the chapter. I have also italicized Lavater's interpolations and emendations of the text, if the portion of Ruth in which it appears is italicized. I have not, however, italicized Lavater's glosses or paraphrases of the text.

For proper names, I have tried to emend the text wherever there is a clear misspelling. I have also corrected the diacritical marks on Greek words wherever they are wrong. I have capitalized proper names even where Lavater does not capitalize them.

Not all paragraph divisions are original, but all headings and sub-headings are. All the material in brackets is mine, with two exceptions. In some cases, following standard editorial practice, parenthetical terms and content within a parenthetical phrase have been placed in brackets. In other instances, Lavater has included German expressions in parentheses. I have translated such expressions within parentheses and preserved the original German text in brackets within the parentheses. All footnotes are also mine. Some footnotes indicate where I have emended the text and others indicate errors in the original text. When Lavater's original Scripture references contained an error, I have silently corrected these, unless the error had some additional significance worth noting. Nevertheless, this translation is not a critical text and so does not include a comprehensive critical apparatus. Other footnotes are explanatory and yet others are references to extrabiblical books. My citations of classical sources follow modern citation conventions, usually those in the *Oxford Classical Dictionary*, wherever possible. To assist the reader, I have often added a short title of the extrabiblical source to which Lavater refers. Scripture references appear in footnotes only when the text contains a direct quotation, reference, or clear allusion to a particular passage of Scripture. If a work is only cited without a specific reference, it does not appear in a footnote, but does appear in the proper index. All references in the body of the text are original.

The bibliography and the ancient sources index are mine. The early modern sources cited in the bibliography and the footnotes are not necessarily the versions of the texts that Lavater used, though the editions cited are generally from the period in which Lavater was writing. I have also modernized the place names in the publication information for the early modern sources, and I have generally identified authors and publishers by their most popular names, which are not always the Latin names included in Lavater's text. The ancient sources index includes Greek, Latin, and English titles, though I have translated all titles in the body of the work, unless a work is generally known by its Greek or Latin title. I have noted wherever I have been unable to locate a text to which Lavater refers, and I have included what information I have in the index.

In the Scripture index, all and only the references followed by descriptions or citations are original to Lavater's index; the descriptions and citations are Lavater's as well. I have retained them because Lavater appears to have thought these passages were especially important in his commentary. All the other Scripture references in the index appear either in the body of the text (and so are original to Lavater's commentary, though he omitted them from his index) or are found in the footnotes (and so were included by me). It is important to note what the Scripture index does not include. It does not include references that appear in titles of works, references to erroneous citations, or references to Ruth, except when Lavater refers to passages in other chapters of Ruth outside the chapter he is discussing. The bibliography and Scripture index, however, include references from the appendix.

The subject index is also original to Lavater's text. Of course, the order of the entries has been altered since I translated the terms into English and alphabetized them accordingly. Occasionally, I have combined some entries under one term if the entries had the same key term in the original index. Yet wherever the original index contains the same subject more than once, under different key terms, I have retained each entry for this subject.

I wish to express my gratitude to all who directly or indirectly contributed to the completion of this volume. First, many thanks to the brothers and sisters at Covenant of Grace Associate Reformed Presbyterian Church in Winston-Salem, North Carolina. Hearing the preached Word with you, praying with you, singing with you, and participating in the Lord's Supper with you has been encouraging and refreshing, especially in our unusual times. Many thanks also to my friends to whom this book is dedicated for attempting to lead the church to the old paths of the Reformed catholic tradition, of which this book is a part, and for encouraging preaching and teaching on many of the subjects contained in it. I wish to thank Dr. Jonathan Gibson, who introduced me to the works of Ludwig Lavater and who kindly agreed to write the foreword to this volume. At Westminster Theological Seminary in Philadelphia, Dr. Gibson has continued the biblically faithful tradition of Reformed Old Testament exegesis. Many thanks also to the people at Reformation Heritage Books, including Dr. Joel Beeke, Dr. Jay Collier, and Dr. Drew McGinnis. It has been a pleasure to work with them. Finally, I cannot express more gratitude to any mortals than to my parents, who have constantly and enthusiastically supported my work. I hope this commentary will edify all who read it.

Most importantly, may this commentary point the reader to Jesus Christ, the descendant of Boaz and Ruth.

—Michael Hunter
Kernersville, North Carolina
May 7, 2022

"Precious Jewels"
Ludwig Lavater's Homilies on Ruth
Jonathan Gibson

Introduction

Ludwig (Lewis) Lavater (1527–1586) is not a name commonly associated with the magisterial Reformers. Indeed, one will search in vain for his entry in some encyclopedias of the Reformation.[1] And yet, Lavater played a significant role in the Swiss church of the sixteenth century, continuing the important reforms of Huldrych Zwingli and Heinrich Bullinger in Zürich, especially with respect to church liturgy and polity. Lavater served at the Grossmünster church in Zürich as archdeacon for thirty-six years and then for a short time as antistes (head minister) before his early death. He was also a prolific scholar, publishing a wide range of books from biographies and theological treaties to commentaries and homilies; he even wrote a popular work on demonology.[2]

Lavater was born into a noble family at Kyburg Castle on March 1, 1527. His father, Hans Rudolf Lavater (1492–1557), served as the *Landvogt* (magistrate) of Kyburg in the municipality of Horgen, a canton of Zürich. Hans Lavater was a pious Protestant and ardent defender of Zwingli's reforms, while his wife, Anna Reuchlin, was from a pious family that had sat under Zwingli's preaching from as early as 1519 and

---

1. E.g., *The Oxford Encyclopedia of the Reformation*, ed. Hans J. Hillerbrand, 4 vols. (New York: Oxford University Press, 1996).

2. James Isaac Good, *History of the Swiss Reformed Church since the Reformation* (Philadelphia: Publication and Sunday School Board of the Reformed Churches in the United States, 1913), 13.

was supportive of his reforms before the Reformation even dawned.[3] Hans served as a prominent soldier in the Swiss army, leading the battle of Kappel in 1531. Despite the defeat, he escaped unhurt but later suffered recriminations by the Zürichers, eventually spending time in prison. However, he was released shortly thereafter following an investigation that vindicated him of any wrongdoing in the Kappel defeat. Hans's commitment to the Protestant faith was evidenced as early as 1524 when upon a visit to Rome to enquire about Swiss soldiers not receiving their salary, he refused to bow before the pope and kiss his feet, despite being encouraged to do so.[4]

Being raised in a pious Christian home, Ludwig Lavater expressed faith from an early age, his biographer Johann Wilhelm Stucki noting 1538 as his "year of salvation."[5] Although initially raised in Kyburg, Lavater received his education in Kappel and then Zürich before traveling abroad for further studies in Strasbourg, Paris, Wittenberg, and Lausanne. He returned via Italy to Schwamendingen in the Zürich countryside, where he began preaching as a candidate for the ministry. He then supplied the pulpit for a short time at Horgen when the antistes of the city church became unwell. He later moved to Zürich to serve in the Grossmünster church, still as a ministerial candidate. When the minister of the Fraumünster church fell ill, he provided pulpit supply there for a time (including at Pentecost). Around this time he also met and married Margaret Bullinger, daughter of Heinrich Bullinger. The young couple were wed on May 8, 1550. Soon afterward, having proved himself fit for the ministry, Lavater was ordained to the role of archdeacon in the Grossmünster church in Zürich, a position he held for thirty-six years.[6] On December 29, 1585, when Rudolf Gwalther became incapacitated, Lavater was appointed antistes of the Zürich

---

3. Johann Wilhelm Stucki, preface to *Nehemias, liber Nehemiae, qui et secundus Ezrae dicitur, homilis LVIII*, by Ludwig Lavater (Zürich: Officina Froschoviana, 1586), fol. β1r; cf. also Irena Backus, *Life Writing in Reformation Europe: Lives of Reformers by Friends, Disciples and Foes* (Aldershot, U.K.: Ashgate, 2008), 112–13.

4. Good, *History*, 12.

5. Stucki, preface to *Nehemias*, fol. β1v.

6. Stucki, preface to *Nehemias*, fol. β4v–γ1r.

church. However, he did not serve long in the role, dying on July 15, 1586, just shy of sixty years old.[7]

Although generally neglected in works on the Swiss Reformation, Ludwig Lavater left an indelible mark on the Zürich church as a reformer, scholar, pastor, and preacher.

Lavater the Reformer

As a churchman, Lavater helped to stabilize and solidify the reforms begun by Zwingli and carried on by his father-in-law, Heinrich Bullinger, and Zwingli's son-in-law, Rudolf Gwalther. In some ways, Lavater continued the ministries of each of these men: the church reforms of Zwingli, the commentary writing of Bullinger, and the homilies of Gwalther. Regarding church reforms, Lavater made a particular contribution in the area of liturgical rites, publishing *Short Work on Rites and Regulations* in 1559, which proved important in tracing the early customs of the Reformed church.[8] Lavater also sought to reintroduce singing in the Zürich churches, an element of worship that had been abolished (along with the organ) in an overreaction to papal rites.[9] His appointment as antistes of the Zürich church in 1585 created the possibility for his desire to be realized, but his short tenure meant that singing did not return to church services in his lifetime. However, the fact that his short work on church liturgy was republished in 1702 indicates that he remained an influential voice in ecclesiastical reform for some time.

Lavater the Scholar

Lavater believed that his advancement as a scholar was due to his learning from other Reformers. In Strasbourg, he came under the influence of Martin Bucer and Jacob Sturm; in Wittenberg, he sat under the teaching of Philip Melanchthon; while in Zürich, he was significantly impacted by men such as Heinrich Bullinger in New Testament, Konrad Pellikan

---

7. Good, *History*, 13.

8. One can read a modern translation by Michael Hunter in *Reformation Worship: Liturgies from the Past for the Present*, ed. Jonathan Gibson and Mark Earngey (Greensboro, N.C.: New Growth, 2018), 213–46.

9. Good, *History*, 13.

in Hebrew and Greek, and Theodor Bibliander, Peter Martyr Vermigli, Josias Simler, and Johann Wolf in Old Testament.[10] Lavater earned a standing among these theological greats through his own scholarly publications. After Bullinger and Gwalther, he became the third most published author in Zürich.[11] The bulk of his writings were comprised of homilies or commentaries, strongly favoring the Old Testament over the New Testament.[12] Lavater also ventured into other areas: he wrote biographies on Heinrich Bullinger and Konrad Pellikan, and produced a hugely popular work on demonology, for which he gained the nickname "Ghost-Lavater" (*Gespenster-Lavater*).[13] In 1563, he produced a major contribution on the sacrament of communion: a treatise on the origins and progress of the sacramental controversy between Luther and Zwingli from 1523 to 1563.[14] Indeed, his scholarly work as a theologian was so respected that when his brother-in-law Josias Simler died in 1576,[15] he was elected professor of theology at the Zürich Academy. Lavater, however, declined the appointment, preferring to remain in his ministerial post.[16] Further afield, Lavater's work drew the admiration of Theodore Beza, disciples of Vermigli, and John Jewel, bishop of Salisbury. These men were particularly impressed with Lavater's commentaries: Beza stated that they contained the characteristic mark of

---

10. Stephen M. Coleman and Todd M. Rester, eds., *Faith in the Time of Plague: Selected Writings from the Reformation and Post-Reformation* (Glenside, Pa.: Westminster Seminary Press, 2021), 212.

11. Christian Moser, "A Mirror of Virtue: Commentaries on the Book of Ruth in Sixteenth-Century Zürich," in *Following Zwingli: Applying the Past in Reformation Zurich*, ed. Luca Baschera and Bruce Gordon (London: Routledge, 2014), 124.

12. Lavater published homilies and commentaries, not really distinguishing between the two, on the books of Proverbs (1562), Joshua (1565), Ezekiel (1571), 1–2 Chronicles (1573), Ruth (1578), Genesis (1579) (Lavater completed Vermigli's commentary by commenting on the last eight chapters), Job (1582), Esther (1583), 1 Samuel 25 (1584), Ecclesiastes (1584), Judges (1585), Nehemiah (1586), Ezra (1586), and James 5 (1587).

13. Moser, "Mirror of Virtue," 124.

14. Ludwig Lavater, *Historia de origine et progressv controuersiae sacramentariae de Coena Domini ab anno nativitatis Christi M.D.XXIIII. usq[ue] ad annum M.D.LXIII. deducta* (Zürich: Froschauer, 1563).

15. Simler had married another daughter of Bullinger.

16. Good, *History*, 13.

"an absence of digressions and ambiguities," while Jewel said that Lavater's commentary on Solomon's Proverbs helped him to understand aspects of the book for the first time.[17]

Lavater the Pastor

When Lavater declined the chair of theology at the Zürich Academy, it revealed that at heart he was a pastor before he was a scholar. This was certainly reflected in his ministry. Not only did he disciple young men in the Reformed faith—Johann Wilhelm Stucki, biographer of Reformed figures in Zürich, and Markus Bäumler, composer of the Zürich catechism, as just two examples[18]—he also demonstrated practical love and care for the poor and destitute, including refugees and travelers from England, France, and Italy.[19] In addition to these ministries, Lavater was described as a model and mirror of Christian character and good works in the church: "Examples of nearly all the virtues could be drawn from him," wrote his biographer.[20] This is perhaps best exemplified in his visiting the sick and dying without request, and in his offering saving comfort to criminals while they awaited execution.[21] Even in his scholarship, he employed his intellectual acumen in service of the church and city, addressing the exigences of pestilence, scarcity, and famine, and offering both practical and spiritual advice.[22] Arguably, it was Lavater's lived experience through such times that shaped the pastoral care for which he came to be renowned.

17. Backus, *Life Writing*, 115.

18. Good, *History*, 13.

19. Coleman and Rester, *Faith in the Time of Plague*, 213.

20. Stucki, preface to *Nehemias*, fol. γ4v, cited in Coleman and Rester, *Faith in the Time of Plague*, 213.

21. Backus, *Life Writing*, 116.

22. See, for example, the collection of Lavater's sermons in *Disease, Scarcity, and Famine: A Reformation Perspective on God and Plagues*, trans. Michael Hunter (Grand Rapids: Reformation Heritage Books, 2021). See also Lavater's sermon on 1 Chronicles 21:9–15, "The Merciful Hands of the Lord," in Coleman and Rester, *Faith in the Time of Plague*, 214–30.

Lavater the Preacher

Lavater began preaching in his early twenties and continued until his untimely death in 1586 at sixty years old. Our knowledge of Lavater's preaching comes to us firsthand from his friend and biographer, Johann Wilhelm Stucki. Interestingly, Stucki published his biography of Lavater not as an independent work but as the preface to Lavater's posthumous commentary on Nehemiah because he wanted to spotlight his skills as a preacher.[23] While Stucki had a high regard for Lavater the person and warmly complimented his moral virtues, it was Lavater the preacher whom he wished to leave as a lasting impression on the interested reader. He described his sermons as follows:

> [They] were prepared without adornment or colouring, not for show but for edification, for the use of the flock. They were adapted for both the learned and the simple ears, and full of doctrine and consolation. He stuck remarkably well to the maxim, "whatever you teach, be concise," and eagerly respected both brevity and clarity (which is a great art indeed), for he would say that especially in the winter cold any speech or sermon by any man, however eloquent, was more of a burden than of use to the public. I should add that his ordering of material and method was so excellent that any man who was not altogether slow or stupid could encompass and retain his entire sermon in his mind and memory.[24]

Lavater's preaching was so respected that Konrad Pellikan, professor of Old Testament at the Zürich Academy, would attend his sermons and make requests for written copies afterward.[25] This brings us to Lavater's *Book of Ruth Explained in Twenty-Eight Homilies.*

Homilies on Ruth

Lavater published his twenty-eight sermons on Ruth in 1578, presumably preaching them the year before at Grossmünster in Zürich. The

---

23. Backus, *Life Writing*, 112.

24. Stucki, preface to *Nehemias*, fol. γlv, translated by and cited in Backus, *Life Writing*, 114.

25. Backus, *Life Writing*, 114. Backus believes that Pellikan's requests account for the corpus of Lavater's homilies that we have today.

sermons enjoyed some success beyond the city of Zürich. In 1586 they were translated into English by an eleven-year-old boy from London named Ephraim Pagitt;[26] in 1601 the Latin edition was republished in Heidelberg.[27] While the book of Ruth was generally neglected in the Reformation era, Lavater was not alone in teaching and publishing on it in the context of the Zürich church. He was one of at least four scholars who taught or published on Ruth—Pellikan (1531, 1533, 1543), Bibliander (1537, 1549), and Wolf (1562) all preceded him.[28] The book of Ruth was popular among the Züricher pastor-theologians for the simple reason that it helped to promote a distinct Christian ethic for a city undergoing significant reforms.[29] The content of the book fitted hand and glove with the moral mandates of the Zürich magistrates, which included, *inter alia*, regulations for eating, drinking, clothing, and appropriate relations between the sexes.[30] Familiarity with the book of Ruth reveals how well suited it is to speak to such matters.

Lavater preached his sermons in his native tongue of German, but he wrote them up and published them in Latin.[31] Lavater's homilies follow almost entirely the order of his sermons, but they were supplemented with material to profit the academy as well as the church. Their academic depth is evidenced in Lavater's engagement with the original Hebrew and comparison with early versions (Septuagint and Vulgate) and modern versions (Münster and Zürich). His wide engagement with Jewish and Christian interpreters (e.g., Eusebius and Nicholas of Lyra), along with frequent quotes from Roman philosophers and poets (Seneca, Plutarch, Virgil, Cicero, Plautus, Pliny, Juvenal), reveals his breadth of extrabiblical knowledge. Yet, given his overarching goal of practical

---

26. *The book of Ruth expounded in twenty eight sermons, by Levves Lauaterus of Tygurine, and by hym published in Latine, and now translated into Englishe by Ephraim Pagitt, a childe of eleuen yeares of age* (London: Robert Waldegrave, 1586).

27. Moser, "Mirror of Virtue," 124.

28. Pellikan published a few commentaries on Ruth, while Bibliander taught on the book at the Zürich Academy but never published his preparatory notes. Moser, "Mirror of Virtue," 124.

29. Moser, "Mirror of Virtue," 122.

30. Moser, "Mirror of Virtue," 135.

31. Moser, "Mirror of Virtue," 134.

application, he does not lose the reader in the details. Taking his cue
from 2 Timothy 3:16 and Romans 15:4, Lavater believed that the short
book of Ruth could be compared to "precious jewels" of "exceptional
worth," which supplied "the greatest usefulness to all parts of life." In
this regard, Lavater's preaching reflects a kind of proto-Puritan style
that sets forth the practical implications of the text at great length. As he
commented, "God sets before us examples of the saints so that, having
them constantly before our eyes, we will copy them in our lives."[32] One
of Lavater's *Leitworten* is "virtue," which appears throughout his homilies. For Lavater, the nine prominent characters in the book—the main
ones being Elimelech, Naomi, Ruth, the unnamed relative-redeemer,
and Boaz—serve as models of Christian virtue, either positively or
negatively, providing examples and guidance for interfamily and master-
servant relations. Even when it comes to the tricky issue of Ruth's
conduct with Boaz under the cover of night, Lavater interprets the epi-
sode along the line of moral example, presenting Ruth by way of how
not to act in this instance.[33]

Lavater's overall approach might draw the comment—perhaps even
criticism—that his sermons constitute a species of moralistic preaching.
Certainly, Lavater's work lacked the kind of rich typology that was present in the Middle Ages, in which Boaz and Ruth pointed the reader to
Christ and His church.[34] However, the Zürich preacher does frequently
refer to Christ in his sermons, embedding his moral imperatives in the
larger framework of assumed gospel indicatives, and by the end of the
book he arrives at Christ through the genealogy of David. In Lavater's
own words, "the scope and primary intention of this history is to show
the genealogy of David and, therefore, of our Lord and Savior Jesus
Christ, who according to His flesh descends from the seed of that line.

---

32. See below, p. 118.

33. In this regard, he deviated from his predecessors who generally found noth-
ing suspect in Ruth's conduct with Boaz at the threshing floor (Moser, "Mirror of
Virtue," 127). A marginal note in Wolf's commentary encapsulates the general position:
"The example of Ruth should be followed in everything" (cited in Moser, "Mirror of
Virtue," 130).

34. Moser, "Mirror of Virtue," 127.

Christ is the scope and the end of the Law and the Prophets."[35] In sum, while Lavater's sermons certainly focus on the moral, they are not without reference to the Messiah.

Conclusion

In closing, it is an honor to introduce this new, readable translation of Lavater's homilies on Ruth. Michael Hunter has made accessible for scholars a text that will no doubt stimulate further research into this much-neglected Zürich *Prediger*. More importantly, Hunter's translation has provided pastors with a helpful resource for sermon preparation on the book of Ruth. The length of Lavater's publication, twenty-eight sermons in all, serves as an encouragement (and challenge) for pastors to slow down and think more deeply about how the sacred writings of the Old Testament are profitable for teaching, rebuking, correcting, and training in righteousness (2 Tim. 3:16), while at the same time not ignoring their christological trajectories (2 Tim. 3:15). If pastors take the time to read Lavater's sermons on this "precious jewel" of a short book, they will find that it indeed supplies "the greatest usefulness to all parts of life," as Lavater believed. But more than that, pastors will discover the book of Ruth to be "crammed with many different doctrines and comforts," as they encounter "God the Best and Greatest"[36]—a God who providentially orders the whole of our lives for our good and His glory, just as He did for Naomi and Ruth.

---

35. See below, p. 9.
36. See below, pp. 3, 9–10.

The Book of Ruth
Explained in
Twenty-Eight Homilies

Dedicatory Epistle

To a man who has distinguished himself by long-standing nobility and virtue, Mr. Battista à Salis of Rhaetia, his most honorable lord,

Greetings.

Since indeed those, noblest man, who usefully interpret even one or two passages of sacred literature and publish this interpretation for public use deserve at least some thanks, much more should the zeal and diligence of those be approved who, explicating sacred books in their entirety from their sources, apply them to general usefulness in human life. And so no one, I hope, will consider it a fault in me that I am publishing the book of Ruth, crammed with many different doctrines and comforts, explained at this time in several homilies. I call them homilies because I am following almost the same order in this text that I followed from the pulpit in the public explication of this book, and I treat the same subjects, with a few changes. For I have inserted some things that can be set forth with greater profit in the schools than in the churches. It will not be difficult for honest readers to see this. Moreover, I purposely did not want to dwell too long on individual passages, but only to write down brief summaries of the sermons, so that I would not lead students of sacred literature too far from the diligent reading of the sacred text itself and of other useful books, about which matter we have also spoken elsewhere.

The argument of this book itself invited me to dedicate my homilies, or, rather, this little commentary, to you, noblest man, although we have never met. For this book treats especially of the amazing and memorable conversion of Ruth the Moabitess, of whom Saint Matthew makes honorable mention in Christ's genealogy.[1] And indeed when I was thinking about publishing these homilies, suddenly the message was brought to us that God, our heavenly and most merciful Father, by His great compassion had converted you to the profession of pure doctrine by the occasion of a dangerous and very serious disease from which you suffered! Nothing more desirable than this could have happened to us who teach the gospel at Zürich. For we do not doubt that God determined to use the very remarkable example of your wonderful conversion, a more illustrious example than which your churches have scarcely had, for the glory of His name and the benefit of His church, both in your nation and also elsewhere. And so, when this opportunity was offered, I wanted, both on my behalf and on behalf of the ministers of our church, to congratulate you and to exhort you to persist steadfastly in the truth of doctrine that you have come to know. And so we congratulate you, and congratulate you truly, because the most pleasant light of the gospel shone on you as you sat in darkness and the shadow of death[2] and because God gave you a mind to profess publicly your faith received from His Word. Likewise, we exhort you to continue in that faith, to continually make greater progress in it, and to serve and profit the church of God by your authority, which is very great not only among the people of Bregaglia but throughout all Rhaetia, by your care and by your counsel. There were and still are many in the honorable and illustrious Salis family, gifted with great power of mind and body, who in Rhaetia, your fatherland, have held the highest civil offices with great praise, have discharged honorable legations to various princes and republics, and have acquired distinguished and immortal praise for themselves by admirably doing great deeds in war and peace. Although these things are great and admirable, nevertheless, far greater is your praise and glory, because you have embraced the gospel of our Lord Jesus Christ by true faith, through which we are included in the number of the sons of God (which is true and eternal nobility) and are

---

1. Matt. 1:5.
2. Ps. 107:10; Matt. 4:16; Luke 1:79.

made partakers of the inheritance of heavenly possessions with all the saints, if we persevere in it to the end. May God the Best and Greatest condescend mercifully to preserve you, most honorable man, your wife, the most excellent woman, and your most precious children, together with all the other noble and illustrious men of your most honorable family, and to fill you all more and more with His gifts. The pastors of our church and the professors of our school, and especially the most honorable man Mr. Rudolf Gwalther, send very many greetings to you and yours. I commend to you men of excellent piety and doctrine, Mr. Johannes Martius, of your church at Soglio, and Mr. Scipio Lentulus, of the church at Chiavenna, vigilant and trustworthy pastors, my respected and honorable fellow-priests, whom I desire to be very well. But as for you, most honorable man, I urgently ask you to pardon me because I have dared to address you in this public text. At Zürich, in the year from Christ's birth 1578, in the month of July.

To your excellence,
Most respectfully,
Ludwig Lavater, Minister of the church at Zürich

Introduction

Title of the Book

This short book takes its name from Ruth, a most excellent woman, not because she wrote it, but because the narrative deals mainly with her. For it recounts that she was a Moabitess, on what occasion she converted to the Israelite religion, what she did, and likewise how after marrying Boaz, a man of great authority, she gave birth to Obed, David's grandfather. So the short book of Esther takes its name from Queen Esther, the main character, about whom the narrative in that book is told. The books of Samuel (to say nothing now about others) are also named for the main character. For even if we willingly concede that the prophet Samuel wrote the first book up to chapter 24, nevertheless, it is certain that he could not have progressed further. For at the beginning of chapter 25 his death is described, and the remaining six chapters to the end of the book contain events that happened only after his death. The second book, which is also named Samuel, deals only with those events that happened after his death and, therefore, could not have been reported by him in writing. Rather, it seems it is called Samuel because it follows the story of David, whom Samuel, by the command of God, anointed as king, and because it was written and published by one of his disciples, such as Nathan or Gad, under the name of his teacher. Some are of the opinion that this book of Ruth was written by Samuel. Others are of the opinion that it was excerpted from the large book *Chronicles of the Kings of Judah and Israel*, which is mentioned several times in the books of Kings and which was lost without the loss of doctrine necessary for salvation. That it is not the book of Chronicles or Paralipomenon,[1] which still exists, I have demonstrated in my commentary on that book.[2]

But I cannot easily say who excerpted this short history from the previously mentioned book or who wrote it, whether Ezra or rather some prophet who lived in the time of the judges or afterward. Nor does knowing this matter very much. Whoever it was, it should be enough for us that this book by universal consent is numbered among the canonical books of Sacred Scripture, which by the inspiration of the Holy Spirit were written by holy men and were handed down by God to His church and were miraculously preserved through so many crises for our comfort and instruction. If you have a document granting an extraordinary privilege guaranteed by the seal of an emperor or king, you do not worry at all about the name of the writer or the pen that he used in writing it. So when it is settled by the unanimous consent of all the pious that this book has the Holy Spirit as its author, we should not be concerned much about the instrument that He used in sealing it.

Argument

The argument or subject of this book is as follows. When a famine arose, Elimelech, together with his wife, Naomi, and their two sons, moved from the town of Bethlehem to the region of Moab. There, when their father was dead, the sons took Moabite wives. After several years passed, they too died in exile, survived by their mother and their wives. At this time, Naomi, who had been informed that God had made His people's land fertile again, began a plan to return to her fatherland. Both her daughters-in-law joined her. She urged both of them to remain among their people. And so Orpah returned to her people. But Ruth, since she could not at all be separated from Naomi, came with her mother-in-law to Bethlehem at the beginning of the harvest. The people of Bethlehem wondered what Naomi's arrival meant. Meanwhile, Ruth, in order to

---

1. Paralipomenon is the title given to Chronicles in the Vulgate. This title follows the LXX, in the which the books of Chronicles are called Παραλειπομένων ("of things passed over").

2. Ludwig Lavater, *In Libros Paralipomenon sive Chronicorum, Ludovici Lavateri Tigurini commentarius* (Zürich: Froschauer, 1573), fol. 1r.

support herself and her mother-in-law, went out to gather ears of grain, and it happened by the providence of God that she came to the field of Boaz her relative. When he came to the field and learned from his overseer who she was, he addressed her kindly and ordered his domestic servants and his reapers not to harm her. After thanking him, she returned home loaded up with the grain he had given her and related to her mother-in-law, in order, everything that had happened. Naomi counseled her to go secretly to Boaz's barn, to lie down at his feet while he was sleeping, and to ask him to be her husband according to the law of God that commands a brother or relative to marry the wife of his dead brother or relative who lacks a male descendant. Ruth obeyed her mother-in-law and asked Boaz about marriage. He responded that some other man was more closely related to her, but that if he were to give up his right, he would marry her. And when on the following day that relative renounced his right, with the acknowledgment of the judges, Boaz married her and from her fathered Obed, the grandfather of David.

Parts
This whole history appears to consist mainly of two parts. First, a recollection of the miseries of Naomi and Ruth, then the change in their fortune, that is, how God made rich again those whom He had thrown into poverty.

Scope
The scope and primary intention of this history is to show the genealogy of David and, therefore, of our Lord and Savior Jesus Christ, who according to His flesh descends from the seed of that line. Christ is the scope and the end of the Law and the Prophets. Further, we will hear later that this story happened in the time of the judges of Israel. Therefore, it is rightly subjoined to the book of Judges.

Usefulness
Although this book is small, nevertheless, it contains many distinguished qualities and supplies the greatest usefulness to all parts of life, and therefore it can be compared to precious jewels, many of which are

small but nevertheless have exceptional worth. The maxim about Sacred Scripture that appears in St. Paul's second epistle to Timothy, chapter 3, applies to all the sacred books and therefore also to this one: "All Scripture is given by inspiration of God and is profitable for doctrine, for reproof, for correction, for instruction in righteousness, that the man of God may be perfect, furnished unto every good work." Likewise, in Romans 15: "Whatsoever things were written aforetime were written for our learning, that we through patience and comfort of the Scriptures might have hope."

So that the usefulness of this text can be better perceived, we will comment on some main points that are set forth in it. To be sure, a discussion concerning individual points will follow more fully in their own places. First, as all the sacred books contribute to the knowledge of God, so does this one. For it teaches that Christ, the Son of God, descends from Jewish and gentile sinners and, therefore, that He belongs to both. It teaches that the providence of God the Best and Greatest governs everything and that marriages, too, are arranged between brides and grooms under His direction. Ruth, desiring to gather ears of grain to get nourishment, happened upon Boaz's field, which was the occasion for her to become his wife and Obed's mother. We will see that God plagues the pious with various troubles (poverty, bereavement, exile, famine) and often brings affairs to the point that it can seem to be all over for them. But if they are not broken by the evils, but patiently endure everything, waiting for God's help and calling on Him, the evils are often turned into a brighter fortune, even in this life. In addition, we will gather from the story that God also cared about the gentiles. Among His elect He also had Jethro, Naaman the Syrian, the widow of Zarephath, the Ninevites, and others. Not that we are saying they were saved outside of Christ. He wanted Rahab and Ruth to be joined to the Abrahamic seed so that at the appointed time the Messiah would be born from them. Spouses, mothers-in-law, daughters-in-law, widows, heads of households, slaves, and hired servants have illustrious examples to imitate. We will learn that foreigners, the poor, our relatives, and likewise, recent converts to the true religion must be treated kindly and must not be harmed either by words or deeds. We also have in Boaz a clear example of keeping a promise. Likewise, we learn that rewards are provided for virtues, even in this present life. Therefore, no one should say it is just the same whether we act well or badly.

Characters in This Book

Nine prominent characters are introduced in this short little work: Elimelech, Naomi, Mahlon, Chilion, Orpah, Ruth, Boaz, his overseer, and the relative who gave up his right. In each of these, examples of our duties are set forth to us, which by God's help we will comment on in their own places.

Let us give enormous thanks to God for His unspeakable kindness, that He desired for the sacred books to be written, to be preserved through so many fierce storms, and to be read aloud in the church from the sources, and let us study them day and night, rejecting and neglecting useless books about fables, which are worn out in the hands of the stupid.

Ruth 1:1–2

1 *It came to pass in the days when the judges judged that there was a famine in the land (of Israel). And a (certain) man of Bethlehem-Judah went to sojourn in the land (field) of Moab, together with his wife and his two sons.*

2 *And the name of the man was Elimelech, and the name of his wife Naomi, and the name of his two sons Mahlon and Chilion, Ephrathites of Bethlehem-Judah. And they came into the region of Moab and dwelt there.*

Division of the Chapter

The following items are especially discussed in this chapter. Elimelech, in a time of famine, travels to the Moabites and dies among them. After his sons marry Moabite girls, they too die. The widow Naomi returns to Bethlehem. Both her daughters-in-law accompany her to a point. But Orpah then returns to her own people. Ruth clings to her mother-in-law when she returns to her fatherland. Everyone marvels at Naomi's return. Finally, the time when she returned home is noted.

The Time of Elimelech's Journey

The first part, or the first section, of this chapter shows how Elimelech with his wife and two sons moved from Bethlehem to the region of Moab in a time of famine. It covers many things in a few words. First, it indicates when this story happened, namely, in the time of the judges, that is, of Israel. But it is uncertain under which judge, of whom many are enumerated, these things happened. Some refer this story to the times of Ehud, others to the times of Deborah and Barak, others to the times of Jephthah, who finally overcame the Moabites after the many disasters that they had inflicted on the Israelites (from which some think this famine that is mentioned here arose). If you say, "Elimelech would not have had a place among the Moabites when they had been conquered in battle; they would have torn him to pieces at the time," they will respond that the Moabites were so oppressed and crushed that they would not have dared to harm the Israelites. Jephthah ruled the people for six years. His story appears in Judges 10–12. Ibzan followed him. The doctors of the Hebrews think Ibzan was Boaz, David's great-grandfather, so that he had two names. He ruled Israel for seven years (Judg. 12). Josephus includes this story in the times of Eli.[1] Lyra shows in his comments on chapter 1 of this book that this does not agree with the chronology.[2] But it makes no difference to our salvation to know the moment in time that these things happened. Otherwise, the Holy Spirit would not have left it out. It should be enough for us to know in general that this story must be referred to the times of the judges.

The Cause

As far as it concerns the cause that motivated him to leave his father-land, it seems it was a famine, because the text says that a famine had arisen in the land of the Israelites. The holy fathers often moved from one place to another in time of famine to better support both themselves and their families. In Genesis 12, Abraham in a time of famine went to Egypt, which they call the world's granary. In chapter 26, when a famine arose, Isaac went to Gerar to Abimelech, but God, appearing to him in a dream, warned him not to go to Egypt but to stay in those places of which He would tell him. The story about Jacob, or Israel, is well known, namely, that he sent his sons to Egypt for food several times.[3] Afterward, when the famine had lasted for a long time, he went with his

---

1. Joseph. *AJ* 5.318.
2. Nicholas of Lyra, *Biblia mit Glossa ordinaria, Postilla litteralis von Nicolaus de Lyra und Expositiones prologorum von Guilelmus Brito* (Venedig: Paganinus de Paganinis, 1495), fol. 278v.
3. Gen. 42–43.

whole family down to his son Joseph.[4] To these examples can be added that Elisha tells the Shunammite woman, whose son he had raised from the dead, to go to another region, because God was going to summon a famine that would last for seven years (2 Kings 8). This woman followed the prophet's counsel and so was saved in a time of famine. For the same reason Elimelech, together with his family, migrated to the region of Moab, which perhaps had an abundance of grain at the time. The Hebrews, as Lyra mentions, contrive another reason.[5] For they say that Elimelech was a wealthy and powerful man. Since the famine at the time was severe, his many relatives and the poor demanded from him what they needed to live. Therefore, so that he would be delivered from this annoyance and so that he would not squander his wealth, he left his only fatherland and went with his family to the region of Moab, where he was reduced to extreme poverty and died, together with his sons. If he had traveled abroad for this reason, as it is evident some people sometimes do, he could not be excused. For as it says in the Proverbs of Solomon, chapter 21, "He who stops his ears at the cry of the poor, he also shall cry to the Lord, but shall not be heard." For He is the righteous avenger of the poor and afflicted. What happened to the rich royal official is well known to everyone from Luke 16. But someone could wonder, with good reason, from where the Hebrews get these things. They allege many strange stories in their explanation of sacred literature. Truly, since they rejected Jesus Christ, who is the light of the world,[6] they deserve to grope around in the darkness. Christians also have turned their ears to strange stories when the doctrine of the gospel has been suppressed and removed.

Famine

Concerning famine, in the writings of the prophets it is included among the four scourges with which God chastises men. Now they are these: disease, famine, war, and evil beasts. How serious the calamity of famine is we gather at least from the fact that it very often drives men into exile.

---

4. Gen. 46.
5. Lyra, *Biblia*, fol. 278v.
6. John 8:12.

God certainly sends famine for the sins of a people where and when He wants. Not that we must conclude that those who are oppressed by famine are worse than others. For He also afflicts pious men with famine, not to destroy them, but to test them with this tribulation, as also with other calamities, and to exercise their faith. Indeed, they take care of their affairs by lawful means, without violating true religion, and they conduct themselves far differently from the impious who are entangled in the same evils. The Hebrews allege that God punished the Israelites with this terribly severe famine because once Joshua and the elders who had seen the miracles of God were dead, they became more remiss in executing God's commands. For from the history of the judges it is clear that the Israelites spurned His laws, turned to idols, and were afflicted with various disasters.

Bethlehem-Judah

The sons of Elimelech are called Ephrathites from Bethlehem-Judah, which the text so names to distinguish it from another city of this name in Galilee, in the allotment of Zebulun. In Matthew 2, the chief priests and scribes of the people, when Herod asks where the Messiah was to be born, also respond, "In Bethlehem of Judea." This city is also called Ephrathah. For in Genesis 35 we read that Rachel died in childbirth on the way that leads to Ephrathah, that is, Bethlehem, and that Jacob erected a tombstone over her grave. For the ancients had their graves next to public roads, to which so many epitaphs written for travelers testify. As far as it concerns the etymology of these names, Bethlehem means, "House of Bread," that is, in the Hebrew idiom, "an abundance of crops." For it was located on soil that was fertile and abounding in grain. "It has been a real lard pit and a good, fertile land" (*Es ist ein rachte schmalzgrüben und güte schnabelweid gewesen*), as we say. Some think Bethlehem is called "House of Bread" because of the mystery that Christ, who in John 6 calls Himself "the bread of life," had to be born there. Moreover, Ephrathah, writes Jerome, means καρποφορία (*karpophorian*), that is, "fruitfulness."[7] Therefore, he says, this city is named both Ephrathah

---

7. Jerome, *Opera*, ed. Desiderius Erasmus (Basel: Froben, 1516), vol. 6, fol. 67v–68r.

and Bethlehem because of the fitting meaning of the names. Yet there are those who think that Ephrathah received its name from Caleb's wife, Ephrathah,[8] which is not satisfying to me, because long before her the city was called by this name. This city also had a third name, for it is called the City of David in Luke 2: "And Joseph went up unto the City of David, which is called Bethlehem." Then an angel said to the shepherds, "Unto you is born this day in the City of David a Savior, which is Christ the Lord." It was called this partly since it was David's fatherland, partly because he restored it, and partly because Christ the Son of David (who also is simply called "David" by the prophets) was born there.

Ephrathite

Zuph in 1 Samuel 1 is called an Ephrathite since he lived in Mount Ephraim. But some think that these were called Ephrathites after their fatherland, Ephrathah, so that an Ephrathite and a Bethlehemite are the same thing. So Isai,[9] the father of David, is called an Ephrathite because he was born in Bethlehem, which long ago was called Ephrathah. For in 1 Samuel 17 we read, "David was the son of an Ephrathite man of Bethlehem, whose name was Isai." Or perhaps those who were from this family were called Ephrathites *par excellence* ($\kappa\alpha\tau'\grave{\epsilon}\xi o\chi\grave{\eta}\nu$), that is, by antonomasia.[10] The Chaldean translator adds "nobles."[11]

Nobility

Among external blessings is included being born in a distinguished fatherland to noble parents. Those who descend from good and noble families should avoid committing any act unworthy of their ancestors. Those who descend from obscure families should see to it that by their virtues they outshine their ancestors. Moreover, some think that it was

---

8. 1 Chron. 2:19, 50.

9. Lavater refers to David's father as Isai and Jesse.

10. Antonomasia is a figure of speech in which an epithet or patronymic is used instead of a proper name.

11. Tg. Ruth 1:2. "The Chaldean translator" and "the Chaldean periphrast" are Lavater's designations for the author of the Targum, which he occasionally refers to as "the Chaldean version."

specified where they were born so that no one would think that they had
been born in the region of Moab.

Whether Elimelech Did Right in Migrating to the Land of Moab with His Family

What did Elimelech do? He went with his family from Judah to the
region of Moab and lived there. Now you say, "Did he do right in deserting the home of his fathers and going to the Moabites?" Concerning this
act, one can argue both sides. Those who blame him can use the following and other arguments. First, it had been forbidden to the Israelites to
associate with that nation. For in Deuteronomy 23 God enacted a law
that Ammonites and Moabites were not to enter the assembly even to
the tenth generation, not because He wanted to keep them from hearing the Word of God and from true worship, but so that they would
not discharge some office, whether ecclesiastical or political, and so that
they would not have the right of suffrage or of marrying a Hebrew (for
interpreters say that this is what the Hebrew expression means). A twofold reason for that law is given. The first is that they denied passage to
the Israelites, their brothers, when they were coming out of Egypt. The
other is that they hired Balaam the soothsayer to curse the Israelites
(Num. 22–23) and that they made them to sin in the matter of Baalpeor, for which reason many died.[12] Therefore, the fact that Elimelech goes
with his family to that nation that was hostile to God does not seem to
be praiseworthy. Next, he should not have deserted the Israelites and,
likewise, his kinsmen in their afflictions. For as those who desert their
own people in time of war or disease seem to sin, so do those who do
so in time of famine. This is especially so since it can be inferred from
Naomi's words that he was rich. Deserters have always been held in bad
repute. Who today would not disapprove of the decision of those who
go over to the enemies of the gospel in times of danger? Likewise, what
they did seems to contradict faith. For Elimelech thinks that he can
escape the punishment of God. The nation of Israel possessed promises
that God would be with them in all troubles. He should have believed

---

12. Cf. Num. 25:1–9; 31:16.

those promises, considered God's providence, prayed, and expected a good and happy outcome to the famine. God certainly could have preserved him in so fertile a land no less than in the region of the Moabites. What he did also contradicts fortitude and magnanimity. For he should have endured anything rather than desert the tabernacle and the worship of God and migrate to a profane nation. In addition, he exposes his wife and children to a clear danger of idolatry. For everyone ignores how dangerous it is to live in the midst of idolaters. To live among men of our faith is not always devoid of danger. What then if we join ourselves to the impious? Some argue from the outcome that he did not do right, since he paid a penalty for deserting his fatherland. For he fell into extreme poverty, which he was fleeing, and together with his sons he died in exile. But this happened to Jacob, Joseph, and very many other good men, so that we must not make a judgment about someone's faith and morals from the outcome.

Those who defend the act can bring forward the following arguments. First, it seems that he did what he did, not by human counsel and without the command of God, but by the examples of the pious, which we cited above. The necessity produced by famine also forced them to become exiles more than once. Next, God must not be put to the test. The promises should not have made them lazy and careless, and Elimelech was obligated to look out for himself and his own family. Without harming his own family, he deserted his fatherland to provide for them what they needed to live. In addition, what he did turned out well. For in this way the glory of God was illuminated, and His promises were fulfilled. Although one could make this argument, God often uses for good the failings of His own people and by His own goodness turns even those things that are evil to a good end.

Nothing Certain Can Be Established about This Act
It is certain that pious and holy men sometimes fall into great sins. But since we do not know whether he migrated to the Moabites because he was prompted by contempt for the law or by avarice, as the Hebrews think, or whether he was prompted by a warning from God or a private revelation, or by other necessary causes and, likewise, how he conducted

himself in the foreign land, we will neither praise nor condemn his act. When the Scriptures do not accuse men, neither ought we to accuse them. And when matters are ambiguous, we should rather believe better things about men. It is possible that he retained the liberty of his religion. Certainly, under gentile kings the Jews seem to have retained their religion, as also today under Christians. For the cruelty of those kings toward the Jews was not as great as that of some kings and princes today, who want to be called Christians, against those who profess purer doctrine. Here perhaps it is relevant that it is written that Elimelech sojourned in the field of Moab and dwelt in the field of Moab. Some German versions have "in the field" (*im faeld*). Later it says several times that Naomi returned from the fields or the open country. שָׂדֶה (*schadaeh*) means "field" and, likewise, "region," "land." Perhaps he wanted to live not in cities, but in the fields, so that he would be corrupted less. For in cities opportunities to sin are daily put in our way. Hence long ago many withdrew to their farms and to solitary places. Jonadab, as we read in Jeremiah 35, counseled his sons the Rechabites to dwell in tents and to engage in the shepherding business so that they could serve God better.

We Must Not Migrate to Places Where False Religion Flourishes

In general, we say from the Word of God that those places must not be deserted in which the pure voice of the gospel publicly resounds. For it is very dangerous to live where no room is given to purer doctrine. For if in those places in which the exercise of pure religion is practiced you frequently engage with those who do not love the true faith, and although you nevertheless listen to the sacred sermons, you still are made a little more remiss in doing so, what will happen in those places where there is no mention of Christ and true religion, and likewise where so many things that can undermine our faith continually meet our eyes?

How We Should Conduct Ourselves among the Impious

But if necessity itself forces us, as sometimes happens, to live in those places in which impiety reigns, we must take care that we do not deny

Christ. Joseph lived a holy life in the court of Potiphar the Egyptian,[13] and later, when he was in charge over all Egypt, he called his father and brothers to him because of the severity of the famine.[14] Severe necessity forced David to flee with six hundred men to the king of the Moabites, although most interpreters criticize this flight (1 Sam. 27). Nebuchadnezzar carried off Daniel, his companions, and very many others, as in our time the Turks carry off large bands of Christians into perpetual servitude, who, whether they want to or not, are forced to live among idolaters.[15] Yet they should endeavor to live blamelessly among the wicked. In Jeremiah 29, Jeremiah teaches his people how they should conduct themselves in Babylon under Nebuchadnezzar. There are those who commonly say, "When in Rome, do as the Romans do." They tell people to accommodate themselves to the times. But Christ, in Matthew 10, demands from His faithful a confession of faith. We must strongly rebuke those who for the sake of gain and other trivial reasons voluntarily leave Jerusalem and go to Babylon.

Hospitality Must Be Shown to Foreigners
Let us learn from the example of the Moabites to show hospitality to pious men. For although the Moabites were hostile to the Israelites, nevertheless, we nowhere read that they harmed Elimelech or his family. If you say that they had been so oppressed by the Israelites that they did this unwillingly, nevertheless, it is evident that they showed hospitality also to David's parents when they were weakened by old age (1 Sam. 22). The Egyptians also showed hospitality to Christ and His mother.[16] The Lord everywhere has committed foreigners to our care. Men live in exile for many reasons. We cannot always remain in our fatherland, even if we would very much want to. Therefore, let us not show ourselves more unmerciful than the gentiles in this regard. Always consider that your people also are not indigenous (αὐτόχθονος), but that they were aliens and foreigners. Consider, likewise, that there are

---

13. Gen. 39.
14. Gen. 45:4–13.
15. Dan. 1:1–7.
16. Matt. 2:13–15, 19–21.

surprising revolutions in circumstances and daily changes in empires and that grievous wars easily arise in which many are driven out of their homes and estates. Therefore, let us remember the vicissitude of human affairs and conduct ourselves rightly toward others. Elimelech is forced to go away with his family. But if you say he was wrong to have done this voluntarily and with no urgent necessity, nevertheless, it is evident that many good, pious men in all ages have done this who had to change their country and leave their homes unwillingly. In Isaiah 16, God threatens the Moabites that they are to be driven out of their home, and He indicates the reason: they either did not receive with hospitality the Israelite war refugees, or they betrayed to the Israelites' enemies those whom they received.

Wives Should Follow Their Husbands
Women also have an example to imitate in Naomi, who followed her husband into exile. Sarah also did not desert Abraham because of adverse fortune when he was sojourning, although more than once she fell into great danger because of him and through his fault. Other pious ladies also have patiently endured exile and other troubles with their husbands. Yet if men despise true religion and migrate to places where pious women cannot live without violating their conscience, they should not expose themselves to obvious danger. What do you think those women would do who prove themselves difficult if their husbands want to move, for important reasons, from one street to another, what, I say, do you think they would do if they were to have to undertake a long journey with the greatest difficulties and dangers for the sake of their husbands? It is certainly troublesome to live among people you do not know, but sometimes the hard spear of necessity forces us.

Ruth 1:3–5

3 *And Elimelech, Naomi's husband, died. And she was left, and her two sons.*

4 *And they took them Moabite wives. The name of the one was Orpah, and the name of the other Ruth. And they dwelled there about ten years.*

5 *Mahlon and Chilion died also both of them. And the woman was left (bereaved) of her two sons and her hsuband.*

If anyone wants to engage fruitfully in reading sacred literature, first he must observe the sense and scope of each passage. Then he must relate individual points to the confirmation of his faith and to the correction of his morals, as to the scope. As far as it pertains to these few words, our author says that Elimelech died, leaving Naomi with her two sons, who married Moabite wives. Mahlon, as it is noted in chapter 4 below, married Ruth, Chilion married Orpah, and they remained in exile for ten years. Afterward both of them died. But Naomi survived her husband and sons.

Whether Ruth Was the King's Daughter

The Hebrews, whom some Christian interpreters follow, say that this Ruth was the daughter of Eglon, king of the Moabites, whom Ehud (who is also called Aioth) stabs in Judges 3. But it is not likely that the king gave his daughter in marriage to a poor Hebrew exile or that he allowed her to live in poverty. Nor does the chronology seem to agree. Moreover, the Jews are accustomed to speak magnificently about their people and to feign some nobility, like those who, though they are obscure and poorer than Codrus,[1] nevertheless lie among strangers about their great wealth and sometimes about the eminence of their family.[2]

In General, Let Us Be on Guard against Entering into Relationships with the Impious

Regarding this passage, the question can be raised whether these two men, since they were Israelites born in Bethlehem, did right by marrying Moabite women. It was specified in the laws of God that they were not to enter into such marriages. In Numbers 25, the women of the Ammonites enticed the Israelites to fornication and idolatry. Hence the Israelites were obligated not to enter into covenants and marriages with the Ammonites or with the Moabites (Deut. 23). So for the same reason it was unlawful for the Jews to marry other unbelievers. Exodus 34: "And lest perhaps thou take of their daughters unto thy sons, and their daughters go a whoring after their gods, and make thy sons go a whoring after their gods."

Idolatry Is Compared to Fornication

Idolatry (I may note in passing) is represented everywhere in sacred literature by fornication. For God has, so to speak, betrothed to Himself not only the whole church, but also its individual members, like a bride. Therefore, they should depend on Him alone. But if they chase after others and abandon Him, they commit adultery. This metaphor best expresses the nature of idolaters. For adulteresses and adulterers think day and night about their disgraceful love affairs. They neglect care for their household and pour out their wealth on those with whom

---

1. Codrus was a mythical or semi-mythical king of Athens. During his reign, the Dorians invaded Attica, assured by a prophecy from the Delphic oracle that they would be successful if they did not kill the Athenian king. When Codrus learned of the prophecy, he disguised himself as a woodcutter and provoked some Dorian soldiers into killing him, thereby saving Athens. The expression here is a proverb found in Erasmus, *Adagia* 1.6.76.

2. Lavater held the view, common among European Christians of the medieval and early modern periods, that Jews were characteristically dishonest.

they commit adultery. They excuse the vices of those with whom they commit adultery. They cannot be taken away from their love. They cannot tolerate those who warn them. Deuteronomy 7: "Neither shalt thou join thyself in marriage with them (the seven proscribed nations). Thy daughter thou shalt not give unto his son, nor his daughter shalt thou take unto thy son. For she will turn away thy son from following me, and they will worship other gods. Therefore, the anger of the LORD will be kindled against you and destroy you suddenly." Joshua 23 repeats the same thing in that great assembly that Joshua held shortly before his death. Likewise, Judges 3 and 1 Kings 11. That these laws must be understood as concerning not only the seven proscribed nations but also others is understood from the general cause that is annexed to the law. For it says that they will be turned away from the worship of the true God. They certainly run into this danger whenever they join in marriage with idolaters. Ezra, in chapters 9 and 10,[3] and, likewise, Nehemiah, in chapter 13, are also angry with the Jews and say that those who married Moabites and Ammonites violated the law of God. We read the same thing in Zephaniah 2.[4] Nor are examples lacking that show how unhappy these unequal marriages are. Solomon, contrary to the royal law (Deut. 17), married many foreign women, among whom the Scriptures include Ammonites and Moabites (1 Kings 11), whom he allowed to erect temples to their gods. And he no doubt adduced many plausible reasons as a defense of his act. But he threw himself and his people into the greatest difficulties. From a Moabite wife he fathered Rehoboam,[5] who was very wicked and was a large reason for the severing of the kingdom. Jehoshaphat entered into a relationship with the impious family of Ahab. For he gave Athaliah, Ahab's daughter, to Jehoram in marriage.[6] No doubt he seemed to himself and to others,

---

3. Lavater cites the chapters from Ezra but refers to the book as 1 Esdras. First Esdras, however, only has nine chapters.

4. Although Zeph. 2 pronounces judgment on the Moabites and Ammonites, the text does not address the Jews' marriages to Moabites and Ammonites. The reference may be to Mal. 2.

5. Scripture actually identifies Rehoboam's mother Naamah as an Ammonitess. Cf. 1 Kings 14:21, 31.

6. 2 Kings 8:16–18, 25–26.

who had persuaded themselves that in this way the divided kingdom could be restored to its former condition, to have done this according to prudent counsel. But the whole family of Jehoshaphat came close to being utterly destroyed because of this marriage. In 2 Chronicles 21, it says that Jehoram, Jehoshaphat's son, lived no differently from Ahab. The reason is added: "For he had the daughter of Ahab to wife." Impious women not only encourage their husbands to idolatry, but also instill it in their children along with their milk. But we must not take these passages to mean that it was in no way permissible for the Israelites to marry foreigners, even if they had been converted to the true faith. In Deuteronomy 21, there is a law that a captive could be married by a Hebrew on certain conditions. Salmah, who is also called Salmon, a prince of the tribe of Judah, married Rahab, a Canaanite.[7] Boaz married this Ruth, who was inserted into Christ's genealogy (Matt. 1). David had as a wife Maacah, the daughter of the king of Geshur.[8] We must not suppose that those marriages were unlawful.

And so that we might draw more closely to the matter, whether those two brothers did right or not in marrying Moabite wives, nothing certain can be established. Those who are of the opinion that they did wrong urge that Scripture says, "They took them Moabite wives," and they say that their mother did not give them those wives. But it can just as easily be said that they were able to take these wives for themselves with their mother's consent. Next, they say that the brothers did not father children from them, which was considered among the Israelites to be a disgrace, and that the Lord threatens with bereavement those who violate marriage laws (Mal. 2). Likewise, they say that they died a premature death, which was also included among the punishments for sins. But these arguments are weak. I would agree rather with those who say that they sinned because they took Moabite wives who had not yet converted to the faith and worship of the one God. For I infer from the fact that Orpah could not really be turned to the true faith by her long-lasting social intercourse with believers that she returned to the gods of

---

7. Matt. 1:5.
8. 2 Sam. 3:2–3.

her fathers. Lyra, on the last chapter of this book, infers that Ruth also had not yet embraced the true religion from the fact that Naomi tried to persuade her to return too, which she would not have done if she previously had been converted, since she would not have advised her to apostatize from the faith and worship of the one true God.[9] But we will discuss this elsewhere. Moreover, God did not want them to marry Ammonites and Moabites, not only because they were idolaters, but also for other reasons (Deut. 23). But Naomi afterward confesses that both of these women showed marital fidelity to their husbands. The two sons should have returned to their fatherland and taken wives there. For they were not unaware that the Israelites were prohibited by law from marriage with foreign peoples and that this law had been repeated more than once. Yet it was more dangerous if Israelite girls were to marry Moabites and other foreigners. In the New Testament also marriages with idolaters are condemned. In 2 Corinthians 6, Paul says we must not be yoked with unbelievers, which pertains especially to marriage. For among the Latins marriage is signified by a yoke, because spouses are subdued as though under one yoke. Although you may understand these words of Paul in a general sense, that we should not have companionship with unbelievers, nevertheless, it can be inferred from this that much less are we to marry them. When the apostle says in 1 Corinthians 7 that a believer is not to desert an unbelieving spouse, he is speaking about a marriage that has been entered, not about entering a marriage. Therefore, we must avoid joining ourselves to the impious for the sake of wealth, power, or other temporal advantages. We must at least have regard for the children, who, because of an unequal marriage, are commonly endowed with a bad character. In Genesis 6, those descended from the holy fathers married wives descended from Cain because of their beauty, from whom were born the Nephilim, that is, apostates, despisers of religion. Superstitious mothers corrupt their children with false opinions that they hold tenaciously. Moreover, they can do this easily since they are with them every day and spare no effort to do it. In Judges 3, there is another example of Israelites who married idolaters. Many recent

---

9. Lyra, *Biblia*, fol. 281r.

examples can be produced of those who in this way threw themselves and their children into the greatest dangers to their wealth, their reputations, and their souls. Therefore, parents should remember these dangers and should be careful not to give impious wives to their sons and much less impious husbands to their daughters, in which there is greater danger. Children should not choose for themselves such spouses against their parents' will. Although many say that they can turn their wives to true worship, nevertheless, they should know that they are not wiser than Solomon, who no doubt hoped that he could accomplish the same thing, but he was subdued by feminine charms and forsook God.[10]

Everyone Is Going to Die

From the fact that it says that Elimelech and both his sons died, it should enter our mind that all men are going to die (Heb. 9). In the Scriptures, it is called "the way of all flesh," on which men may not linger as they wish.[11] As many as came before us are all dead. In Genesis 5, those aged patriarchs who lived before the flood are listed, and of each one it says that he died. Other dangers can be removed to some extent, but the danger of death cannot be avoided. When a man's time comes, he must die, whether he wants to or not. And if someone else were to want to die in his place, it would not be allowed. Indeed, most die sooner than they expect. Not only those who are weakened by old age, but even young men sometimes suddenly die. Who would have thought that Naomi would outlive her sons? We do not know when, where, or how we are going to die.

This should encourage us when the fatal hour is imminent. For who would not gladly join himself with so many travel companions? Who has dared to demand that God allow him alone to survive? If your loved ones die, you should also consider that they go before you and that

---

10. 1 Kings 11:1–8.

11. See 1 Kings 2:2 in the Douay-Rheims Bible. The Vulgate, Theodore Beza's Latin version, and Leo Jud's Latin version all read *terrae* (earth), not *carnis* (flesh). According to Marbury B. Ogle, "The Way of All Flesh," *Harvard Theological Review* 31, no. 1 (January 1938): 41–51, *carnis* appeared in medieval liturgical material and subsequently replaced *terrae* in some medieval Latin manuscripts of Scripture.

you soon will follow. There are certainly stronger comforts in the Scriptures, but these also must not be despised. If you are afflicted by various weighty troubles, you should also consider that you are going to die, and perhaps shortly. Therefore, you are not to commit suicide, but are patiently to await death. Next, since we hear that we must await death, we should equip ourselves with what we need, as those who are about to make a journey usually do. We should avoid wicked deeds, and we should be zealous for piety and an innocent life. Those to whom every mention of death is troublesome deserve rebuke. For who would expect that a man would serve well in war who is terrified of a drawn sword in peace? Danger is certainly never overcome by avoiding it.

In Manifold Troubles, We Must Hope for Good
Now since Naomi herself, though surrounded by many evils, does not lose courage, we also, when we are thrown by God into very serious calamities and miseries, should not despair or accuse Him.

1. Widow
A woman, if for no other reason than that she is a widow, is miserable. For the husband in the Scriptures is called the head of his wife.[12] A body without a head is not a man, but a torso.

2. Bereaved
Widows are sometimes despised even by their own people. This evil is somewhat mitigated if a husband leaves behind him children who are a comfort and help to their widowed mother. But the death of her children also followed the death of her husband, Elimelech, so that Naomi appears to have been utterly destitute of human help and protection.

3. Poor
To these is added poverty, for the wealth that they had possessed seems to have diminished little by little because of their migrations and other reasons unknown to us. Now, what is more despised than a poor widow?

---

12. 1 Cor. 11:3.

4. Old Woman

Add to these that she was already old, and such cannot properly support themselves. They are fretful and subject to many diseases. Old age is in itself a disease.[13] Old women are commonly considered unworthy to live, and they are attacked with many insults.

5. Exile

To this pile of evils was added exile among the Moabites, a savage, insolent, and superstitious nation hostile to the Israelites. If she had been bereaved of her husband and children in her fatherland, she would have had her kinsmen and relatives to comfort her. If she had been exiled among people of her nation, it would have been troublesome. How much more among these?

6. Conscious of Her Wrong

But if, as some think, they went to the land of Moab in violation of the Word of God, she also felt bites and pricks to her conscience, and it entered her mind that she fell into these evils by her own fault. Despite the convergence of these evils, Naomi did not throw away her faith, for she was not unaware that this is the lot of the saints in this world, to be vexed by many severe afflictions.

Reasons for Tribulation

During severe hardships, we must consider that they do not fall on us by chance, but by God, a very merciful Father, for our benefit and, likewise, that He mitigates evils and can utterly remove them, if it is for our good. We must consider what we deserve for our sins and also that God has been accustomed often to throw His own people into extreme evils so that He might bestow greater happiness on them later. In addition, others also have their own burdens. We must not say that no one has ever been thrown into so many evils, when, as Paul says, we have not yet resisted to the point of bloodshed.[14] God subdues us with great evils so

---

13. Ter. *Phor.* 575.
14. Heb. 12:4.

that we will aspire to eternal life, in which we will finally be liberated from all evils.

There are also other purposes for the troubles that God sends on His own people. Satan tries to persuade us by adversities that God hates us and, therefore, that it is necessary for us to look out for our own affairs. But we must patiently await help from God, who also in His own time at last mercifully delivered Naomi from great evils.

Ruth 1:6–9

6 *Then she arose with her daughters-in-law and returned from the region of Moab. For she had heard in the region of Moab that the* LORD *had visited his people in giving them bread.*

7 *Therefore, she went forth out of the place where she was, and her two daughters-in-law with her. And they went on the way to return unto the land of Judah.*

8 *And Naomi said unto her two daughters-in-law, "Go, return each to her mother's house. The* LORD *deal mercifully with you, as ye have dealt with the dead, and with me.*

9 *The* LORD *grant you (namely, a husband) that ye may find rest, each of you in the house of her (future) husband." And she kissed them, and they lifted up their voice, and wept.*

Now the text deals with Naomi's return to her fatherland. In the first place, it mentions that when she learned that the Lord had restored fertility to the Israelites, she began her journey as soon as possible to return to her fatherland. Both of her daughters-in-law joined themselves to her and followed her to a point, for no other reason, as it seems, than to leave their fatherland and travel together with her to Judah.

Fertility from God
We learn from this passage from where abundance comes. For Scripture says that God "visited" (this word is taken in a good and bad sense) His people and gave them bread, that is, crops, fruits, and other necessities

for sustaining life, all of which are included in the word "bread" among the Hebrews, as also in the petition, "Give us this day our daily bread."[1] Therefore, God gives us all that we need. Moreover, as He gives us abundance out of His mercy, so He sends on us scarcity out of His justice. He certainly works through secondary causes, to which, nevertheless, He is by no means bound. Therefore, we must pray that He will deal with us not according to what we deserve, but according to His immeasurable mercy.

Places in Which True Doctrine Does Not Resound Must Be Abandoned

But we must also imitate Naomi's clear example. For as, when the scarcity had been removed, she immediately withdrew from an idolatrous nation to the people of God as to a haven, so also as often as the opportunity is offered to us to flee to those places where we can serve God with a pure conscience, we should embrace it with both hands. And especially if in our fatherland there is public preaching of the Word of God. David, in his exile, especially laments that he cannot attend the sacred assemblies, and as a deer very eagerly searches for streams of water when it is chased by hunters, so his soul panted for God.[2] In 2 Samuel 2, after hearing about Saul's ruin, David immediately consults the Lord, whether he should go up from Ziklag to a city of the tribe of Judah, considering nothing preferable than to return home even at the first opportunity. After being commanded by God, without delay he went up to Hebron with his wives and fellow soldiers. If we live in those places where there is freedom of religion, we can scarcely compel ourselves to do our duty. What, then, will happen in those places where there is no mention of the Word of God and where we observe so many depraved examples with our own eyes? Therefore, if by some necessity you fall in with impious men, as soon as you can properly do so, change your situation. For we must have greater concern for eternal life than for everything else. Those Israelites have a bad reputation, and deservedly

---

1. Matt. 6:11; Luke 11:3.
2. Ps. 42:1.

so, who did not embrace Cyrus's kindness to return to their fatherland[3] but preferred to die in Babylon rather than abandon their houses. We also should allegorically leave the region of Moab and Babylon, that is, idolatry and wicked deeds (Rev. 18).

Mother's House

Naomi urges her daughters-in-law that each of them should return to her mother's house. She calls it the "mother's house" not because their fathers were dead, for later, in chapter 3, Boaz praises Ruth because she left her father and mother and went to the land of Israel, but because children, and especially female children, frequently stay with their mothers and are closer to them. Genesis 24 calls Rebekah's house the house of her mother, not of her father.

For what reason she advised them against traveling to Judah, we will say later in its place.

To Show Mercy

She prays for favor on them, first, that the Lord will bless them, and that He will deal kindly with them just as they showed mercy to the dead and to her. The word חסד (*chaesed*) means "piety, clemency, kindness, beneficence," not any beneficence, but what proceeds from ardent affection. That expression frequently occurs in the Scriptures, and commonly אמת (*emeth*), "truth," or "faithfulness," is added. In Genesis 24, Abraham's servant says, "If now ye agree to deal mercifully with my master, tell me," that is, "If you want to treat him kindly, to deserve well of him, and to give your daughter to be his son's wife." In 1 Samuel 15, it says concerning the Kenites that they "dealt mercifully with all the children of Israel, when they came up out of Egypt," that is, they showed them kindness. Therefore, they were saved while the Amalekites were destroyed. In 2 Samuel 3, Abner says to Ishbosheth, "I have shown mercy unto thy house," that is, "I have shown it kindness." In chapter 10, David says, "I will show mercy unto Hanun the son of Nahash, as his father showed mercy unto me," and David sends envoys to comfort him

---

3. Ezra 1:1–4.

concerning the death of his father. He was moved by the kindness of Hanun's father; therefore, he wanted to return thanks.

What did these widows do? They loved their husbands while they lived, and they cared for them with every kind of service as is proper for honorable wives. They spoke respectfully about the dead and so ordered their lives that those who were now dead did not have a bad reputation because of them. In addition, for the sake of their husbands, they honored their remaining mother-in-law with what kindnesses they could, and so they showed mercy toward the dead. Certainly, no one should think that they, out of some absurd mercy, instituted some sacred rites or poured out some prayers for the dead for their salvation. For Ruth at least knew that the souls of the dead who had faith in the Messiah are at rest. Priests who perform the mass urge men to deal mercifully with the dead, that is, to take care that masses are celebrated weekly, monthly, annually, and so forth, for the expiation of their sins that they committed, so that their souls will be delivered from purgatory. But although God instituted so many different kinds of sacrifices, nevertheless, (as Peter Martyr has observed) we read about nothing that was instituted for those who are tormented in purgatory, which He absolutely would have done if souls were suffering torments in purgatory.[4] From sacred literature it is certain that after this life there are only two reception areas for souls, namely, a place of rest and a place of torments. A third place that they call purgatory is a human figment. If someone wants to bestow some kindness on the dead, he should show kindness to their widows, children, and relatives, and likewise, he should proclaim the glorious deeds of the dead. And he should not do this because the living have asked him to.

Another thing that Naomi wishes for her daughters-in-law is that each one will find rest in the home of her husband. That is, she desires for them good fortune and also a peaceful marriage and good, amenable husbands with whom they can pass their lives comfortably without want (which is a common burden in marriage) and, likewise, without quarrels and blows. Later, in chapter 3, Naomi said to Ruth, "I shall seek rest for thee, that it may be well with thee," that is, "I will be on the lookout for a good husband for you."

Hardships of Spouses

She did not think that in marriage they would be free from every trouble. For marriage has its own hardships, as there are various diseases, difficult childbirths, transgressions, funerals, or otherwise sad misfortunes regarding children, and very many other things of this sort. But God, as Naomi was not unaware, wants to be present in pious marriages and to alleviate their hardships. Moreover, such spouses as Naomi desires for her daughters-in-law are certainly given by God. Young men and young women should not by superstitious lots inquire into what sort of wives and husbands they should expect to have, but rather they should pray to God that He would provide for them in this regard, and they should depend on His providence.

From Naomi's wish or prayer, we gather that she believed that God cares about the affairs of mortals, adorns good deeds with rewards, and assails bad deeds with punishments.

What We Must Desire for Others

Next, we learn what we must pray and desire for others, and especially for those who show us great kindness, namely, all those things that pertain to spending life happily. The apostles also begin their epistles with a prayer for divine grace and peace. The Satirist somewhere reproaches the foolish prayers of those parents who desire for their children wealth, beauty, and other things of this sort, not those things that are of chief importance.[5] Certainly, external goods apart from goods of the soul profit us little. In addition, those who curse their children care poorly for them and themselves, as we see commonly happens. Even if you bless them, they are for the most part miserable. What then will happen if you repeatedly curse them?

We see in addition what is to be expected for those who conduct themselves rightly and admirably toward others. God adorns love, faith,

---

5. This designation perhaps identifies Juvenal as the satirist *par excellence*. Juv. 14.

and other virtues with rewards. If you support your parents when they are weakened by old age and render to them all the duties of a child, so also your children will take care of you in your old age. But if you afflict them, so you will experience your children as an affliction. And whether you want to or not, you will say, or at least think, "I am treated fairly, since I was impious to my parents." The same thing must be said about others toward whom we have not been merciful.

The Duty of Spouses

We must also note the duty of spouses. Naomi praises her daughters-in-law because they discharged all the duties of humaneness to her sons. Other women should also do the same toward their husbands. If they conduct themselves rightly, most women can have good and amenable husbands, but if not, they create considerable troubles for themselves and others. She desires rest for them, that is, a peaceful marriage. And so spouses should not quarrel and fight with each other, but live harmoniously. For peace and harmony in marriage is especially praised. Concerning the duty of spouses, we read many things in the epistles of Paul and Peter, which it is not necessary to recite here.

Naomi kissed her daughters-in-law, and they shed very abundant tears, about which we will say something later in its place. Naomi repeatedly calls her daughters-in-law her "daughters" in this book, who loved her more than their fatherland, parents, and kinsmen. Good God,[6] how rare today are mothers-in-law and daughters-in-law who get along! Frequently disputes between them arise for trivial reasons. Many women wish their mothers-in-law would go alone to the farthest borders of the Garamantes.[7]

---

6. The exclamation *Deus bone* is not used in an irreverent way. Lavater earnestly appeals to God to note the impenitent sins of God's people.

7. The Garamantes were a people who lived in what is now Libya. Our expression "all the way to Timbuktu" is similar to Lavater's expression here.

Ruth 1:10–13

10 *And they said unto her, "Surely we will return with thee unto thy people."*

11 *And Naomi said, "Turn again, my daughters. For what reason (why) are you going with me? Are there any more (sons) for me in my womb, that they may be your men (husbands)?*

12 *Turn again (I say), my daughters. For I am too old to marry. But even if I should say (could say), 'I (still) have hope,' even if I should marry a husband tonight and should also bear sons,*

13 *Will ye tarry for them till they are grown? Will ye stay (will ye delay on account of them) so that ye will not have a husband (ye will not marry husbands)? Nay, my daughters, since I have much greater bitterness than you, because the hand of the LORD is gone out against me."*

When Naomi sets out on her journey to her fatherland, both her daughters-in-law not only accompany her to a point for the sake of duty, but also resolve to travel together with her to Judah. But she deters them from their plan and tells them to go back home, adding her reasons. For she says she is already too old to resolve to marry a husband again and to give birth to sons who might marry her daughters-in-law according to the law of Moses and who might raise up seed for their brothers [i.e., Naomi's sons]. Naomi certainly would not have sinned if she had married someone else, although she was an old woman. For marriage is instituted not only to avoid filthy lusts and to produce offspring, but also for the sake of mutual comfort and support. For God said, "It is not good that the man should be alone. Let us make him an help."[1] Many widows marry again so that they will more easily obtain for themselves what they need to live. But if now at a worn-out age she had married a young man, she would have been accused of wantonness and frivolity. Elderly widows ought rather to think about the pleasures of the other life than the pleasures of this life and new marriages, and to prepare themselves for it, which they can do quite better if they are single than if they have husbands.

The elderly learn from this example to be mindful of their old age and to give up childish games at last, as the proverb goes.[2] Next, she says that if marriage were suitable and it had entered into her mind to marry another and she immediately bore male offspring by him, nevertheless, it would not be a good plan to wait for them until they had grown up and, meanwhile, to neglect opportunities to marry others who would be willing to marry them. Sometimes girls wait until those whom they want to be their husbands reach a suitable age, which is dangerous, just as it is dangerous that prepubescent boys and girls are joined in marriage by their parents in some regions. For afterward, when they have grown up, they either do not consent to the marriages or their desires easily change. Tamar, Judah's daughter-in-law, also waited until Shelah, Judah's third son, had grown up so that he would raise up the name of his two brothers who had died without children (Gen. 38). Naomi adds that she is burdened with anguish and grieves intensely because of them and that her sorrow is going to increase. Or rather she means to say this: "I would grieve more than you if your circumstances were in a bad state because of me *because the hand of the LORD is gone out against me*. God stretches out His hand against me, that is, I am oppressed by Him with poverty and other troubles. What would you do with me since I cannot provide anything that will profit you?" She is not disposed as those who, if they are oppressed by evils, wish all others were oppressed by the same evils and, likewise, who desire to serve their own interests through the

---

1. Gen. 2:18.
2. The expression *nuces relinquere* literally means "to give up the nuts." Children would play with nuts. So the expression means to give up childish ways or childish games.

evils that befall others. Many people have an opportunity to provide an advantageous marriage for their handmaids—no rather, even their own children—but they do not do this, so that they will not have to employ others and incur greater expenses.[3] I will say nothing about those who drive their own children into disgraceful business so that they, meanwhile, can indulge their appetite.

Naomi recognizes that she did not fall into those difficulties by chance but confesses that the hand of God is stretched out against her. For no afflictions would befall believers unless God had decreed to trouble them through those afflictions. To think about this often is very useful for patiently enduring all things. We will hear later what she accomplished by this speech.

Why Naomi Orders Her Daughters-in-Law to Return Home

"But why," you say, "when both her daughters-in-law willingly offer themselves as companions, does she push them away from her? Would it not have been useful for them to be led away from idolatry to true religion and to be delivered as from a fire?" I respond that Naomi certainly desired for both of them to be converted to the worship of the true God, but she wanted by her dissuasion to test their steadfastness. Perhaps she did not sufficiently perceive their minds. For we must not immediately trust in the first affections of men, especially of girls, who easily change their minds and sometimes succumb to trivial temptations. Being a prudent woman, she feared that if perhaps something were to befall them in a foreign land other than they expected, they would immediately fall back into idolatry. How often have we seen men who have embraced the gospel, when they do not obtain what they had dreamed, fall back into their former errors with great offense to others? Yet "it had been better for those apostates not to have known the way of righteousness, than, after they have known it, to turn from that which was delivered

---

3. Some parents did not want their children or handmaids (who were like daughters) to marry because the children and handmaids would have their own households and would no longer provide the parents with free (or at least cheap) labor. The parents would then have to hire someone outside the household to do the same work, but often at greater expense.

unto them as a holy commandment" (2 Peter 2). Christ Himself, in
Luke 14, tells those who would follow Him to consider what awaits
them, by a double analogy. Likewise, in Luke 9 He says that after the
hand is put to the plough, one must not look back to the things that
are behind. In chapter 17, He recalls to our minds the example of Lot's
wife, who was transformed into a pillar of salt. They do wrong who try
to push others into the Christian religion by human devices or empty
promises. For if afterward they come to know that matters are different
than they heard, many of them persecute the true religion with deadly
hatred. We must deal with them with arguments that are drawn from
the Word of God. Therefore, how much do they sin who drive men
to a profession of false religion by promises, deceit, threats, and torments? In Matthew 23, Christ our Savior says, "Woe unto you, scribes
and Pharisees, hypocrites! For ye compass sea and land to make one
proselyte, and when he is made, ye make him twofold more the child
of hell than ye are." For they trained those who devoted themselves to
their sect to be the most hostile enemies of Christ. There are those who
today are zealous to lead the Jews to their religion and who throw them
into graver ruin, teaching them, contrary to the law, that God has commanded them to worship idols, to believe the Messiah is embodied in
bread, and so forth. Also, no one is to be pushed into other vows from
which there is no return. Wives must not be forced on unwilling young
men, and husbands must not be forced on young women. For consent
is required in marriages. Much less are they to be driven into perpetual
celibacy by enticements, or some other artifice, by force or by threats.
If Naomi could have had male children, nevertheless, she would not
have wanted, on account of the risk, for her daughters-in-law to wait
until they had grown up. But she already desired suitable husbands for
them. Much less would she have wanted them to vow perpetual widowhood in the passion of that stage of life. In the Council of Saragossa, it
is recorded that young women who dedicated themselves to God were
not to be veiled unless they proved they were at least forty.[4] Later, they

---

4. *ACS*, can. 8, ll. 75–78. The line numbers here correspond to the line
numbers in Felix Rodríguez, "Concilio I de Zaragoza: Texto crítico," in *Primero*

were veiled when they reached the age of thirty, and when true doctrine had at last utterly collapsed, every woman indiscriminately and without exception began to be veiled, even those of a tender age. The apostle in 1 Timothy 5 forbids a widow younger than sixty to be supported by the ministry to the poor, but he wants the younger widows to marry, to bear children, and to be housewives. Today a noose is also thrown over children of a tender age. For many who would later be more fit for marriage are unwillingly thrust into monasteries, which has produced various monstrosities of shameful deeds. But there is sin not only in the fact that at a simple stage of life they are enclosed in a monastery, but in the fact that this whole kind of life, as it is in use today, is repugnant to sacred literature. Although men see and understand this, nevertheless, they fiercely defend their inventions.

But someone might contend that Naomi advised them to return to their fatherland because they would be able to live more comfortably among those they knew than among strangers, but not to probe their minds. We respond that if this is so, she sinned no less than those who today urge those who wish to desert their fatherland, in which they cannot worship Christ according to the desire of their heart, not to do this, but to believe in their hearts what they will, and who say that it is just the same whatever they believe, provided that they avoid atrociously wicked deeds, and that they must obey the magistrate and wait for better times. For Christ requires from His faithful an open confession (Matt. 10). We should extend the kingdom of God and acquire disciples for it. Nevertheless, we must do this prudently, not rashly. But everyone especially ought to take pains to instruct their children and households rightly in the true religion.

Concilio Caesaraugustano: MDC aniversario, ed. Guillermo Fatás Cabeza (Zaragoza: Institución Fernando el Católico, 1981), 9–25.

Ruth 1:14–15

14 *And they lifted up their voice, and wept again. And Orpah kissed her mother-in-law, but Ruth clave unto her.*

15 *Unto her she (her mother-in-law) said, "Behold, thy kinswoman is gone back unto her people, and unto her gods. Return thou also after her."*

What Naomi accomplished by her speech to her daughters-in-law, or rather, what happened after she commanded them to return home, next is brought to mind. Orpah returned to the house of her mother, but Ruth clung to her mother-in-law. We will hear what can be gathered from these verses for our edification. After Naomi urged both of them with many arguments to return home, again they wept profusely. This was an indication of the great sorrow that they experienced because they would have to be separated from each other. For sorrow elicits tears. As blood flows if we are wounded in our body, so if we are wounded in our soul, tears burst forth, for which reason some call tears "the blood of the soul." They did not sin by weeping, as neither today do those who shed tears when they are separated from good friends.

The Stoics said that it was not fitting for a brave man to shed tears, for this was an indication of a soft and effeminate soul. But sacred literature teaches otherwise. For there are many examples in it not only of women, but also of very brave men who testified to their sorrow with tears, and they are not said to have sinned in that regard. Joseph wept four times when his brothers came to him in Egypt to buy grain.[1] David, who conquered and killed a lion, a bear, and giants, wept so profusely when Ziklag was laid waste and his wives were taken that his strength deserted him; his soldiers did the same (1 Sam. 30). In 2 Samuel 15, David wept as he ascended the Mount of Olives. Peter also wept profusely.[2] Paul and all whom he had summoned to Miletus wept in Acts 20. Christ our Savior Himself wept more than once.[3] Therefore, that Stoic absence of emotion (ἀπαθεία) is not acceptable to God. Nevertheless, as in other things, so also in tears, we must not exceed moderation, and we must not weep for every supposed reason. For indeed, not all weeping can be excused. Seneca, although he himself was a Stoic, nevertheless says that one must weep, not wail.[4]

But it is for our comfort that in this short book it is written twice that these poor women wept profusely, for we infer from this that God cares about the tears even of the very poor. In Psalm 56, David testifies that God gathers his tears, and indeed the tears of all the pious, in His bottle or flask and records them in His book. Good God, how few daughters-in-law are there today who shed tears if their mothers-in-law depart from them to other regions or even from this life! Or if they shed tears, they can be called crocodile tears.

Kissing

Orpah kissed her mother-in-law. In Palestine and all of Syria they frequently used a kiss, and as also other nations do today, so they received and dismissed their guests and friends who came to them with a kiss and, likewise, greeted with a kiss those whom they met on the way. In Luke 7, Christ reproaches Simon the Pharisee because when He came Simon did not greet Him by giving Him a kiss. Orpah, saying farewell to her mother-in-law, kisses her. Now a kiss is a sign of friendship and benevolence, as well as of veneration, faithfulness, and obedience. Plutarch writes in the *Life of Cato of Utica* that when Cato was departing

---

1. Gen. 42:24; 43:30; 45:2, 14–15.
2. Matt. 26:75; Mark 14:72; Luke 22:62.
3. Luke 19:41; John 11:35; Heb. 5:7.
4. Sen. *Ep.* 63.1.

from his province, the soldiers reverently kissed his hand, which at that time was a kind of honor given only to emperors, and very few of those.[5] Pomponius Laetus, in his *Compendium of Roman History*, writes as follows: "The emperors in former times offered their hands to be kissed by nobles, and afterward they raised them up with their hands to kiss their mouth. The common people kissed their knees. Diocletian decreed in an edict that everyone, without discrimination of descent, was to fall prostrate and kiss his feet, to which he added something worthy of veneration by adorning his shoes with gold, gems, and pearls. They say that Gaius Caligula previously did this."[6] Later, the Roman pontiffs, who, like those tyrants, want divine honors to be given to them, also offered their feet to others to be kissed. The Cumaean Sibyl proclaimed this in sermon 8: Ἔσσετ᾽ ἄναξ πολιόκρανος, ἔχων πέλας οὔνομα πόντου· κόσμον ἐποπτεύων, μιαρῷ ποδὶ δῶρα πορίζων. That is, "There will be a king with a white head or helmet, having a name near to the sea,[7] inspecting the world, and conferring gifts with polluted foot."[8] Those to whom he offers his feet to be kissed must consider this a great gift. Saint Paul, in the last chapter of 1 Corinthians, says, "Greet ye one another with an holy kiss," excluding the vices of immodesty and hypocrisy, but he does not prescribe a law by these words such that this custom of kissing each other should be accepted in every nation. In 2 Samuel 20, Joab killed Amasa after kissing him. Judas betrayed the Son of God

5. Plut. *Cat. Min.* 12.1.

6. Pomponius Laetus, *Romanae historiae compendium ab interitu Gordiani Iunioris usque ad Iustinum III*, in *Opera Pomponii Laeti varia* (Mainz: Schoeffer, 1521), fol. 14r–15v.

7. Lavater translates ἔχων πέλας οὔνομα πόντου as *nomen habens vicinum ponto*, rather than *nomen habens vicini ponti* (i.e., "having the name of the nearby sea"), or something similar. The original reference is to Hadrian, whose name (Ἁδριανός) sounds similar to "Adriatic" (Ἁδριατική), the "nearby sea." Lavater appears instead to interpret the oracle as a prophecy about the Roman pontiffs generally. Thus, a possible explanation for how Lavater understood the reference to the king's name being "near to the sea" is that the Greek word for "sea" (πόντος) and the Latin word for "sea" (*pontus*) sound similar to the Latin word for "Pontiff" (*pontifex*). This interpretation would explain Lavater's translation of the oracle.

8. Sib. Or. 8.52–53.

with a kiss.[9] Today it is very common that men falsely accuse in private those whom they kiss, that is, whom they fawn over in their presence. We must believe that Orpah kissed her mother-in-law with a sincere mind, not as that son about whom there is a fable, who, pretending that he wanted to kiss his mother when he was being led to his punishment, moved his mouth, bit her ear, and tore it off.[10]

Necessary Steadfastness

It says that Orpah returned to her own people. But if, as is somewhat probable, she had at least some taste of true religion, she is a type of those whom the Lord in the gospel calls "temporary" ($\pi\rho\sigma\kappa\alpha\acute{\iota}\rho\upsilon\varsigma$), who profess the true faith for a time but afterward are subdued by the hope of prosperity or the fear of adversity and jump back again.[11] It is not enough to have laid some foundations of true religion, but we must build on it until that spiritual building is finished. It is not enough to run, unless we reach the goal. "He that shall endure unto the end," says the Lord, "shall be saved," not he who begins well and makes some progress.[12] Lot's wife, who, when she looked back, was turned into a pillar of salt, is an example to us.[13] If Orpah had come to Judah, it seems that she would not have persevered. But whether she perished in her errors or afterward converted, or repented, without losing the truth, we do not know. Nor are we to raise questions about that issue and others of this sort that are not at all edifying.

Ruth clung to her mother-in-law and could not be separated from her by any arguments. A similar example appears in John 6 concerning Christ's apostles. When many were forsaking Him, He asked them whether they also wished to go away. Then Simon Peter responded, "Lord, to whom shall we go? Thou hast the words of eternal life. And we believe and know that thou art the Christ, the Son of the living God."

---

9. Matt. 26:49; Mark 14:45; Luke 22:47.

10. This story is found in one of Aesop's Fables. See *Fabellae Aesopicae quaedam notiores, et in scolis usitatae*, ed. Joachim Camerarius (Leipzig: Valentin Bapst, 1552), 113.

11. Matt. 13:21; Mark 4:17.

12. Matt. 24:13.

13. Gen. 19:26; Luke 17:32.

We must pray to God that He will also not allow us to be led away from true religion either by flatteries or by threats and terrors.

Baalpeor

When Orpah had departed, Naomi again urged Ruth also to return home, for her sister-in-law had returned to her people and to her gods. But what gods did the Moabites worship? Besides others, mainly, as we read in Numbers 25, Baalpeor whom some, such as Isidore and Theophylact, according to the testimony of Giraldi in his *History of the Gentile Gods*, have interpreted as Priapus.[14] Others have interpreted him as Saturn. And some have said that Baal was indeed the name of the god himself, but that Peor was the name of the mountain or place where he was worshiped. The idol Peor takes its name from "making naked," for פער (*paar*) means "to lay bare," "to make naked," namely, because, as the author of the obscene poem says, Priapus's male member was always laid bare, never covered by clothing. For he introduces him speaking as follows: "You ask why my obscene part is without clothing? I ask, Why does no god cover his own signs?"[15] The worship of this idol was so vile that modesty does not allow us to speak about it in the sacred assemblies. From this we gather how far men fall when the light of truth is lost.

Chemosh

They also worshiped the god Chemosh. Indeed, in 1 Kings 11 it is written that Solomon built a high place for Chemosh, the abomination of Moab, on the Mount of Olives. The fact that in Judges 11 Jephthah makes Chemosh the god of the Ammonites does not contradict this passage, for this god appears to have been worshiped by both nations. Who Chemosh was is uncertain. כמס (*kamas*) means "to hide." From this indeed some infer that he was Pluto, the god of the underworld, or the subterranean realm. Giraldi seems to indicate that Venus Astarte

---

14. Giglio Gregorio Giraldi, *De deis gentium varia & multiplex historia, libris sive syntagmatibus XVII comprehensa* (Basel: Johannes Oporinus, 1548), 111.

15. *Priap.* 8.1–2.

was called Chemosh, who was worshiped by the Sidonians and also by the Moabites in the form of a star.[16] There are some who think that Baalpeor and Chemosh were one and the same god, with whom I do not agree, because it is certain that the gentiles worshiped many gods. Some think that Chemosh was the god of feasts and revelry, who is called Κῶμος by the Greeks, no doubt because the Greek alludes to the Hebrew word.[17]

Milcom

Neighboring regions also had their own gods or idols. The Ammonites had Milcom (2 Kings 23;[18] Jer. 49), which sounds like their word for "king."[19] Perhaps he was called this because he was chief among the many tutelary gods that they worshiped. In 1 Kings 11 the god of the Ammonites is called Molech. Some think he is Saturn. What if Molech and Milcom are the same god?

Ashtaroth

The Philistines had Ashtaroth, that is, Juno, or Venus (1 Sam. 7).

Baalzebub

The Ekronites worshiped Baalzebub, that is, the lord of the fly (2 Kings 1). He seems to be the same as the one who is called "Fly-catcher" (Μυίαγρος) by the Greeks. Pliny calls him Myodes in his *Natural History*, but Achores in the old edition.[20] Gregory of Nazianzus calls him Ekron.[21] (The god Ekron is named for Ekron, the Philistine city, where he was mainly worshiped.) Jupiter is also named Ἀπόμυιος,

---

16. Giraldi, *De deis gentium*, 376–77.

17. The Greek Κῶμος sounds similar to the Hebrew כמס.

18. I have revised all of Lavater's references to 3 and 4 Kings (in which he is following the Vulgate and LXX) to 1 and 2 Kings, respectively.

19. In Jer. 49:1, 3, the MT has "their king" (מַלְכָּם). The LXX, Peshitta, and Vulgate translate the text as though it has "Milcom" (מִלְכֹּם) instead. The Hebrew and Aramaic word for "king" (מֶלֶךְ) sounds similar to "Milcom."

20. Plin. *HN* 29.34 and *HN* 10.40. *HN* 29.34 calls the god "Myiodes" rather than "Myodes." *HN* 10.40 calls the god "Myiacores."

21. Gregory of Nazianzus *Or.* 5.29.

Muscarius, from chasing and driving out flies. For a multitude of flies brought great discomfort to the Phoenicians. Therefore, they sacrificed to that god and prayed to him, that he would drive them away.

Dagon

The Philistines also worshiped Dagon, about whom Judges 16 and 1 Samuel 5 speak. The Hebrews note that he resembled a man in the upper part, but a fish in the lower part, as Neptune and the Sirens are depicted. For דג (*dag*) means "fish." Others say that he was portrayed as a human with a female face. In Greek, they call him Δερκετώ (*Derceto*), or Δερκή (*Derce*). Eusebius, in book 1 of *The Preparation of the Gospel*, says, "Dagon discovered grain and the plough, and therefore he was called Jupiter 'the Husbandman' (Ἀρότριος) and was worshiped among the Phoenicians."[22] This seems to agree beautifully with the Hebrew etymology. For דגן (*dagan*) means "grain" or "wheat."

Love of the Fatherland

But this was a great temptation for Ruth. For no one willingly deserts his fatherland and friends, nor does piety advise that this should be done unless weighty and necessary reasons force us. Our fatherland draws us to itself, according to Ovid's statement in book 1 of his *Letters from the Black Sea*: "Our native soil leads us all with some sweetness and does not allow us to forget it."[23]

Next, men are so disposed that they can scarcely be led away from the religion of their fatherland. God, in Jeremiah 2, amplifying the sin of the defection of His people, says that if they run throughout the world, they will not find another nation that would exchange their gods for other gods, and nevertheless His people exchanged His glory for something worthless, for those that are not really gods. All nations tenaciously hold on to their own gods, which they chose for themselves. For this reason, it is a very laborious business to turn men from the worship of false gods to the worship of the true God. Therefore, it would not

22. Euseb. *Praep. evang.* 1.10.37d.
23. Ov. *Pont.* 1.3.35–36.

have been surprising if Ruth also had refused to worship another god and to embrace a new religion. In addition, examples, especially household examples, greatly move the souls of men. If those who are dear to us return to idolatry, especially if many great men do this, men, however much they love true doctrine, begin to waver. And so it would not have been surprising if Ruth, shaken and broken down by these "battering rams" of her mother-in-law, had returned to her own people. But Naomi's intention never seems to have been to tempt Ruth to defection, but to test her steadfastness and, likewise, to take care that she would not afterward be able to say that she had been forced by her mother-in-law to receive the Israelite religion.

Souls Must Be Strengthened against Defection

In cases of this sort, our souls must be strengthened by contrary examples, promises, and threats drawn from the Word of God. In Matthew 10, the Lord says, "He that loveth father or mother more than me is not worthy of me, and he that loveth son or daughter more than me is not worthy of me." So is he who prefers his fatherland, his religion, and other things to Christ. We must not look at what others do, whether many or few, but rather how rightly they act and what God demands of us. We must wear Him out with constant prayers so that He will strengthen and preserve us in the true religion by His Spirit.

Seventh Homily

Ruth 1:16–18

16 *And Ruth said, "Entreat me not to leave thee or to depart from thee. For whither thou goest, I will go. And where thou lodgest, I will lodge. Thy people shall be my people, and thy God my God.*

17 *Where thou diest, will I die, and there will I be buried. The* LORD *do so to me, and more also, unless death (alone) part me from thee."*

18 *And so when she saw that she was steadfastly minded to go with her, then she left speaking unto her.*

Ruth could not be persuaded by any reasons to forsake her mother-in-law. But like lime on which cold water is poured, she was made more eager and more excited by dissuasion, and she testified with many words that she was unwilling to depart from her, no rather, that she was ready to endure every fate with her, and that she would embrace the Israelite religion and flee the superstition of the gentiles, as will appear from her words. *"Entreat me not to leave thee,"* that is, "Do not get in my way. Do not trouble me with dissuasion. Do not hinder me from going with you." *"Whither thou goest, I too will go."* "I am prepared to suffer any difficulties with you." But since Naomi had said that Orpah had gone to her people and to her gods, she adds, *"Thy people (probably "are," or "shall be"), my people, and thy God, my God."* "I do not acknowledge another people or another God than the people and God of Israel, whom you worship, and in whom you place all your hope and trust. Nor afterward will I worship Baalpeor or Chemosh, the gods of my nation, or those of other nations."

Shared Tomb

"Where thou diest, will I die, and there will I be buried." It is the character of men, that they wish to be buried in the tombs of those whom they hold dear and do not wish to be separated from them even after death. We read in Genesis that Abraham bought the field of Ephron of Heth, in which there was a cave, which he turned into a tomb for himself and his family.[1] There he first was buried, and then Isaac.[2] Jacob also did not want to be buried in Egypt, but bound Joseph by an oath to bring his corpse to the land of Canaan and to bury him in the tomb of his fathers (Gen. 47; 49). Tobias said to his son, "When I am dead, bury me with honor, and honor your mother, and also bury her by me with honor in my tomb."[3] At the end of book 10 of Virgil's *Aeneid*, Mezentius, however impious, asks Aeneus to allow his body to be interred in the tomb of his son Lausus.[4] It is considered a curse to lack the honor of burial and not to be interred in the tomb of one's fathers. On the other hand, it is considered a blessing to be buried with honor. When true doctrine collapsed, superstitious men thought that magnificent burials gave some benefit to the souls of the dead.

Ruth Uses an Oath

Ruth adds an oath by which she confirms that she will not leave her mother-in-law: *"The LORD do so to me, and more also, unless death create a division between me and thee."* She does not simply swear, but curses herself if she does not keep her oath. That oath formula is common in the Scriptures: "God do so to me, and more also." But the formula does not express what evils those who use the formula call down on themselves, or to what awful things they devote themselves if they break their oath. For by those aposiopeses[5] the Holy Spirit wants to teach us that we must deal cautiously in swearing and that we must beware lest our

---

1. Gen. 23.
2. Gen. 25:8–10; 49:29–32.
3. Tobit 4:3–4.
4. Verg. *Aen.* 10.903–6.
5. Aposiopesis is a rhetorical figure in which the speaker abruptly breaks off his speech.

tongue outrun our mind. For here that saying ought especially to have a place, "Tongue, where are you going?"[6] It is to be observed that pious men often used oaths both in the Old and in the New Testament, not in all matters, but only in weighty and difficult matters. The forms that they used are also noted, for they are not of one kind. This formula that Ruth uses shows that in the end they will all perish who violate their oath and so profane the holy name of God. In addition, the saints really did what they promised by oath, as also Ruth did. There are some who interpret these words, "*God do so to me,*" conditionally. "If God from now on grants me strength and ability as He has done so far, I will be constant." The former sense, that it is an oath formula, is simpler.

There is set before us in this passage a distinguished example in Ruth, first of conversion to God, and of confession of faith. Denying her nation and religion, she confesses that she will join herself to the true God and to His people. Rahab's confession in Joshua 2 was similar: "for the LORD your God, he is…"

Next, she is an example of love toward God and neighbor. Since she had learned, no doubt, from her father-in-law, her mother-in-law, and her husband, and especially by the inspiration of the Holy Spirit, that the God of Israel is the true God, leaving Baalpeor and the other gods and goddesses of the gentiles, she hurries to that land where the true God is worshiped, and she does not allow her journey to be hindered by the comforts of this life. It certainly could have been more pleasant to live among her own people and easier, as it seemed, to get herself a husband. Nevertheless, she preferred (as we read about Moses in the letter to the Hebrews)[7] sooner to suffer afflictions with the people of God, than to enjoy the temporary pleasures of sin, esteeming the reproach of Christ greater riches than the treasures of Moab. If she had lacked faith, she would have returned to the idolaters because of the slightest glimmer of

---

6. Erasmus, *Adagia* 2.2.39. The references to Erasmus's *Adagia* correspond to Desiderius Erasmus, *Desiderii Roterodami Erasmi opera omnia emendatiora et auctiora, ad optimas editiones praecipue quas ipse Erasmus postremo curavit summa fide exacta, doctorumque virorum notis illustrata,* vol. 2, ed. Johannes Clericus (Leiden: Petrus Vander Aa, 1703).

7. Heb. 11:25–26.

hope of a more splendid marriage, of wealth, and of other comforts. She heard the Word of God with profit, and so can be compared to the well rooted tree[8] and to the house built on the rock (Matt. 7).

We also have an example of love toward neighbor. Our neighbor is whoever needs our help and attention (Luke 10). Naomi was worn out by old age, cares, and sicknesses and so needed others' assistance. Therefore, Ruth, who had received considerable favors from her, was unwilling to leave her, and although she too was destitute of necessities, nevertheless, depending on the goodness of God, she was not willing to desert her mother-in-law, whom she considered a mother. Good God, how few are there today (I am not even just talking about daughters-in-law) who show the same benevolence to their mothers-in-law! But what's more, how few are the children who are so disposed toward their parents who are worn out by old age! Many cannot be persuaded by any reasons, however weighty, to be present with their parents when they are afflicted with diseases and to serve them. But even when the affairs of the parents are still in a good condition, they dread their presence, if their parents are a little too strict. Rare are those who think that children cannot do as many favors for their parents as they received from them. They often abandon their parents in the greatest dangers. The reason for this is that they are destitute of both faithfulness and love.

In the fact that Ruth denies the religion of her fatherland and embraces the religion of Israel, the calling of the gentiles is prefigured, who have left their superstitions and have gone to the God of Israel.

After Naomi sees that her daughter-in-law is entirely determined to accompany her, she is no longer willing to trouble her. But now that she has seen and tested her steadfastness enough, she gladly receives her as a companion on her journey. She would have wanted the other also to have been converted to the worship of the true God. Without a doubt, she rejoiced that God had joined to her, who was afflicted in so many ways, so faithful a daughter. For it would have been very troublesome and difficult for her to make this journey without a faithful companion.

8. Ps. 1:3.

She teaches us by her example not to be troublesome to those who have determined to do good, but rather to oppose those who attempt evil, so that we might restrain them from their intention. And however stubborn they are, nevertheless, we must not yield an inch.

Let poor and afflicted men draw out this comfort, too, that God can stir up men to help and nurture them. And when they seem to themselves most abandoned, nevertheless, let them not allow themselves to be driven to despair by the enemy of mankind.

Ruth 1:19–22

19 *So they two went until they came to Bethlehem. And it came to pass, when they were come to Bethlehem, that all the city was moved about them, and they said, "Is this Naomi?"*

20 *She answered them, "Call me not Naomi, (but rather) call me Mara (bitter), for the Almighty hath greatly afflicted me with bitterness.*

21 *I went out full, but the LORD hath brought me back empty. Why then call ye me Naomi, since the LORD hath afflicted me, and the Almighty hath harmed me?"*

22 *So Naomi returned, together with Ruth the Moabitess, her daughter-in-law, (which) had returned out of the region of Moab. And they came to Bethlehem in the beginning of barley harvest.*

How Naomi and Ruth came from the region of Moab to Bethlehem in Judah, what happened to them there, and likewise, at what time of year they made this journey is described in these few words, which contain very much doctrine and comfort.

First, both of them are said to have gone on a journey until they came to Bethlehem. Ruth, who was younger and therefore less burdened, does not run ahead of her who was weakened by old age, but she waits for her. And it must not be doubted that she relieved the discomfort of the journey to her mother-in-law with pleasant conversation and whatever other means she could.

It is the duty of younger people, even when they go on a journey with older people, to have concern for them. This phrase also seems to indicate that they did not linger on the journey, but went straight to Bethlehem. For it is not suitable for women to delay for long on the roads.

At their arrival, the whole city was moved. הום (*hum*), in the *niphal* conjugation, means "to make a tumult, an uproar, or noise." In 1 Samuel 4:5, when the ark was brought into the camp, the Israelites are said to have shouted so that the earth was moved. The Septuagint renders it καὶ ἤχησεν, "and it resounded," just as also in this passage. In 1 Kings 1:45, when the king was chosen, the city was in a tumult or shaken with an uproar. In Matthew 21, when Christ entered the city of Jerusalem, "the whole city" (πᾶσα ἡ πόλις), says the evangelist, ἐσείσθη, that is, "was moved." So in this passage the city was moved. That is, they were astonished and had various conversations about the arrival of these poor women. They crowded together to see them, as happens in many cities, sometimes too shamelessly, if some strangers enter a city. They marveled at the change of circumstances.

Hence it appears that this woman Naomi was very famous and that Elimelech her husband was a distinguished man. For there is no great gathering of people on account of the arrival of men of low condition. Moreover, they said, "*Is this Naomi?*" נעם (*naam*) means "to be lovely, delightful, and pleasant." The sense is, "This is not that very noble woman who has endured so many evils, is it? Even this lovely and pleasant woman? She certainly does not accord with her name. We were Trojans.[1] Good God, how much has she changed!" Although there were some who said these things with good intentions and meanwhile marveled at such a great change, nevertheless, it is probable that most mocked her because she had lost her beauty and also her wealth while seeking a better condition, as are the manners of the common people. Now it intensely torments us if others mock us when we are in a bad condition and do not rather sympathize with us. We see that even the strongest men are greatly upset by mockery.

---

1. The expression *Fuimus Troes* first appears in Verg. *Aen.* 2.324. In the original context, Panthous, the priest of Apollo, speaks these words after the fall of Troy to express that they were once Trojans, but are no more. The words indicate a fall from prosperity to misery. Likewise, the expression here indicates that Naomi, in accordance with her name, was once beautiful and pleasant, but is so no more.

Incidentally, we also learn that beauty is a fragile good, which is destroyed by diseases, old age, mistreatment, and in many other ways. Therefore, we must not trust too much in beauty. There also exist among the pagans excellent maxims on this subject.

She asks that from then on they call her not Naomi, but rather Mara, that is, "bitter, sad, and afflicted," because of the bitterness with which she was afflicted by God Himself. And this, which she said in a word, she afterward explains more fully: *"I went out full, but the LORD hath brought me back empty."* "I had a husband, children, and wealth; now I am destitute of all these things. And therefore, I do not accord with my name. My affairs are no longer in the condition they were in when I was in the flower of my age and beauty. God presses and humbles me with various troubles. Therefore, another name suits my condition."

The Pious Are Not Without Tribulation

From these words we learn that wherever on earth they go, whether they are at home or elsewhere, the pious will not be without their own tribulation. When Naomi returns to her fatherland, she is received with sneers. In the region of Moab, too, she no doubt had to see and hear many things that gravely wounded her soul. God certainly grants His own a temporary respite, but He wills that in the meantime they collect their minds and prepare themselves for future struggles. Indeed, we ought not to request from God that we might live without tribulation, since those children "whom he loveth he chasteneth" (Heb. 12). "All that will live godly suffer persecution" (2 Tim. 3). "We must through many afflictions enter into the kingdom of heaven" (Acts 14). Therefore, let us not consider it evidence that God is angry if He burdens us with various troubles.

Patience

In the second place, we must see how Naomi conducted herself in that new tribulation and in the other troubles with which she was heavily oppressed. With patience she overcame all evils. She allows those who mock her to call her Mara instead of Naomi, if they so wish. She utters nothing impiously against God or reproachfully against man. The old

woman could easily have found some things with which she might have
attacked those who were coming against her, by saying, "How impudent are you? What is the meaning of this throng? Have you never seen
poor and afflicted women? Do you have nothing to do at home? Are you
rejoicing in others' troubles? You are certainly proving your foolishness,
or rather, your malice." But she does not use harsh words, but deals with
them calmly. And she freely confesses that her own affairs have been put
in a bad situation.

She Acknowledges That God Is the Author of Her Afflictions
How was she able to disregard the voices of the people and lightly bear so
many evils when we are all impatient by nature? First, she acknowledges
and confesses that these things did not happen by chance, but that God
is the primary author of these troubles, who rightly regulates all things
according to His good will and who wrongs no one. She says, "*God hath
brought me back.... He hath afflicted me.... He hath harmed me.*" She
accuses neither the Moabite women, nor her husband or children, nor
fortune. She attributes all these things to the Lord. If we believe that
God, who is our just and most merciful Father, inflicts tribulation on
us, we are more patient. Joseph is an example to us, who said that he
had been sent to Egypt by God,[2] and likewise David, who said that God
had commanded Shimei to curse him.[3] We must not think about what
sort of people they are who harm us with words or deeds, but what sort
of people we are, by what causes we have provoked the wrath of God
against us, and what we deserve, and submit ourselves to Him. If we
attend only to secondary causes, we will never be at peace in our souls.

Next, she acknowledges that God has sent these troubles on her for
good, not to destroy her. For she says that He humbled her. This word
means "to afflict, to humble." For humility follows from affliction. Hard-
ship gives understanding. Naomi was not without her vices. Perhaps,
as often happens, she did not recognize how distinguished a husband
she had before he died. The same could be said about her children, her

2. Gen. 50:20.
3. 2 Sam. 16:10–11.

wealth, her good health, and her other blessings. Or else she was proud of them and trusted too much in them. God snatches from us those things in which we place our hope and trust, so that we will wholly depend on Him alone.

Usefulness of Tribulation

In the Psalms, David says, "It is good, LORD, that thou hast humbled me."[4] Great is the usefulness of this tribulation, which should move us to patience. God often prepares a way for greater things by afflicting us. It is as if someone demolishes an old house to construct a new and more splendid one. In addition, Naomi says twice that she has been afflicted by the Lord, Shaddai, the Almighty, who can easily turn adverse circumstances into favorable circumstances. In all afflictions you should consider that God is omnipotent, and so it is not difficult for Him, if He wills and if a blessing on His children demands it, to deliver them from the greatest evils. He makes the poor rich. He gives health to the sick. No, rather, He raises the dead and often adorns the despised with great authority. In addition, He sometimes brings His own children into the greatest difficulties so that afterward they will recognize Him alone as their deliverer and give Him thanks.

In the last place, it is noted at what time of year Naomi returned to her fatherland, namely, in the springtime, when the barley harvest was beginning. Around the feast of Passover they began to reap the barley. The Chaldean translator says that they arrived on the first day of Passover, when the Israelites began to reap a bundle of the firstfruits, which was barley.[5] It is also written in Leviticus 23 that the Israelites, on the fifteenth day of the month Nisan, offered a bundle of ears of the firstfruits of their crops. Moreover, the Hebrew interpreters also affirm that this bundle was barley. This matter is mentioned because of the story in the following chapter, how Ruth gathered ears of grain and became acquainted with Boaz.

---

4. Ps. 119:71.
5. Tg. Ruth 1:22.

We Ought Not to Miss an Opportunity

Next, Naomi teaches by this example that we should not neglect an opportunity, which is, as Cicero says, "a time that has in itself a suitable aptness for doing or not doing something."[6] This is very important in beginning and finishing business. For everything, as Solomon says in Ecclesiastes, has its own time.[7] Paul, in Ephesians and Colossians, tells us to redeem the time, a metaphor taken from buyers.[8] He who allows an opportunity to slip away can no longer seize it afterward. The old man in Plautus says, "When you are a young man, then when your blood is vigorous, it is fitting for you to give attention to obtaining wealth."[9] Young men, when the opportunity is offered, should learn literature and true religion. They should not put it off to other times, which are less suited to learning these things. When Naomi first hopes that she can gather a living from the field, she returns to her fatherland; she does not put the matter off until all the crops and produce have been gathered. Solomon, in Proverbs 10, says, "He that gathereth in summer is a wise son; but he that sleepeth in harvest is a man that causeth shame." In chapter 20: "The sluggard will not plough by reason of the cold; therefore shall he beg in summer and not have bread."

6. Cic. *Inv. rhet.* 1.27.40.
7. Eccl. 3:1.
8. Eph. 5:16; Col. 4:5.
9. Plaut. *Merc.* 3.2.7–8.

Ruth 2:1–3

1 *Now Naomi had a kinsman of her husband's (Naomi's husband had a kinsman), an industrious man of the family of Elimelech, whose name was Boaz.*

2 *And Ruth the Moabitess said the following unto Naomi: "Let me now go, please, to the field so that I might glean ears of corn after him in whose sight I shall find grace." And she said unto her, "Go, my daughter."*

3 *So she went, and came, and gleaned (ears of corn) in the field after the reapers. And she happened by chance to light on this part that belonged unto Boaz, who was of the family of Elimelech.*

On what occasion Ruth converted to the true faith and followed her mother-in-law into Judah is explained in the previous chapter. Now this chapter recounts how she became acquainted with Boaz. Besides a distinguished example of divine providence, there are also set forth to us by the Holy Spirit in this chapter examples of many duties or virtues in Ruth, her mother-in-law, Naomi, and likewise also Boaz and his family.

Who Boaz Was
First, it is revealed that Boaz was related to Elimelech and was a man of חיל (*chail*), which means "power," "strength of soul and body," and likewise "wealth." He was, so it appears, a wise, manly, and wealthy man, which is set forth in advance as important background information for the rest of the narrative. The Hebrew and Chaldean interpreters think that this Boaz was the judge Abesa, or Ibzan, because in Judges 12 it

says that after Jephthah, Abesa of Bethlehem judged Israel.[1] As far as this relationship is concerned, Bibliander, in his books *On the Demonstration of the Gospel* (which are not yet published), drawing from the chronicles of the Hebrews, comments that Elimelech and Nahshon were brothers.[2] But Lyra, in his commentaries on this book, remarks that Elimelech and Salmon, Boaz's father, were brothers, about which we will also say something later.[3]

Gleaning
Ruth asks her mother-in-law for permission to go into the field to gather ears of grain. The Greeks call gleaning καλάμων συλλογὴν and gathering ears of grain καλαμᾶσθαι, which was permitted by the law (Lev. 19): "When thou reapest the harvest of your land, thou shalt not wholly reap the corners of thy field, and neither shalt thou gather the gleanings (of the remaining ears of corn) of thy harvest. Also, thou shalt not glean thy vineyard, neither shalt thou gather seeds of grapes (that fall down), but thou shalt leave them for the poor and stranger. I am the LORD your God." Afterward, in chapter 23: "And when ye reap the harvest of your land, thou shalt not wholly reap the corners of thy field when thou reapest, neither shalt thou gather what remaineth when thou reapest, but thou shalt gather it for the poor and stranger. I am the LORD your God." Deuteronomy 24:

> When thou reapest thine harvest in thy field, and hast forgot a
> sheaf in thy field, thou shalt not go again to fetch it. But it shall
> be for the stranger, for the fatherless, and for the widow, that the
> LORD thy God may bless thee in all the work of thine hands.
> When thou beatest thine olive trees, thou shalt not carefully
> search the boughs after thee, but it shall be for the stranger, for
> the fatherless, and for the widow. When thou gatherest the grapes
> of thy vineyard, thou shalt not look for clusters after thee, but thou
> shalt leave it for the stranger, for the fatherless, and for the widow.

---

1. Tg. Ruth 1:1, 6; 4:21.
2. I have not been able to identify the work to which Lavater refers, or whether it was even published.
3. Lyra, *Biblia*, fol. 279r, 280r.

And thou shalt remember that thou also wast a bondman in the land of Egypt, and therefore I command thee to do this thing.

In addition, in Leviticus 25 He commands that the seventh year be a Sabbath of the Lord. They were neither to sow nor prune vineyards, but they granted to the poor and to strangers that which grew of its own accord. They did likewise in the year of Jubilee. In Matthew 12, the Pharisees do not accuse Christ's disciples, who were making their way through the cornfields on the Sabbath and were picking ears of grain and eating them, of theft or robbery, but of violating the Sabbath. Now even though it was permissible for strangers and widows to gather ears of grain, nevertheless, Ruth was not willing to do it without consulting her mother-in-law.

What Daughters-in-Law Should Do
Daughters-in-law learn from the example of this woman in what stature they should hold their mothers-in-law and how much honor they should give them. She does not disregard her mother-in-law, though she had lost her husband and had no children by him and was, moreover, forced to support her. She was not otherwise disposed toward her than if she had actually been her own mother. The commandment of the Lord about honoring parents also includes fathers-in-law and mothers-in-law. Honor also consists in daughters-in-law consulting their mothers-in-law, when they wish to go on a journey or do other things that are of some significance. There are today few daughters-in-law, no rather, even daughters, who behave so modestly toward their parents. If they should support their mothers as Ruth supported her mother-in-law and, moreover, should consult with them about doing things, good God, how many quarrels would they remove! If parents willingly and from natural affection, which they have toward their children, warn them about what they must do or avoid, are not the parents, nevertheless, overwhelmed with reproaches! How many sons are there who at night against their parents' will leave home and wander around in the streets! How many daughters run out to all kinds of shows and dances!

Naomi kindly responds, "*Go, my daughter.*" Mothers-in-law who are consulted by their daughters-in-law should not laugh at them or attack them with bitter words, but should respond kindly, so that they will feel that they are like daughters to them. Again, she calls her "daughter." She does not verbally abuse her. It is certainly useful and proper for foreign widows, especially if they are young and beautiful, to stay at home, not to go out of their houses alone, and not to wander in the streets, so that they will not come under suspicion of indecency or be violated, as we read about Dinah, Jacob's daughter.[4] Necessity, which is the last and greatest weapon, urged her to go out of her house and make a living for herself and her mother-in-law. Parents should not be too rigid toward their children. They should allow children to obtain from them what is appropriate.

Ruth entered the field and gathered ears of grain. She does not idly await food from heaven, she does not steal others' things, she does not prostitute her body to get what she needs, but she applies herself to honest labor and, indeed, to very hard labor. For it is difficult and laborious to harvest and gather crops and, likewise, to look for ears of grain through the fields when the sun is hottest. Moreover, she did not want to be troublesome to anyone by gathering ears of grain. She promises that she will gather in the field of the one in whose sight she has found favor, that is, to whom she is pleasing, by whose good grace this can be done. She also seizes the opportunity to make a living. Unlike many women, she did not have to be forced to work, but she willingly and industriously did what she had to do.

On Labor

Pious women should imitate this distinguished example of labor and humility. In Ephesians 4, Paul writes, "Let him that stole steal no more. Let him labor, working with his hands the thing which is good, that he may be able to give to him that needeth." It is not that he imposes on everyone the need to labor with their hands, but he says that we must endure all the most difficult hardships rather than use deceit, fraud, and various tricks, which are included in the word "theft." Now there is not one kind of labor. There is labor that requires the mind rather than the

---

4. Gen. 34:1–2.

body: to pronounce judgment, to manage a church or school, to practice medicine, and so on. For he who does not think that judges, preachers, teachers, and physicians labor is no less absurd than if someone feels that on a ship only those who pump out the bilgewater and drive the oars labor, and not the one who sits at the helm on the poop deck. Next, there is labor that especially demands bodily strength, and this is not of one kind. For there are different crafts and businesses. As each and every member in the body has its own function, so in the body of the republic every man is assigned his labor, and it would not be useful for everyone to practice one craft. The apostle commands us to work τὸ ἀγαθὸν, something good and honest. For there are useless skills (ματαιοτεχνίαι), such as those of tight-rope walkers and vagabond beggars,[5] and evil skills (κακοτεχνίαι), such as those of monopolists, moneylenders, magicians, and pimps, for whom it would be better to do nothing than to exercise their skills and labors. There are those who only serve men's desires. God commends to us honest labor. Before the fall, He gave to Adam a paradise to be cultivated.[6] He would not have wanted him to be idle, but to cultivate the garden, which Adam could have done without trouble. After the fall, God wanted him to eat his bread in the sweat of his face and with hard labor to cultivate the land, which produced thorns because of his sins.[7] In Proverbs 6, Solomon stirs us up to labor by the example of the ant, and through mimesis he imitates the speech of sluggards, whom we can scarcely drag out of bed. The wise men of the gentiles also commend labor and condemn idleness. The Massilians, as Valerius Maximus testifies, shut their gates to all who through some pretense of religion were seeking food without labor.[8] If the same thing had been done in several previous ages, we would not have so many orders of monks.[9] Moreover, every man ought

---

5. The "vagabond beggars" (*agyrtae*) often had a religious character (e.g., mendicant friars).

6. Gen. 2:8, 15.

7. Gen. 3:17–19.

8. Val. Max. 2.6.7.

9. Lavater is referring to the mendicant orders.

to undertake not only honest labor in his vocation, but also at a lawful time, not on holy days, and likewise, while his strength permits. Nor is there a reason that any man should wear himself out through immoderate labor. Likewise, what you get through your labors must be ascribed to the blessing of God. In 1 Thessalonians 4 and 2 Thessalonians 3, the apostle adds the reason why pious men must labor industriously, namely, so that they can relieve the needy and so that they can have what they need and not be a burden to others, as healthy beggars, Anabaptists,[10] and other idle men are.

Nothing Happens by Chance

By chance she comes into the field of Boaz, or it happens as an accidental or fated event. The word מקרה (*mikraeh*) means "an accidental, fated, or chance event." 1 Samuel 6:9 says about the ark, "If it goeth up to Bethshemesh, then it hath done us all this evil, but if not, then we shall know that it is by no means his hand that smote us; it was a chance that happened to us." If you consider Ruth's will, it was fortuitous that she entered that field. But if you consider God's plan, He led her into it as though by the hand. What seems to us to happen by chance does not happen apart from God's providence. The point can be demonstrated by an example taken from the law of God, Exodus 21 and Deuteronomy 19. If two men are felling trees and an axe slips out of the hand of one and kills the one next to him, he did this unintentionally, and therefore, asylum was opened to him, but as far as it concerns God, He handed the other man over for certain reasons. Jerome, in his comments on Jeremiah 12, says that nothing good or bad happens randomly and without providence, but that all things happen by the judgment of God.[11] As it says in the Proverbs of Solomon, lots are governed by God.[12] If a sparrow does not fall to the ground apart from the will of God, what can

---

10. Lavater is presumably alluding to the Anabaptists' communities of goods, in which members of the community had no private property, but shared everything.

11. Jerome, *Explanatio Sancti Hieronymi Presbyteri in Jeremiam Prophetam*, vol. 4 of *Sancti Eusebii Hieronymi Stridonensis Presbyteri Operum*, ed. Dominic Vallarsi, 2nd ed. (Venice: Zerletti, 1767), 926.

12. Prov. 16:33.

happen by chance in human affairs that does not happen by the certain plan of God?[13] Moreover, we see that God directs those men who undertake honest labor and blesses them. We will hear more later on this subject, for Ruth was pleasing to Boaz and his family.

---

13. Matt. 10:29–31; Luke 12:6–7.

Ruth 2:4–7

4 *Meanwhile, behold, Boaz came from Bethlehem, and said unto the reapers, "The LORD be with you." They said unto him, "The LORD bless thee."*

5 *Then said Boaz unto his servant that was set over the reapers, "Whose damsel is this?"*

6 *The servant that was set over the reapers answered and said, "It is the Moabitish damsel that came back with Naomi out of the country of Moab.*

7 *She said, 'I pray you, let me glean, and I will glean (ears of grain) after the reapers among the sheaves.' And she came and hath continued from the beginning of the morning until now. Now she tarrieth in the house for a little bit."*

We said above that Ruth, after previously getting permission from her mother-in-law, gathered ears of grain behind the reapers, and by chance, or to speak more accurately, by the providence of God, she entered into the field of Boaz, her kinsman. Now what happened there the Holy Spirit carefully explains in these and the following verses.

Blessing
First, it is reported that Boaz, coming to the field from Bethlehem, greeted his reapers, who responded, "The LORD bless thee." The word "blessing," which appears everywhere in sacred literature, does not have one meaning. For sometimes it means "to praise" and "to give thanks," as

when David, in 1 Samuel 25, says to Abigail, "Blessed be the LORD God of Israel, which sent thee this day to meet me." Sometimes it means "to pray for good things," as the patriarch Jacob, in Genesis 48, blessed his children, that is, prayed that it would be well with them. In Genesis 37, Jacob, when he came to the king and departed from him, blessed him, that is, greeted him and bid him farewell, thanked him, and wished him well. When it is attributed to God, it means "to do well," since God works by speaking. Proverbs 10 says, "The blessing of the LORD, it maketh rich," that is, God increases and preserves wealth. In reading Sacred Scripture we must consider what the simple use of this word is, as when in this passage they say, "*The LORD bless thee.*" The meaning is, "May He give you an abundant harvest and, likewise, other good things, both of the body and of the soul."

Greeting

We have an example in this passage of a greeting. The custom of greeting is not only very ancient, but also very useful for gaining and strengthening love, which our Savior earnestly commends to all the pious. An angel also greeted Gideon with the following words when he was threshing wheat: "The LORD is with thee, mighty man of valor" (Judg. 6). It is included among the duties of the priests to bless the children of Israel. A solemn blessing is contained in Numbers 6. Some Anabaptists deny that men are to be greeted, citing what Christ said to the seventy disciples in Luke 10: "Salute no man on the way." But He meant nothing else than that they should not allow themselves to be distracted from their duty under the pretext of a greeting. Or if you understand it literally, it was a personal or special command, not a general one. When the angel greets the Blessed Virgin, he uses the same formula that Boaz uses in this passage. Christ Himself also greeted his disciples, saying, "Peace be unto you."[1] The apostle Paul begins his letters with a greeting and closes them with greetings.[2] He puts down the names of those whom he wishes to greet and, likewise, of those who wish well to others. If we greet others,

1. Luke 24:36; John 20:19, 21, 26.
2. Rom. 1:1–7; 16:1–24; 1 Cor. 1:1–3; 16:19–24; 2 Cor. 1:1–2; 13:11–14; Gal. 1:1–5; 6:18; Eph. 1:1–2; 6:23–24; Phil. 1:1–2; 4:20–23; Col. 1:1–2; 4:10–18; 1 Thess.

whether by speech or in writing, through ourselves or through others, it is incredible how much this does for uniting souls. Nevertheless, we must beware of doing this with a hypocritical mind. It is part of courteousness and politeness to greet others and to bless them. If wealthy and powerful men address the poor in a friendly manner, the poor are very touched, seeing that they are not despised by the wealthy and powerful. Nor must we doubt that Boaz's greeting was very pleasing to the reapers. There are those who, out of hatred and ill will, disdain to greet others; the commandment of Christ ought to enter their minds, that we should pray for our enemies and bless them.[3] How often does it happen that those who do not want to greet each other and afterward are torn apart and separated from each other would want nothing more than to live together and to discharge all the duties of politeness to each other?

Heads of Households Should See What Their People Are Doing

An example of a good householder in regard to domestic economy is also set forth. He goes out to his reapers and inspects what is being done in the field. For the master's presence is very useful for managing something well. According to Pliny, in his *Natural History*, the ancients said that the master's eye is very fertile in the field.[4] Aristotle, in his *Economics*, writes about someone who, when he was asked what the best manure was, answered, "The master's footprints."[5] Even if someone has good and faithful servants or serfs, nevertheless, when the masters are away, they do everything more carelessly and negligently. Titus Livy also elegantly said that those things do not usually turn out very prosperously that are done with others' eyes.[6] On this subject, consult Erasmus's proverb, "The forehead is better than the back of the head."[7] Negligent heads of households destroy both themselves and their families. These

---

1:1; 5:26–28; 2 Thess. 1:1–2; 3:16–18; 1 Tim. 1:1–2; 6:21; 2 Tim. 1:1–2; 4:19–22; Titus 1:1–4; 3:15; Philemon 1–3, 23–25.

3. Matt. 5:44; Luke 6:28.

4. Plin. *HN* 18.8.

5. Arist. *Oec.* 1.6.3, 1345a5–6.

6. This exact expression does not appear in Livy, but a similar expression appears at 26.22.6.

7. Erasmus, *Adagia* 1.2.19. Cf. Cato, *Agr.* 4.

things can also be applied to more powerful offices, namely, to kings and bishops, that they will not do everything by others' hands, ears, and eyes, while in the meantime they indulge their desires.

Boaz asks his servant, whom he had set over the reapers (Josephus calls him "the overseer of the fields" [ἀγρονόμον]),[8] about Ruth, namely, who she is and whose wife or daughter she is. He does not ask as some of the young men ask, so that they might violate the women, but since he saw that she was a stranger and troubled. His steward responds that she is a Moabitess who had recently come with Naomi, and he bestows on her great praise. It did not enter his mind that she would be his wife. But see how wonderfully God leads her!

Heads of households ought to imitate the fact that Boaz sets a servant over the reapers who prescribes to each man his duty so that everything will be done in order and who is without doubt an industrious man. For unless in large families individuals know what they must do and have their own overseers and leaders, affairs will not be managed very successfully. As in an army order is necessary, so in a household. The servant carefully observed Ruth so that he could answer his master when he asked about her. So servants should carefully observe all things that concern them so that they can give an account to their masters about everything.

The Servant Praises Ruth

We also must note that he praises Ruth. He did not, as the envious usually do, find fault with or diminish the things in her that deserve praise. Nor does he hate or insult her because she is a foreigner. Those who deserve praise ought to be praised for their virtues. Virtue is not to be hated. Often, the poor who are commended to the rich by the latter's servants receive great favors from them. This kind of duty is required of us, that when we ourselves cannot help pious men by our wealth or counsel, at least we intercede for them with others who can, which can be done without troubling us.

Moreover, he states two things about Ruth that are worthy of praise and that we ought to imitate. One is that she asked them for permission

---

8. Joseph. *AJ* 5.324, 325. Josephus, however, uses the term ἀγροκόμος.

to gather ears of grain. The law of Moses expressly allowed strangers and widows to gather ears of grain. Nevertheless, she is not willing to use that privilege if the masters of the field are unwilling, but only if she does it with their good grace. There are many who, though the owners are unwilling and opposed, against divine and human commands concerning theft and robbery, enter others' fields and meadows, gather their crops, destroy their hedges, and do them great harm.

The other thing that he commends in her is that she is industrious and diligent; from morning until now, that is, until noon, she attended to her labor. As soon as she had eaten, she returned to work. "Now she tarrieth in the house for a little bit." Münster renders it, "After she took a short break in the cottage."⁹ The Zürich version has, "She sat in the little cottage for a very short time."¹⁰ Some understand it to mean that she was in the house not even a moment. The ancient translator and the Septuagint held this view.¹¹ Others understand it to mean that she always stood, except for a short time when she either returned home or tarried in the little cottage (which perhaps was in the field so that they could get shade and collect their strength). For those places are very hot in harvest time. She was not one of those girls who wander idly through the streets or spend the whole day looking out their windows. But rather she was of the sort that is celebrated in the last chapter of Solomon's Proverbs about whom it mentions, among other things, that she attended to her labors day and night. This should be considered more valuable in women than extraordinary beauty. There are few children today, and few hired servants, who are as persistent in their labors as she was.

---

9. *Biblia Sacra utriusque testamenti*, trans. Sebastian Münster and Desiderius Erasmus (Zürich: Froschauer, 1539), fol. 285r.

10. *Biblia Sacrosancta testamenti veteris & novi, e sacra Hebraeorum lingua Graecorumque fontibus, consultis simul orthodoxis interpretibus, religiosissime translata in sermonem Latinum*, trans. Leo Jud, Theodor Bibliander, Konrad Pellikan, Petrus Cholinus, and Rudolf Gwalther (Zürich: Froschauer, 1543), fol. 120v. For an informative discussion of this version and Münster's version, see Bruce Gordon, "Remembering Jerome and Forgetting Zwingli: The Zurich Latin Bible of 1543 and the Establishment of Heinrich Bullinger's Church," *Zwingliana* 41 (2014): 1–33.

11. The "ancient translator" (*vetus interpres*) refers to Jerome, the translator of the Vulgate.

Ruth 2:8–10

8 *Then said Boaz unto Ruth, "Hearest thou not, my daughter? Go not to glean in another field, neither go from hence, but abide here fast by my maidens.*

9 *Let thine eyes be on the field that they do reap, and go thou after them. Have I not charged the servants that they shall not touch thee? And if thou art athirst, go unto the vessels, and drink of that which the servants have drawn."*

10 *Then she fell on her face, and bowed herself to (prostrated herself upon) the ground, and said unto him, "Why have I found grace in thine eyes, that thou shouldest take knowledge of me, seeing I am a stranger?"*

This passage explains how Boaz addressed Ruth and how she behaved toward him. Boaz addresses her with friendly words, calling her "daughter" because of his age and status, for he was old and belonged to the order of elders. When Scripture commands sons and daughters to respect their parents, it means, among others, younger people also, whose duty it is to reverently honor their elders, especially their magistrates. Next, he commands her not to gather ears of grain in others' fields. For perhaps, so that she would not be troublesome to him, she would have wanted to glean not only in his field, but in others' also. Since he knows that she is an extraordinary woman, he wants to do her favors. He does not send her away to others, as some usually do, who, though they easily can and should support their poor relatives, deny this care to them. He commands her not to go from the place where she already was to another, but to stay with his girls and follow them, partly so that if she were alone in some field of his, she would not be exposed to harm, from which his men easily could have defended her, and partly so that if she were with his servants, who no doubt passed the time with pleasant conversation, jokes, and singing, she would gather ears of grain with less trouble. For it is useful for men who are sad and disturbed frequently to spend time with others, talk with others, and as much as possible avoid solitude. *"Hearest thou not, my daughter?"* that is, "that I have commanded you not to gather in someone else's field?" The Germans also say, "Did you hear it?" (*Hast du es gehört?*), when they earnestly give some command to others and impress it on them. In addition, he promises her protection against his servants. *"Have I not,"* he says (that is, he most certainly has), *"charged the servants that they shall not touch thee?"* The Hebrews express in a question what they vehemently want to affirm. Below, at 3:1, it says, *"My daughter, shall I not seek rest for thee, that it may be well with thee?"* First Samuel 10:1 says, "Is it not (that is, the situation is such as I told you) because the LORD hath anointed thee to be captain over his inheritance?" In 1 Samuel 23, the traitors of Ziph say to Saul, "Doth not David dwell with us in strongholds in the wood?" So I understand what the Samaritan woman in John 4 says, "Is not this the Christ?" to mean that it certainly is the Christ.

Impudent Servants Act with Impunity in Harvest Time

During the harvest and vintage, great liberty, or rather license, is granted to workmen to lighten their labors, but they sometimes abuse that privilege, shamefully violate pure and chaste virgins, and insolently do many things. His servants also could have done the same; therefore, he promises that he will restrain them from hurting her.

Duty of the Head of the Household

Now it is the duty of the head of the household to guard the chastity not only of his daughters and maidservants, but also of other virgins, that he not say anything obscene by which they might be inflamed to act shamefully. He should instill in them how shameful whoring is and how defiled daughters are embarrassed by public disgrace. He should turn them away from all the things (from depraved conversations, companionship with men who are under suspicion, shameful shows and dances, and so on) by which they can be incited to lust, especially if he sees that they are lascivious and impudent. There are some who say that this protection is applied to daughters in vain. But young people often sin out of ignorance. Of how much wickedness do they make themselves guilty who prostitute their maidservants (whose chastity they are obligated to protect and whose parents they practically are) to others, or who defile them themselves! Likewise, he ought to beware lest the bodies, reputations, or wealth of his neighbors or any others are harmed by his domestic servants.

He ought to restrain not only his domestic men, but also his animals (such as dogs, horses, cows, and so on) from being troublesome to others. In the law it says, "If the ox were wont to push with his horn in time past, and it hath been testified to his owner, and he hath not kept him in, but that he hath killed a man or a woman, then the ox shall be stoned, and they shall also put his owner to death."[1] Likewise, "If fire break out and come upon the ears of corn and take hold of the stacks of corn, or the standing corn in the fields, he that kindled the fire shall make restitution."[2] "If a man shall open or dig a pit, and not cover it… the owner shall give money for the beasts."[3] The Lord commanded the roofs on houses, which were flat, to be walled so that no one would fall off.[4]

He adds that if she is thirsty, she should go to the vessels and drink from the water that the servants have drawn. There is a great scarcity of water in those places. Palestine indeed has its own rivers, streams, lakes, and springs. But nevertheless, in many places the springs dry up in the very hot environment so that sometimes water must be sought far away. In 1540 this also happened in many places in our own Switzerland, which abounds in water. In Genesis 26, Isaac's servants dug wells, which he had to cede to others for the sake of peace. In Exodus 2, Moses helps

---

1. Ex. 21:29.
2. Ex. 22:6.
3. Ex. 21:33–34.
4. Deut. 22:8.

Jethro's daughters, who were drawing water for their flocks, when the shepherds oppose them, because there were no other springs in those places. It is a great kindness that Boaz tells Ruth to take a drink from his vessels, that is, his flasks or bottles. Just as *arma* are taken broadly among the Latins (I may note in passing), namely, for instruments of nearly any art (there are military *arma*, scholastic *arma*, culinary *arma*, and so forth), so קלים (*kelim*) among the Hebrews means "instruments, weapons, ornaments, furniture, or clothes." There seems to be an emphasis on his statement, "*that which my servants have drawn,*" that is, not without labor. "Even if they should say that they drew it by their own labor and wish to drive you away, nevertheless, I want you to drink, with no one standing in your way." Afterward, he orders her to eat with his reapers.

Example of Humanity toward the Afflicted
There is set before us in this passage an excellent example of humanity toward the poor, widows, strangers, and especially recent converts to the true faith. On how the latter are to be treated, see Romans 14 and 15. Boaz first addresses Ruth in a friendly manner. He does not wait until she asks him for something. He promises her protection and drink. He grants her more than she would have dared to ask, and he does so with a benevolent spirit.

What was the reason for this humanity and kindness toward Ruth, whom he did not yet know would be joined to him in marriage? Since by faith she had the favor of God, she also experienced the benevolence of men. God even reconciles enemies to those to whom He wishes well, as Solomon says in Proverbs 16. Next, he learned from the report of his steward that she was endowed with extraordinary virtues and, therefore, was worthy of favor and benevolence. If the steward had spoken badly about her, perhaps Boaz would have fostered a hatred toward her. In addition, she was endowed with faith, which is the source of good works, and he saw with his own eyes the industry of this girl in gathering ears of grain.

We must imitate Boaz's humanity. We must assist and treat kindly the poor and strangers. We must defend new converts to the faith against the wrongs to which they are exposed. Next, if we want to have the benevolence and friendship of men, we must especially take care that God favors and is reconciled to us.

Second, it shows how Ruth behaved toward him. First, she fell on her face and bowed herself to the ground. She shows that she does not deserve for Boaz, a distinguished man, to treat her so kindly. השׁח means "to bend down, lower oneself, drop down," and in the *hithpael* form הותשׁה means "to bow down, to bend the head or the rest of the body, to fall prostrate at someone's feet." The Greeks translate it προσκυνεῖν.

Adorare

The Latins generally render חשׁתוה by the word *adorare*. In Exodus 20, in the second commandment of the Decalogue, against images and idols, it says, "Thou shalt not bow down thyself [*adorabis*] to them." Idolaters shout that they do not adore images and that they are wronged if these rumors are spread about them. But they do not know, or certainly do not want to know, what it means to "adore." The Hebrew word means "to bow down and fall prostrate before them." But surely they will not deny that they do this, will they? Therefore, they cannot be excused of idolatry.[5] Among the Latins, *adorare* also means "to bend one's knees, to show honor by prostrating oneself." Now they had a common custom of throwing themselves at the feet of those to whom they wished to give honor. We only bend our knees, unless we enter the presence of great princes, and even then we only fall on our knees before them as suppliants.[6]

Next, she is astonished at and highly values his kindness because, though she is a foreigner, nevertheless, she is favored by him. For exiles and the poor are generally despised by the rich and powerful.

---

5. Lavater is particularly accusing Roman Catholics of committing idolatry through their veneration, or adoration, of images.
6. See the Introduction, p. xvi. In 1524, Hans Lavater, Ludwig Lavater's father, refused to bow down and kiss the pope's feet, despite being instructed to do so.

Ruth's Gratitude

In Ruth we have an illustrious example of humility, gratitude, and modesty. She gives evidence of her humility, partly by an external sign, namely, her bodily gestures, that is, bowing down and lowering herself, and partly by her words. For she says, *"Why have I found grace in thine eyes, that thou shouldest take knowledge of me* (or, *that thou dost know me)?"* It does not mean "to know to a slight degree" (as Martin Borrhaus, the accurate and learned interpreter of the Sacred Scriptures, notes),[7] but "to know affectionately and to have concern for someone." She confesses that she is unworthy of those favors. Humility is an extraordinary virtue, the opposite of which is pride.

Gratitude

She shows her gratitude in the fact that she does not disregard the favors done for her, nor does she diminish them. She does not say, "Now what is this, that you tell me to gather ears of grain? Doesn't the law of God grant this to the poor? And why do you offer water to one who thirsts? Water is for public use. Why do you not rather, since you are so rich, give to me, a poor woman, some excellent gift?" The favor he did for her was certainly not so great in itself. Nevertheless, since it comes from a great and honorable man and a benevolent spirit, she highly values it. The proverb says, "A friend is the best of gifts." By her gratitude she caused Boaz to become more prepared and ready to alleviate her poverty. Those who need others' help should carefully observe this example. They should not be impatient if they do not immediately receive everything they ask for. They should not disregard the things that are conferred on them. They should not threaten that they will take anything by force. Rather, they should consider that others also have their own burdens and that by their importunity they do very great harm both to themselves and to others. For the fountain of favors is obstructed by ingratitude.

---

7. Martin Borrhaus, *In sacram Iosuae, Iudicum, Ruthae, Samuelis & Regum Historiam, mystica Messiae servatoris mundi adumbratione refertam, Martini Borrhai commentarius* (Basel: Johannes Oporinus, 1557), 281.

Modesty

This girl's modesty appears from the fact that she lowers herself to the ground and does not impudently look at Boaz and, next, from the fact that she says little. Modesty is the most praiseworthy thing in a woman. For, as Cicero says, "Modesty is the guardian of all virtues, flees disgrace, and obtains the greatest praise."[8] This modesty, therefore, caused her not to look rather wantonly at Boaz and not to speak with him for too long. Even the gentiles condemn both these vices in women. The Satirist says, "She would be brazen and the sort of woman who also could keep company with men and could speak with commanders in military uniform in her husband's presence with a bold face and unsheathed breasts."[9] The proverb says, "Silence adorns women."[10] The following verse appears in Sophocles: "Silence graces women" (Γυναιξὶ κόσμον ἡ σιγὴ φέρει).[11] Women who eagerly mix in conversation with men they do not know make themselves suspect.

---

8. Cic. Part. or. 79.

9. Juv. 6.399–401.

10. Cf. Desiderius Erasmus, De civilitate morum puerilium (Leipzig: Nicolaus Faber, 1534), "De Conviviis."

11. Soph. Aj. 293.

Twelfth Homily

Ruth 2:11–13

11 *Boaz answered and said, "It hath fully been reported to me all that thou hast done unto thy mother-in-law after thine husband died, and that thou has left thy father and thy mother and the land of thy nativity and art come unto a people which thou knewest not heretofore.*

12 *The* LORD *will recompense (may he recompense) to thee (payment on account of) thy work, and thy reward be perfected by the* LORD *God of Israel, under whose wings thou art come to trust."*

13 *Then she said, "Let me find favor in thy sight, my lord, for that thou has comforted me,[1] though I be not like unto one of thine handmaidens."*

Ruth marvels that she is known and favored by Boaz and that he addresses her affectionately, though she is a foreigner. For we see that it is generally the arrangement that poor foreigners are despised by the rich and powerful. Then he assigns a reason why he embraces her with favor, namely, on account of her faith in the God of Israel and her love toward her mother-in-law.

Ruth Was Endowed with True Faith
We infer that she was endowed with true faith from the fact that she left her native soil, her parents, her relatives, and the gods of her fathers and embraced the Israelite religion. Abraham's faith is celebrated, who,

---

1. The text does not contain the following clause: *"And for that thou hast spoken unto the heart of thine handmaid."* This clause, however, appears in Lavater's commentary below.

when God called him to a foreign land, immediately left everything and followed Him without turning back.[2] Therefore, she shows that she is in fact a daughter of Abraham, since she preferred on account of true religion to spend her life among foreigners than in her own fatherland. It also appears that she was endowed with true faith from the fact that Boaz says that she had come to trust under the wings of the Lord, that is, that she would spend her life safely under His defense and protection. As many as place their trust in God will not perish. However the devil rages, nevertheless, he cannot snatch them out of God's hand.

Metaphor of Wings in the Scriptures
The metaphor is taken from birds or hens that cover their chicks with their wings, keep them warm, and protect them. David often used this metaphor in the Psalms to show God's zeal in preserving the pious. As the hen clucks and hides her chicks under her wings when the kite ambushes her, so God defends the pious and soothingly calls them to Himself. In Psalm 17, the prophet says, "Keep me as the black of the pupil of the eye, hide me in the shadow of thy wings." Psalm 36: "How precious is thy mercy, O God! Therefore, the children of men put their trust in the shadow of thy wings." Psalm 57: "Be merciful unto me, O God, be merciful unto me. For my soul trusteth in thee, and in the shadow of thy wings I trust, until the grief be overpast." Psalm 61: "I will abide in thy tabernacle forever; I will trust in the covert of thy wings." Psalm 63: "My mouth praiseth thee, when I remember thee upon my bed and meditate on thee in the night watches. Because thou hast been my help, and in the shadow of thy wings I rejoice." Psalm 91 teaches that they are happy who commit themselves to God's care and providence. It says, "He shall cover thee with his wings, and under his wings shalt thou be secure. His truth shall be thy shield and buckler." Isaiah 31 also, in a simile taken from birds or a hen, shows that the city of Jerusalem is to be defended against the Assyrians' attack. "As birds flying," it says, "the LORD of hosts will defend Jerusalem; defending also he will deliver it; and passing over he will preserve it." Christ used this same simile in Matthew 23, saying,

2. Heb. 11:8.

"How often would I have gathered thy children together, O Jerusalem, even as a hen gathereth her chickens under her wings, and ye would not!" The word ὄρνις, the grammarians note, means "bird" in a general sense and "hen" in a specific sense.

From Where She Acquired Faith

But from where did Ruth acquire that faith? Saint Paul, in Romans 10, says, "Faith cometh by hearing, and hearing by the word of God." She probably heard many things from her husband, her father-in-law, and her mother-in-law about the creation, fall, and restoration of man, about the promised Messiah, and so on. Meanwhile, God opened her heart so that she understood what was said and assented to it.

We also see, by the way, that those who forsake idolatry and embrace the true faith retreat as into a haven and refuge. As chicks, if they wander, are exposed to being ambushed and preyed on by hawks and other birds of prey but are defended under the wings of their mother, so those who forsake true religion and seek elsewhere for the protection of salvation throw themselves into manifest danger to their souls. God indeed exercises even His own believers with various afflictions, but at the same time He comforts them. Many think that they are running into the most certain danger to their lives and fortunes if they embrace the gospel and so, against conscience, they hold fast to false doctrine. Nevertheless, vexed by pricks to their conscience, they lead an unpleasant and miserable life.

Another thing that Boaz praises in her is that she loved her mother-in-law, although her husband had departed from this life childless and her mother-in-law was a foreigner. From this it is easy to infer how much she loved her husband. Moreover, by her example she teaches spouses to love each other and to honor each other in all their conjugal duties. For it is known from experience how many good things arise from good marriages and how many bad things arise from bad marriages.

What Good Works Are

It adds that he prayed for Ruth's prosperity. "*May the LORD recompense to thee thy work,*" he says, "*and thy reward be perfected by God,*" that is,

"May God repay you in this and the future life." The papists produce this passage and others like it, many of which appear everywhere in the Sacred Scriptures, to show that we merit eternal life by our good works. By "good works" they mean not only those that are done by the faithful through the Spirit of God and according to His Word, but also the arbitrary works that the foolishness and avarice of men devised. And they go so far that they sell the works that they call "supererogatory" to others for a price. Hence they have placed their hope and trust in their own works and have attributed very much to their own strength. And so they have obscured the doctrine of Christ's merit.

Whether We Merit Eternal Life by Our Works
Therefore, it is useful to know how these passages that mention recompense, reward, remuneration, and so forth are to be understood. Scripture teaches that God forgives our sins and bestows on us eternal life out of mere mercy through faith on account of Christ. A notable passage is in Ephesians 2: "It is the gift of God." Now He promises a recompense for works, not because of their worth, but because of the grace with which God embraces believers. Augustine correctly writes that God crowns in us His gifts, not our merits.[3] For, first, He confers on us His grace so that we will do what is good. Next, out of mere grace He adorns with rewards the good that He Himself worked in us. Eternal life is called a recompense, not properly, nor do the pious expect eternal life as a merit for their works, but as the free gift of God.

Condition of Merit
We certainly do not deny that God is the rewarder of good actions, but by no means do we merit by them such great liberality from Him. For it is the condition of merit, first, that we give of our own. But what do we have that we did not receive?[4] The Lord gives us the will and ability to do right. Next, it is required in merit that we not be bound to do something, but do it willingly and voluntarily. But even if we have

3. August. *Grat.* 6.15.
4. 1 Cor. 4:7.

done everything, nevertheless, we are unprofitable servants (Luke 17). Likewise, it is required that there be some equality or proportion between what is given and what is received. But what equality can there be between our works and eternal life? If you say that we merit eternal damnation for our sins and, therefore, we merit eternal life for our good works, it is not a sound conclusion. For good works come from the Spirit of God, bad works from us. Bad works are completely bad, but good works are defective and imperfect. So it does not follow that just because a man can kill himself, he can make himself alive.

The Use of Good Works

"What, then," you object, "do good works profit?" Very much. For they glorify our heavenly Father. He is praised if those who wish to be called His people live rightly. They make us sure of our election and calling, when, by their testimony, we experience more and more the virtue of Christ in us. They challenge others to holy living. Likewise, as far as it concerns external ministry, the hungry are fed, the naked are clothed, strangers are received into lodgings, and so on. In addition, they testify that we are thankful to God for the blessings that we have received.

Men Are to Be Stirred Up to Virtue by Words and Favors

From this passage we gather that the good works of men are to be praised, proclaimed, and adorned with rewards. The Poet also says, "Virtue that is praised increases."[5] Antisthenes, when he was asked how republics could be preserved, responded, "If rewards were appointed for the good and punishments for the evil."[6] Certainly, we must not strive after virtue so that we might be praised, but on account of God's commandment, though we are stirred up to virtues by praise and rewards. How many are there today who expose themselves to others' ridicule if they flee their fatherland following Ruth's example so that they can freely hear and publicly profess the pure religion? If anyone loves his

---

5. This designation perhaps identifies Ovid as the poet *par excellence*. Ov. *Pont.* 4.2.35–36.

6. The account that most closely matches Lavater's seems to be the narrative that appears in Diog. Laert. 6.1.5.

mother-in-law like a mother, they call him a fool. The same thing also happens in other matters. But in regard to this ingratitude and corruption of the world, we ought to be content with the judgment of a few good men. This example especially teaches us to seek from God that He will render to the pious according to their works and that they will receive a full recompense, just as Boaz prayed.

Moreover, we infer what we are to expect from the Lord if we reject idolatry and serve Him. For the prayers of pious men are not ineffectual but are like promises. This prayer agrees with the words of Christ in Matthew 19: "Verily I say unto you, that everyone that hath forsaken houses, or brethren, or sisters, or father, or mother, or wife, or children, or lands, for my name's sake, shall receive an hundredfold and shall inherit everlasting life." Mark 10 adds, "even in this life, with affliction." The meaning is that the pious are not going to be destitute of the comfort and support that they would have expected from their dearest friends and also that the Lord will confer His grace on them such that a little wealth will be like great wealth. And indeed it is so among true Christians. Jovian and Valentinian were made emperors, who under Emperor Julian had been stripped of their military belts on account of their profession of the Christian religion, and so God, even in this life, rewarded their faith and piety.

The outcome taught that Boaz's prayer was not ineffectual. For since Ruth, for the sake of the God of Israel, forsook everything that she had, she found a hundredfold in this life, for she became the wife of a distinguished man, and her posterity became kings among the people of God. Moreover, in another age she received eternal life, on account of the Messiah in whom she placed her hope.

How Ruth behaved toward Boaz follows. "*She said, 'Let me find favor in thy sight,'*" that is, "May I be acceptable and pleasing to you; may you regard me as agreeable to you." This expression appears in Genesis 33, 34, 47, and often elsewhere. It means "to favor, to gratify someone." "*For that thou has comforted me.*" The emphasis is on "me," namely, a poor, foreign, afflicted widow. For he cheered her up and refreshed her with pleasant conversation when she was sad. The following verse of Aeschylus is famous as a proverb: Ὀργῆς νοσούσης εἰσιν ἰατροὶ λόγοι, that is, "Speech is the physician of a sick soul."[7] *"And for that thou hast spoken unto the heart of thine handmaid."*[8] "That you have spoken with me in a friendly way and have convinced me to have hope." In Genesis 34, it is written that Shechem spoke to Dinah's heart after she was raped and defiled by him, where the Latin version has, "He soothed the sad girl with charming words." He no doubt promised her marriage and tried to comfort her. In Genesis 50, "Joseph said unto his brethren, 'Fear ye not; I will nourish you and your little ones.' And he comforted them and spoke to their hearts." That is, he spoke with them in a friendly way and soothed them with pleasant words. Ruth does not simply say, "me," but, "thine handmaid." So in 1 Samuel 1 Hannah says to Eli the high priest, "Count not thine handmaid for a daughter of Belial." In 1 Samuel 25, Abigail says to David, "Let thine handmaid speak in thine ears, and hear the words of thine handmaid." Again, Ruth recognizes her unworthiness. She does not count herself worthy to be compared with his handmaids or to be numbered among them, no doubt because she came from the gentiles.

Let us also learn to think humbly and modestly about ourselves and, likewise, not to cheat excellent men of the honor owed to them. She calls Boaz her lord and herself his handmaid. There are some uncivil men, such as some of the Anabaptists, who deny that honorific titles are to be conferred on others, since we are all descended from Adam and have one and the same Redeemer.

In addition, we see that since the poor receive great comfort from friendly conversation with the more powerful, the rich do right if they address the poor in a friendly way, especially those who are applying themselves to their work. For the poor see that they are not despised by the rich. Moreover, it is everyone's duty to cheer up and strengthen with comforts drawn from the Word of God those who are struggling with diseases and other evils.

---

7. Aesch. *PV* 380.
8. See p. 87, n. 1 above.

Ruth 2:14–16

14 *Boaz said unto her, "At mealtime come thou hither and dip thy morsel in the vinegar." And so she sat beside the reapers. And he reached her parched corn. She did eat until she was sufficed and left some over (some yet remained).*

15 *And she was risen up to glean. Now Boaz commanded his servants, saying, "Let her glean even among the sheaves and shame her not.*

16 *And be sure to let fall also some of the handfuls for her and leave them that she may glean them. And rebuke her not."*

The holy apostle and evangelist John, in his first epistle, chapter 3, says, "My little children, let us not love in word neither in tongue, but in deed and in truth." For there were always men, and still are men, who certainly promise their help to others at great length, but their deeds do not answer to their words. Boaz was not one of them. For indeed when he came to understand who and what sort of woman Ruth was, he prayed that God would bless her and give her grace. And he not only offered his help to her in words, but also actually gave it. For he commanded her to gather ears of grain in his fields and to drink from his vessels. And when he perceived that she was modest and thankful, he told her to eat with the reapers and to dip her morsel in vinegar. The Greeks call them "sauces" (ἐμβάμματα), which are liquids in small vessels into which we dip bread or other things.

Vinegar

Vinegar was given to the reapers since it has a great power to cool some-one off. I have heard that it is also used today in Italy during the harvest time when it is very hot. They also use wine tempered with vinegar and water, which the Greeks call ὀξύκρατον, acetomel, or honey and vin-egar. Some translate it as *poscam*. The Spaniard Cristóbal de Vega, a very learned man, in book two of his *On the Art of Medicine*, says, "Reapers use, in place of wine, vinegar copiously mixed with water, and it is this that they call *poscam*, diluted to the measure that it can be drunk. If you add to it olive oil and bread, you will produce a cooling food, useful for laborers and for those traveling under the heat of the sun."[1] A greedy man would have said to her, "I did not prepare this food for you, but for my servants." In 1 Samuel 25, when Nabal insolently rejects David's envoys, he says, "Shall I take my bread, and my water, and my cooked food that I have killed for my shearers, to give it unto men, whom I know not whence they be?" Likewise, Boaz commanded his servants to leave part of the ears of grain in the field.

We ought to imitate this example of sincere love. And although we come across many ungrateful men, nevertheless, we should not forget our duty.

We Ought to Supply Enough Food for Laborers

From the fact that Boaz gives his reapers suitable food and drink at the appropriate time—namely, bread, vinegar, parched barley, and water—householders and housewives learn to provide sufficient food for their slaves and hired servants. God in His law even prohibited the mouth of an ox to be muzzled while it is treading out the grain.[2] Solomon, in his encomium for a good housewife (Prov. 31), says, among other things, "She riseth while it is yet night and provideth meat to her household." They who labor much need more abundant food. There are some who indeed force their servants to labor, but do not give them enough food to quiet their growling stomachs. Others do not correctly prepare the food

---

1. Cristóbal de Vega, *Liber de arte medendi* (Lyon: Guillaume Rouillé, 1564), 238.
2. Deut. 25:4.

and do not bring it out while it is edible but prefer for it to spoil. There are some who indeed serve foods but are indignant if their servants eat until they are satisfied. They can be included among those about whom Solomon speaks in Proverbs 23. He says, "'Eat and drink,' saith he to thee; but his heart is not with thee." But what happens? The servants and handmaids, if they see that the masters are so stingy, eat up a lot of food in secret. In addition, those things that they were not willing to give to the laborers are often devoured by dogs and cats.

But if their masters serve what they need, servants should be content and not complain. They should not strive after luxuries. The ancients were content with modest and meager provisions, and you do not hear that they accused their masters. Wages also are to be paid liberally to workmen, especially reapers (James 5).

Ruth does not reject the offered kindness but receives it modestly and with a thankful spirit. And she sits to the side of the reapers and not across from them so that she will not be looked at. She does not thrust herself into the middle of the reapers and throw her hands first into the dish, as the gourmands do, who do not accept what is placed before them, but throw in their hands wherever they see more elegant foods. She waits until either Boaz or others of his household offer her a portion. We must modestly enjoy benevolence toward us, however liberally it is offered by others, contrary to the common saying that "restraint is useless to the poor."

She indeed ate until she was satisfied, but nevertheless, some of the food was left over, which, as we will hear later, she brought to her mother-in-law. She teaches us to use food and drink at least until we are satisfied, yet not to forget the poor. Paul also admonishes the faithful that their abundance will relieve others' want.[3] We should avoid the desire of gluttony and the disgraceful wasting of God's gifts.

Parched Barley

The author writes that Boaz gave to her parched barley. קָלִית, *kaliet*, with the aleph קְלִיא, *cali* (from קָלָא [*kalah*], "he parched"), is baked

---

3. 2 Cor. 8:14.

barley flour. The Vulgate translator translates it as *polentam*. On the method of producing parched barley [*polenti* or *pulenti*], Pliny relates the following:

> They soak barley with water and dry it for one night. On the following day, they roast it. Then they grind it with a millstone. Some sprinkle a little water again on the barley after they have roasted it more thoroughly, and they dry it before they grind it. Others clean the new barley shaken off the green ears of grain, and while it is moist, they pound it in a mortar. And when it has been cleaned, they grind it. So once it is prepared, in the mill they mix with twenty pounds of barley three pounds of flaxseed and half a pound of coriander, with an eighth of a pint[4] of salt, all of which they previously roast. Those who want to keep it for longer store it in new earthen vessels with flour and its bran.[5]

Galen, in book 1 of *On the Powers of Foods*, writes, "Parched barley, which is most excellent, is made from new barley moderately cooked and roasted."[6] The same author says, "Moreover, it is the custom of several, for health, to drink it with must and sweet honeywine mixed together, sometimes even sprinkled only with water, in the summer, two or three hours before going to the bath. And they say that by this drink they feel delivered from thirst."[7]

In Boaz, you have an example of preserving civility at the table. For he is not concerned only about himself but offers food to others also. We have a similar example from our Savior (Luke 24).

After she consumes her food, she then returns to her interrupted labor and continues gathering until evening. She does not take shade as an idle and lazy woman. She is very unlike those who shun work when they are full. This industry and diligence is to be strongly praised in her and all others.

Boaz, charmed by this woman's modesty, commands his servants to allow her to gather ears of grain among the sheaves (which otherwise is

---

4. *acetabulo.*
5. Plin. *HN* 18.14.
6. Gal. *Alim. Fac.* 1.11.
7. Gal. *Alim. Fac.* 1.11.

not allowed), to leave behind a part intentionally, to throw down a part, and not to say that these portions are owed to others, and so shame her or chide her, but to do this so that she can gather a lot and return to her mother-in-law more cheerfully.

Liberality of the Rich toward the Poor
The rich learn from this example that it is their duty to help the needy. God gives a large harvest not so much for the sake of the rich as for the poor. Christ will interpret as conferred on Him whatever you contribute to the use of the poor (Matt. 25). In addition, He blesses your wealth if you regard the poor as entrusted to you. There are many kinds of poor people. But those especially are to be helped who willingly provide for themselves their needs by their own labor, unless a great scarcity of grain hinders them. This example shows how we are to give. He gave Ruth what she needed, not because he was asked, not because he was ordered, but willingly and with pleasure. The Lord requires a cheerful giver.[8] Boaz gives liberally, for after she was satisfied, Ruth saved a part for her mother-in-law. He gives from his own resources and does not do this for ostentation. He could have given her a certain measure of ears of grain. But he considers that it would be more acceptable to her if she should gather them by her own labor. Therefore, he orders the reapers to leave a part for her between their reaping and gathering. In imitation of this distinguished man, we also ought sometimes to give better wages to poor hired servants than is owed them by contract and to do good to those in need even if they do not know it. Arcesilaus's friend was sick and in need, but meanwhile, he was hiding his need, so Arcesilaus secretly put a small bag of money under his friend's pillow to relieve his want.[9] On the duties of the rich, read 1 Timothy 6. How much do they now bind themselves to wickedness who use scarcity to drive the poor completely off their property? The richer men are now, usually the greedier they are. They devise many means by which to excuse their greed. The poor also can give alms, which they call "spiritual," namely, when they comfort and teach others.

---

8. 2 Cor. 9:7.
9. Diog. Laert. 4.6.37.

Ruth 2:17–19

17 *So she gleaned in the field until even and beat out that she had gleaned. And it was about an ephah of barley.*

18 *And she took it up and went into the city. And her mother-in-law saw what she had gleaned. She also brought forth and gave to her that she had reserved after she was sufficed.*

19 *Her mother-in-law said unto her, "Where hast thou gleaned today, and where wroughtest thou? Blessed be he that did take knowledge of thee." Then she showed her mother-in-law with whom she had wrought, saying, "The man's name with whom I wrought today is Boaz."*

Ruth is set forth to us as a clear mirror of many virtues. But her industry, diligent care, and persistent labor are especially commended to us. She gathered ears of grain in the field of Boaz, who told her to sit down with his reapers. After she ate and was full, she immediately returned to her labor from which she had taken a short break. It adds that she attended to her work until evening, and then she beat out what she had gathered, that is, with a staff, and winnowed it.

Threshing

There were two methods of threshing among the ancients that are mentioned in the Sacred Scriptures. One method was done with oxen, the other with staffs with which they beat out the grains. Pliny says, "The harvest is crushed with a threshing sledge on the threshing floor in one place, crushed by horses' steps in another, and beaten with staffs in another."[1] The threshing sledge (I will say in passing) is a type of vehicle with which grain is threshed. It adds that Ruth carried the grain, that is, on her head, which was a great burden. At the end of the chapter, we find that she also gathered ears of grain in the wheat harvest and every day returned at night to her mother-in-law. By her example, she teaches us perseverance in labor and, indeed, in every good work. It is not enough to have begun well, but we must continue eagerly. And while time allows, we must labor; we must not neglect an opportune time. There are some who surrender themselves to idleness to be corrupted. Or if they have been zealous for virtue for some time, they later forsake it.

It should be noted that the Holy Spirit records that she carried the burden herself and did not place it on a pack animal or a wagon. For it shows that God cares about these things, which should comfort those hardworking men who on account of their poverty must bear heavy burdens on their head or shoulders. For indeed, if they do this by faith, they do a good work that is pleasing to God. For God requires of them these ordinary works, not that they should arrange pilgrimages for the sake of religion or put on a monk's hood.

Diligence

But what was the fruit of such labor? There are many who say that they labor in vain. She gathered nearly an *ephah* or *ephi* of barley. If it is converted to the Zürich measure, there were, as Theodor Bibliander estimates, three-fourths of a measure.[2] An *ephah* is a dry measure and contains three *sata* or bushels. A *satum* contains six *cabi*. A *cabus* contains four *logs*. A *log* is the smallest dry and liquid measure, containing six *eggs*. If these are multiplied and you begin with a *log*, a *cabus* will have 24 *eggs*, a *satum*, 144 *eggs*, and an ephah, 432 *eggs*. Now ten *ephahs* make a *homer*, or *corum*, containing 4320 *eggs*, which is the largest measure among the Hebrews, as Münster commented on Exodus 29.[3] Although Ruth could not have gathered so much unless at Boaz's command a part

---

1. Plin. *HN* 18.72.
2. I have been unable to locate a source for this claim in Bibliander's writings.
3. Sebastian Münster, *Hebraica Biblia*, vol. 1 (Basel: [n.p.], 1534), fol. 81r.

had been left for her by the reapers, nevertheless, it is certain that diligence of any sort is very effective in every business. A drop of water by falling continually breaks and hollows out the hardest rocks. Those who are diligent and persistent in their work gradually accumulate property until they have a sufficient abundance. But we must pray to God that He will bless our labors. For unless His blessing is added, all our labors that we complete are in vain. James 4 says, "Ye fight and war (taking a metaphor from war, he is speaking about contentions and quarrels with which they vexed each other), yet ye have not, because ye ask not. Ye ask and receive not because ye ask amiss, that ye may consume it upon your lusts." Many complain that they cannot support themselves by their trade, but nevertheless, they do not diminish their extravagance. They despise God, not acknowledging Him as the author of good things. Solomon in his Proverbs proclaims that God supplies the diligent with what they need and afflicts the lazy with famine. Proverbs 14:23: "In all labor there is abundance, but the talk of the lips tendeth only to penury." Proverbs 19:24: "A slothful man hideth his hand in his bosom and will not even bring it to his mouth," that is, he will not have anything to eat. Proverbs 20:4: "The sluggard will not plow by reason of the winter (or cold); therefore shall he beg in summer and not have bread." And verse 13: "Love not sleep, lest thou perhaps become poor. Open thine eyes and thou shalt satisfy thyself with bread." Proverbs 21:25: "The desire of the slothful shall kill him, for his hands have refused to do anything." But if God sometimes afflicts with famine those who labor strenuously, He does this for certain reasons that we will review elsewhere.

Faithfulness to Her Mother-in-Law

It adds that Ruth showed her mother-in-law what she had gathered and also that she offered and gave to her what she had left over after she was satisfied. It appears that Ruth was remarkably affectionate toward her mother-in-law. For in order to cheer her up she did not show her mother-in-law only a part and secretly feast on the other part. But she showed her all that she had gathered that day and also offered her the food that was left from her sack, bag, or purse. You might easily find daughters-in-law who will give nothing to their mothers-in-law, no, who would even throw their food to dogs, or even eat more than their fill, rather than give anything to their mothers-in-law.

Children Should Support Their Parents
Children should learn to cherish and support their elderly parents. For the word "honor" includes this, among other things, as the Lord Himself interprets it in Matthew 15 when He reproaches the Pharisees and scribes because they were enervating the law of God by their traditions. The gentiles also think it is only fair that we support those who have supported us. Sons and daughters often complain that poverty prevents them from doing this. But if they must spend a lot on wines, expensive clothes, and other worthless things, they never mention their poverty. There are few who care for their elderly parents as is proper. In the history of the gospel, we often read that parents interceded with God for their children so that they would be delivered from diseases, but there is no such story about children interceding for their parents. Very many would wish their parents were dead, whether they are poor or rich. If they are poor and must be supported by them, they are a burden to them. If they are rich, the children wait like vultures for their corpses. Nor are there lacking those who rob their own parents, about whom Proverbs 28:24 speaks: "Whoso robbeth his parents' property is the companion of a destroying man."

Josephus writes that Naomi offered Ruth portions of the food that the neighbors had given her and that she had saved for Ruth.[4] For the words in the text can be taken in both ways. So we infer from this how dear the daughter-in-law was to her mother-in-law, because she did not consume everything but saved a part for Ruth while she was away working. But it seems that it is more fitting for us to take it as referring to Ruth.

Parents Should Demand an Account from Their Children
Naomi asks her daughter-in-law where she gathered the ears of grain. She answers frankly and tells the name of the man in whose field she

---

4. Joseph. *AJ* 5.326.

had been. Naomi teaches parents to have care and concern for their children. Perhaps she thought it was impossible that Ruth had gathered so much by her own labor in such a brief space of time. If children bring something home that they say was given to them as a gift, or if they say that they found it, the parents should carefully inquire about it. For by these steps they come to theft. Parents should demand an account from their children, namely, where they were, with whom, and what they did. If the parents suspect anything, they should ask the children and chastise them when they are caught in a lie. They should also praise those who do right and so kindle in them a zeal for virtue. Teachers and others to whose care and trust young people are committed should do the same. They should diligently require an account not only from the young, but also from adults. I am not advising you to confine children to their homes. But nevertheless, we must take care that if they receive permission and go out, they join themselves with good friends by whose companionship they will turn out better.

Ruth willingly gives an account to her mother-in-law; she does not talk back. She narrates in order what happened to her in the field. Children should do the same toward their parents and those who are in the place of parents, and they should behave in such a way that they can tell without fear what they have done.

Her mother-in-law, before she heard Boaz's name, said, "*Blessed be he that did take knowledge of thee.*" The old translation[5] has, "*who hath pitied thee.*" The word "know" is taken in various ways in sacred literature. Proverbs 12:10: "A righteous man regardeth [knoweth] the life of his beast" (although Solomon uses the word ידע [*iada*], yet our writer uses נכר [*nakar*]), that is, "He has a concern and regard for him, gives him food, grants him rest, or has compassion on his cattle." Verse 10 continues, "But the tender mercies of the wicked are cruel," that is, "They have no concern for them and treat them harshly." So in this passage, "*he that did take knowledge of thee,*" that is, "he who did good to you." She blesses him because he had pity on Ruth. Certainly, the Lord blesses those who show kindness to widows and the poor.

---

5. "The old translation" here and throughout refers to the Vulgate.

Fifteenth Homily

Ruth 2:20–23

20 *And Naomi said unto her daughter-in-law, "Blessed is he of the LORD, who hath not left off his mercy with (to) the living and with the dead." And Naomi added, "The man is our near of kin and is one of our kinsmen."*

21 *Then Ruth the Moabitess said unto her, "He certainly said unto me also, 'Thou shalt keep fast by the young men who are mine, until they have ended all my harvest.'"*

22 *And Naomi said unto Ruth her daughter-in-law, "It is good (honorable), my daughter, that thou go out with his maidens, that they meet thee not in another field."*

23 *So she joined herself to the maidens of Boaz in gleaning (ears of corn) until the barley harvest and the wheat harvest was ended and returned to her mother-in-law.*

The conversation that Naomi had with Ruth is both pleasant and useful. For it contains very many things that are of no little value for our instruction and comfort. Before Naomi had come to know in whose field Ruth had gathered ears of grain, she says, *"Blessed be he that did take knowledge of thee."* But after she heard his name, she uttered this blessing at greater length. *"Blessed be he of the LORD,"* that is, "May God repay him in this age and the age to come." Or, *"Blessed is he,"* that is, "He is acceptable to the LORD; His grace is strong with him." The Lord's blessing embraces both temporal and eternal goods. He who blesses another prays that God will sustain him through the Messiah in whom we are blessed, will forgive his sins, will defend him, and will give him success in all his affairs and guard him from every evil. She gives a reason: "*He hath not left off his mercy to the living and the dead,*" that is, "He has not stopped loving them and doing them favors." I will tell next how Boaz did favors for the dead. She adds that this Boaz is their near kinsman and relative, which Ruth did not know. גואל (*goel*) means "protector," a relative who has the right to help his blood relation and to take vengeance on the one who harmed his blood relation.

Exercising Piety toward the Dead

We draw from these words what is the duty of blood relatives, relatives by marriage, and friends, namely, that they should love each other and compete with each other in doing favors for each other (which favors are not of one sort) and, likewise, that the rich should help the poor. Boaz honored his relatives, living and dead, with love and showed them kindness. How did he do this for the dead? When Elimelech and his sons were still alive, he did them favors, but afterward, when they were dead, for the sake of their memory he showed grace to their widows in as many matters as he could, and he would have done the same toward their children if any had survived. And this is showing piety or mercy toward the dead. Naomi also used this expression above. Certainly, if the dead knew what was being done on earth, they would rejoice in those duties, not if you should try to place them among the gods, establish feast days for them, and pour out prayers to them. Many are concerned too little about the children and widows of their dead friends. Or if they have done something for their sakes once or twice, afterward they leave behind their mercy, that is, they give up caring for them and send them away to others. Boaz was steadfast in friendship.

True Friends

For true friends do not change with fortune. Proverbs 17:17: "A friend loveth at all times." Some examples of this sort of friend are set forth to us in sacred literature. In 2 Samuel 9, after David acquires the whole kingdom, he asks whether someone from Saul's family is still alive to whom he might show mercy, that is, for whom he might do a favor, for

Jonathan's sake. And when Mephibosheth, Jonathan's son, is brought to him, David gives him his father's fields and property. And although he was crippled and lowly, nevertheless, David puts him at his table. It is commonly said that the dead lack friends, but David, for the sake of the memory of Mephibosheth's father, regards him as a son. Therefore, God raised up faithful friends for David also. For during Absalom's sedition, Hushai, Ittai, and others follow David, not his son, however much Absalom's affairs seemed to flourish.[1] Those friends who desert us in adverse circumstances are not true friends, but they are like those birds that fly away when winter is near and finally return in the summer. A sure friend becomes known in unsure circumstances.[2] It is common today for men who are bound to each other by many bonds to fight each other, often for trivial reasons. Friends are not to be despised, however poor and lowly they are, for they can often be of great use to the rich and powerful by their efforts, as in seditions, wars, fires, shipwrecks, diseases, and other evils, public and private. Further, it is required not only of relatives and friends to regard orphans and widows as entrusted to them, but also of all others. Therefore, how much do they sin who for insignificant reasons lie in wait for the children and widows of the dead and take revenge on them when they have been unable to harm their parents and husbands?

What Naomi proclaims about Boaz we can more rightly say about God, because He does not desert those who hope in Him, whether living or dead. Therefore, we too ought to break into praises of God and say, "Blessed be the Lord."

We Should Be Grateful to Benefactors

The other lesson is how we ought to behave toward our benefactors. Naomi acknowledges the kindness shown her. She is grateful toward Boaz and Ruth, and she shows her gratitude by her words and deeds. She blesses Boaz, not with a magic blessing or incantation, but with a heavenly blessing. Imitating this, we should pray for good things through Christ for our benefactors. Many poor men who for a long

1. 2 Sam. 15:17–23, 32–37.
2. Cic. *Amic.* 64.

time have received many considerable favors, whether from relatives or others, grumble, are indignant, and curse them if they suffer rejection even once. If a man gives them as much as he can, they still expect more from him, and not being content, they immediately burn with anger. We ought not only to thank in words those from whom we have received favors and to pray to the Lord for them. But we also ought really to show ourselves grateful. That Naomi afterward looked out for a husband for Ruth we will hear in its own place.

Our Favors Do Not Come to Nothing

Third, from this passage we conclude that the favors we do for our neighbors do not come to nothing. For as Naomi asks God for remuneration for Boaz her benefactor, though he is unaware of it, so at all times there will be some who will praise and receive with a grateful spirit favors done for them and who in their prayers will commend to the Lord the safety of those whose liberality they have experienced. No, rather, if they fail in their duty, nevertheless, the work itself, done by faith, in a certain manner shouts to the Lord. Job, in chapter 31, clearing himself of the most atrocious charges, which were brought against him by his friends, namely, the charges of hypocrisy and impiety, and constructing a narrative of his life lived before this, says, among other things, "Let such and such happen to me if his loins have not blessed me, and if he were not warmed with the fleece of my sheep." Through prosopopoeia,[3] he attributes to the loins warmed by him that they prayed for him, that is, that such a favor would come to the Lord's remembrance, though he who received it was ungrateful. This ought to rouse us to liberality toward the poor. If you compare what Boaz bestowed on the widows with his wealth, it is not so great and magnificent. Nevertheless, it was very useful to them. God also abundantly repaid it. In the gospel, our Savior says in Matthew 10, "Whosoever shall give to drink unto one of these little ones a cup of cold water, only in the name of a disciple, verily I say unto you, he shall not lose his reward." Christ repays small deeds with great rewards, and He does this out of mere grace.

---

3. i.e., personification.

Form of Blessing

Fourth, we also have a formula of blessing: what, from whom, and how we ought to pray for the good of our benefactors, on account of the favors done for us and our families. We said above that the word "blessing" includes temporal and eternal goods. Naomi prays for these good things for her kinsman and from the Lord. And she knows that He can bestow mercy on whomever He will and that He observes and rules over our words and deeds, both good and bad. Those prayers and blessings are not ineffectual. Otherwise, the saints would not use them, nor would the Scriptures teach us to use them. As prayers are not useless, so neither are those wishes that are nothing other than formulas of prayers.

Ruth, continuing to commend Boaz's politeness, says that he commanded her in addition to stick close to his young men until they completed the harvest. But he had said that she should go out with his handmaids. These statements are not contradictory, because both his young men and his handmaids went into the field. For Scripture often places later those things that it passed over in an earlier passage. Some think he said, *"Join thyself to my servants (Join thee thyself around [thû dich umb] my servants),"* as a joke to test her, namely, that she could get a husband. Naomi responded, *"It is good (that is, honorable, pleasing to me), my daughter, that thou go out with his maidens."* She does not try to persuade her to go into another field on the following day. And although she understood that the benevolence of friends is not to be abused, nevertheless, she tells her to return to Boaz's field. Since he was Ruth's relative, Naomi thinks that he will have more concern for her chastity than strangers and outsiders would. For Ruth easily could have fallen in with someone who would not have defended her if she were exposed to danger. The old translation has, *"It is better that thou go out with his maidens."* The reason is added, *"that they meet thee not,"* or, *"that no one withstand thee."* Münster translates it, *"that they not rush upon thee."*[4] The word פָּגַע (phaga) means "to meet, to resist, to oppose," hence, פְּגָרַע (paegara), "bad event or meeting," and likewise, "to entreat, to ask, to rush upon." We say, "Shame would soon befall you" (*Es were dir bald*

---

4. *Biblia Sacra*, trans. Münster and Erasmus, fol. 285v.

erwas begaegnet, ein schmaach widerfaren). "If you were to gather ears of grain in another field, someone could oppose you and say that permission to gather had been given to other paupers. Likewise, some impudent men could force themselves on you, as sometimes happens in the harvest." If you interpret it as "to ask," perhaps the meaning is, "Someone could tempt you into debauchery." It is commonly said that she is chaste whom no one asks. There are some who leave no stone unturned to capture the chastity of married women and virgins. But they, too, will eventually pay a penalty for their impurity. For their children and, likewise, their wives are also often defiled by others by the just judgment of God, or they are inflamed with jealousy toward their wives and so are miserably tormented day and night. Or at least Ruth could have been suspected of wickedness.

Protection for Virgins

Elderly women, following Naomi's example, should rightly form younger women, rouse them by praise to be zealous for virtue, and order them to stay at home and to avoid all occasions to sin. It is commonly said that stalks must be removed from the fire lest they be consumed. Naomi would have preferred for her daughter-in-law to remain at home, but since necessity was forcing her to go out into the field, she tells her to join herself to the handmaids, not the young men. Girls cannot always be at home and are forced sometimes to go abroad or sometimes to take a long journey. But you should urge them not to do this alone but to join themselves to virtuous traveling companions, to avoid conversations with impudent young men, or drunkards, and likewise, suspicious places, and especially to stay at home at night. And they should avoid not only evil, but also the appearance of evil. For indeed, if they fall under suspicion of whoring or committing adultery, they cannot easily clear themselves of it. If they were to be accused of theft, their innocence would be evident to everyone once the thief was caught. But this is far different. Saint Paul in Titus 2 writes, "Teach the aged women likewise (just as was said about the aged men), that they be in a condition that becometh religion, not false accusers, not enslaved to much wine, that they teach honorable things, by which they can make the young women to be modest, to love their husbands, to love their children, to be sober, chaste, keepers of their homes, good, subject to their own husbands, that the Word of God be not of bad repute." It is not enough, he says, for elderly women to live rightly, but he orders them also to form younger women to live rightly, both by their words and by the example of their lives. There are some women who talk with men and go to dances and wild parties, saying that in this way they want to get husbands for themselves. But this way is dangerous and not acceptable to honorable and virtuous people.

Ruth, having regard for her chastity, joins herself to the girls, teaching daughters by her example to obey the good counsel of their parents, which many do not willingly do. But because they are burning and carried away by their affections, they prefer to give ear to flatterers. Afterward, when they fall into many evils, they are led to repentance and lament their own lot too late. But those girls who allow themselves to be ruled by their elders obtain the excellent fruits of obedience.

She stuck with them until the harvest was finished. Perseverance in the same work is to be praised, and moreover, that one might become steadfast, it pays a lot for one to become used to work beginning in one's early years. Those who continually transition from one job to another labor without much profit.

She returned to her mother-in-law, or stayed with her, that is, each night. For it is proper for virgins to spend the night at their homes, not elsewhere. She did not want her mother-in-law to worry about her. Children should not, by wandering around at night, throw their parents into grief, whose sleep they otherwise rather often interrupt. She stayed with her, seeking no other lodging. Today, many girls do not willingly live with their mothers, much less with their mothers-in-law. What if, in addition, they were obliged to support them? Poor virgins who are unwilling to live with their relatives, but wish to live more freely, far from their sight, and to wander wherever their soul carries them, do not have good reputations. But girls should behave in such a way that their blood relatives and in-laws will not deservedly prohibit them from living at home or throw them out of the house.

Ruth 3:1–4

1 *Then Naomi her mother-in-law said unto her, "My daughter, shall I not seek rest for thee, that it may be well with thee?*

2 *Now then is not Boaz of our kindred, with whose maidens thou wast? Behold, he winnoweth the threshing floor of barley at night.*

3 *Wash thyself therefore, and anoint thee. Also, put thy raiment upon thee. And get thee down to the threshing floor. But make not thyself known unto the man, until he shall have done eating and drinking.*

4 *And when he goeth to lie down, thou shalt mark the place where he shall sleep, and thou shalt go in and uncover (the part of) his feet and lay thee down there (at his feet). And he will tell thee what thou shalt do."*

This chapter consists mainly of three parts. The first part contains the counsel that Naomi gave to Ruth to acquire Boaz as her husband. The second part describes how Ruth obeyed her mother-in-law, as well as what she accomplished and how she was received by Boaz and sent away. The third part describes how she returned to her mother-in-law and explained to her in order everything that had happened. Many things are contained in this chapter that pertain to forming a marriage, in which a lot of our happiness and unhappiness in this life consists.

Troubles of Marriage
As far as it concerns Naomi's counsel, first, she promises Ruth her help, that she will look out for a good husband for her. *"Shall I not seek rest for*

thee?" she says; so she calls marriage. She adds, *"that it may be well with thee."* The meaning is, "I will join you to a good and suitable husband, so that you will know where you are to stay and so that thereafter you will not have to obtain what you need by such hard work." She does not promise her a quiet life abounding in luxuries. She does not say that she will have no troubles or miseries, with which the world is full, and for the mitigation of which the Lord instituted marriage. Genesis 2: "He said, 'It is not good (or suitable) that the man should be alone; let us make a help for him.'" God wants it to be well with them, for them to have rest. Many, however, by their own vice, bring the greatest evils on themselves, as when they indulge in suspicions. Indeed, marriage also has its own troubles, especially where there are numerous offspring. Yet they experience more troubles who, despising this institution of God, wallow in lewdness and adulteries. Naomi does not advise her to live thereafter in celibacy. For it was preferable for a foreign widow to marry one of God's people.

In Naomi an example of gratitude is set forth. In the first chapter, she desired a happy marriage for both her daughters-in-law. Now that the opportunity is offered, she loses no time in acquiring a distinguished husband for the girl who deserved the best from her. There are some who only make grand promises but in reality do nothing. Often, when they could do good to their friends without harming themselves, they do not do it, but if others do it, they envy them.

Next, parents should learn to look out for husbands for their daughters and wives for their sons. For this charge belongs to them. Children should not follow their depraved affections in this matter but should take advantage of their parents' counsel. Parents should not tyrannically force their children to enter marriage against their will. Naomi confers with Ruth, her daughter-in-law, about marriage. Marriages into which children are pushed against their will rarely have a happy ending.

The way in which Naomi procured this marriage is added. She instructs her with precepts and teaches her what she ought to do and what she ought to avoid. First, she told her to wash off the sweat and dirt so that she would not smell bad. These washings were common among those nations and were not, in themselves, unlawful. Next, she told her to anoint herself, which also was in use among the peoples of the East, as both the gospel history and others demonstrate. Third, she tells her to put on clothes, that is, more elegant clothes. Fourth, she tells her to go down to the threshing floor and not allow herself to be seen before Boaz had eaten and drunk. At the end of the harvest, the workers appear to have been treated more lavishly, as at sheepshearing. We hold a feast at the end of harvest and vintage (*den schnitt oder freyhauen/den trunten* [the cutting or free-hacking/the meal after the grape harvest]). Likewise, we give more abundant food and drink to those who thresh and winnow the crops in the barn. Naomi tells her to note his bed, or place, and when he begins to sleep, to remove the covering from the place of his feet and lower herself stealthily at his feet. She says that he will indicate what she needs to do according to the law about raising up progeny for a dead brother or kinsman. For afterward he said that there was a nearer kinsman with whom he first had to confer about this business. The law that commands a brother or kinsman to marry the widow of a brother or kinsman who had died without children does not express in what way or by what means he ought to do this, nor did it force a man to do it against his will. Therefore, Naomi uses these stratagems to persuade Boaz more easily and to get him to do willingly and of his own accord that which, according to the law, he should have done anyway. For cleanliness in women pleases men, and husbands often shrink back from their wives because of their dirty clothes. Therefore, women should arrange and adorn themselves. Being alone with a woman, especially at night, attracts many men into marriage. In addition, those who are drunk eagerly do many things that they could scarcely be brought to do sober. Drunk Lot committed incest with his daughters.[1] David, in 2 Samuel 11, wanted to subdue Uriah's steadfastness through intoxication and to impel him to sleep with his wife. Ovid says, "Night, love, and wine urge no moderation. The former is without shame, and Liber[2] and love are without fear."[3]

---

1. Gen. 19:30–38.
2. The god of wine (=Bacchus).
3. Ov. *Am.* 1.6.59–60.

It was certainly right for Ruth to be coupled with Boaz, but there were other ways and means by which she ought to have dealt with him about contracting a marriage. They could have recalled to Boaz's memory the law of God through some honorable man. But perhaps they think it does not matter, since they had persuaded themselves that it was his responsibility to raise up progeny for his dead kinsman according to the law.

But so that no one will abuse this example and wish to contract a marriage within prohibited degrees of consanguinity or affinity, or to defend pimping, or even to excuse his own sins by other errors and wicked deeds of the saints, it must be understood that in the Scriptures four types of examples of pious men are recounted.

First, some deeds are described and set forth for us to imitate, such as faith in Abraham,[4] patience in Job,[5] chastity in Joseph,[6] and ardent prayer in David[7] and others. All the sacred books are full of memorable examples of virtues. How many examples does the Holy Spirit set forth to us in this little book, in Naomi, Ruth, and Boaz? As goldsmiths, painters, and others place works of art before the eyes of their students so that they will imitate them, so God sets before us examples of the saints so that, having them constantly before our eyes, we will copy them in our lives.

Falls of the Saints

Next, there are deeds of the saints contained in sacred literature that are vicious, such as Lot's incest,[8] David's adultery,[9] Jonah's disobedience,[10] the apostles' ambition,[11] Peter's denial,[12] Thomas's little faith (ὀλιγοπιστία),[13] and many other things. These are not recorded by the

---

4. Rom. 4; Gal. 3:6–9; Heb. 11:8, 17.
5. James 5:11.
6. Gen. 39:7–12.
7. The reference is most likely to the Psalms.
8. Gen. 19:30–38.
9. 2 Sam. 11:1–5.
10. Jonah 1:3.
11. Mark 9:34; Luke 9:46; 22:24.
12. Matt. 26:69–75; Mark 14:66–72; Luke 22:55–62; John 18:16–18, 25–27.
13. John 20:24–29.

Holy Spirit so that we will imitate them but so that we will see that men, however holy they are, are corrupt in their nature and that the fact that they excelled in so many singular virtues was due to the goodness of God. These things ought to make us cautious. For if those excellent men fell, what can happen to us, who are by no means to be compared with them? Therefore, according to the admonition of the apostle, "Let him that standeth see that he not fall."[14] And as they did not continue in their wicked deeds but repented, so we also should repent, so that God will forgive our sins and the penalties due for our sins. Likewise, we should receive those who fall and truly repent. True repentance acknowledges the hideousness of sin. By faith, it embraces the mercy of God set forth in His Son and guards against wicked deeds in the future.

Third, the saints in the Old Testament did some things rightly that today it would be sinful to imitate. They circumcised their boys on the eighth day, which is not allowed today since baptism took the place of circumcision. They offered various sacrifices to God, which today have no place. A brother had to marry the widow of another brother and raise up seed for him, which today would be a capital crime. The same can also be said about other ceremonial laws, which were removed by Christ, and also likewise about the judicial laws, in part. Likewise, some things were conceded to the ancients for certain reasons, such as polygamy and a certificate of divorce, which our Savior corrected.[15] These things, therefore, are not to be adopted as examples.

Fourth, there are some unique deeds, such as that Abraham, against the general law, "Thou shalt not kill,"[16] was willing to sacrifice and kill his own son Isaac.[17] Or the fact that the Israelites did not return the gold and silver vessels and the clothes that they had borrowed from the Egyptians.[18] We ought not to imitate these things; we have no command to do the same. In 1 Samuel 14, Jonathan, together with his armor-bearer, attacked the Philistines' garrison in a steep place, which was a matchless

14. 1 Cor. 10:12.
15. Matt. 5:31–32; 19:3–9; Mark 10:2–12; Luke 16:18.
16. Ex. 20:13; Deut. 5:17.
17. Gen. 22:1–18.
18. Ex. 12:35–36.

and heroic deed that did not spring from ambition or greed but from the impulse of the Holy Spirit. He looked to the promise and glory of God and the safety of his fatherland. If someone were not led by a similar Spirit and wished to attempt something similar, he could be called rash. I am omitting other things.

With that said, we will be able to judge more accurately concerning this deed of Naomi and Ruth. We should say, then, that this is a unique deed that is not to be imitated, or that those women were certainly pious and chaste but nevertheless sinned in this way, and that therefore these things are not recounted in the Scriptures so that we will imitate them, but rather so that we will avoid them. Although the outcome was happy, nevertheless, this is to be ascribed not to Naomi's shrewdness, but rather to divine mercy, which often uses our sins for something good. Saint Paul, in 1 Thessalonians 5, commands us to avoid even the appearance of evil. But Ruth was commanded to do what appeared to be evil. Naomi uses those devices by which madams entice young women into wickedness, for they also use baths, sweet-smelling perfumes, and more elegant clothes. Perhaps the outcome would not have been so happy if Ruth had not fallen in with a pious man. If she could not have lain hidden but had been seen by others, who would not have thought that she had gone there to whore or steal? In addition, who will deny that Naomi, as much as it was up to her, threw her daughter-in-law into the danger of being defiled? Moreover, though Ruth was previously pleasing to Boaz, now she could have been displeasing to him because of this deed. Or if he, being inflamed with wine, had had an affair with her, he afterward could have rejected her as a whore. To these considerations must be added that, according to the law, she was owed not to Boaz but to a nearer kinsman, who, unless he had voluntarily ceded his right, would have been wronged. I will say nothing about the fact that men ought to pursue their wives, not the other way around. Although Boaz later praises this deed, nevertheless, we are not to believe that he approved of all its circumstances. Therefore, no one ought to abuse the example of these women and so argue, "If they were allowed to do it, I also will be allowed to do it." For the falls of the saints ought to make us more cautious, not attract us to sin.

There are elderly women who, since they hope that by this means they can bring about marriages between young men and virgins, invite them to nighttime feasts, conversations, and dances and sometimes urge them to use the same bed. There are also virgins who entice young men in various ways and sometimes prostitute themselves to them, saying that they are doing this from an honorable intention, namely, so that they might enter a lawful marriage. But marriages are not to be entered by this way and means, but we are to proceed in the right way. Parents and relatives are to be consulted, and the marriage is to be contracted before honorable men. How many of those clandestine marriages have had a sad and lamentable end?

Those young men also are to be reproved who, so that they can get some girls, promise them marriage but, once they have defiled them, contemptuously reject them as whores and deny that they ever mentioned marriage. Honorable young men are not willing to have as wives those girls who prostitute themselves to them. No, rather, they suspect that they have allowed others also to use their bodies, or that they will do so later.

But what judgment will we make about those who, when they are caught, give as a pretext for their whoring the favorable excuse of marriage, though they have never mentioned it before? Or about madams and pimps who for the sake of profit unite persons whom they ought not to unite?

By the way, we will also note that it says that Boaz was winnowing the threshing floor of barley, that is, the barley that was on the threshing floor. The Septuagint has λικμᾶν, that is, "to separate the chaff from the grain, to sift" (cf. λικμός, "fan, winnowing fork"). It adds, "*at night.*" The Chaldean version has "*in the night air.*"[19] Perhaps he could not winnow it in the day because of the heat. We also read about other holy fathers, such as Abraham, Isaac, Jacob, and Gideon, and likewise, about Roman senators and leaders, that they applied themselves to husbandry, or agriculture, not to idleness, drunkenness, and gluttony. Boaz would have had many men whom he could have commanded to do this work, but

---

19. Tg. Ruth 3:2.

he preferred to take it on himself, partly so that by exercising his body he would enjoy better health, partly so that he would not by indulging in idleness give a place to evil temptations, and partly so that by his example he would rouse his domestic servants to work, for examples are very effective in every way.

Seventeenth Homily

Ruth 3:5–9

5 *Ruth said unto her, "All that thou sayest (commandest) unto me I will do."*

6 *And so she went down unto the threshing floor (the barn) and did according to all that her mother-in-law bade her.*

7 *And when Boaz had eaten and drunk, and his heart was merry, he went to sleep at the end of the heap. And she came in secret. When she had uncovered (the part of) his feet (when his feet were uncovered), she laid herself down.*

8 *And it came to pass at midnight that the man was afraid and bowed himself (either turned himself from side to side, or drew himself in, that is, because of his terror). And, behold, a woman was sleeping at (the place of) his feet.*

9 *And he said, "Who art thou?" She answered, "I am Ruth thine handmaid. Spread thy edge (of thy garment) over thine handmaid, for thou are a kinsman."*

This passage explains how Ruth obeyed her mother-in-law and how she was received by Boaz. She promises that she will do everything, and indeed she does it. In this matter she is not to be accused. For perhaps since she had recently converted to the Jewish religion she thought it was customary to approach him in this way, if she wanted to ask the kinsman of her former husband to be united to her. But if she sinned, she sinned out of ignorance, not that ignorance altogether excuses us of sin. It only mitigates the guilt and does not altogether remove it, as also do good intentions, as they call them. In Genesis 38, Tamar also used deceit to get Judah to be her husband.

The Duty of Children

It is the duty of children to obey their parents and those who are included in this category unless they demand things of them that are contrary to the Word of God, such as if they do not want them to hear the sacred sermons or if they order them to put on the monastic hood or to move to places where pure doctrine is abolished. If they order them to kill or harm someone, to commit theft, to consort with prostitutes, in these and other things of this sort they must not obey their parents. For the laws of God are to be preferred to the mandates of men, however closely connected to us they are. "He that preferreth father and mother to me," our Savior says, "is not worthy of me."[1] Jonathan, Saul's son, was unwilling to kill David when his father commanded him to (1 Sam. 19), though he seemed to be bound to do it by a twofold reason, first, because Saul was his king, and second, because Saul was his father, who commanded him to do this.

In What Sense the Fathers Became "Drunk"

Next, it is written that Boaz ate and drank and had a good time. We also read regarding other holy fathers that they sometimes refreshed themselves with rather abundant food and drink. In Genesis 43, Scripture says of Joseph and his brothers that "they drank and were drunk with him." Here Scripture does not speak about that excessive drunkenness, which it so often condemns, but about somewhat liberal drinking by which they are made merry. Saints Augustine and Jerome also testify in many passages that "drunkenness" [*ebrietatem*] is taken not for intoxication, but sufficiency, as in Psalm 35: "They shall be abundantly satisfied [*inebriabuntur*] with the fullness of thy house," that is, "They will be filled." God had commanded that on solemn feast days they cast aside sadness and cheerfully celebrate His feasts. Under the reign of Solomon, the Israelites came together in very great numbers, eating, drinking,

---

1. Matt. 10:37.

and rejoicing. This must be noted because of some Anabaptists and hypocrites who condemn permissible pleasures and joys. God gives us wine, bread, meats, fish, and other things to use for food and drink. Psalm 104: "God causeth wine to grow that maketh glad the heart of man." We especially must not envy those who perform hard labor if they are made merry with food and drink. In Jeremiah 31, God promises His people that those who would return to their fatherland would abound in those things that pertain to honorable pleasure. Nevertheless, we must beware that we not forget Him when we overflow with His gifts, but we must strive to enjoy His gifts rightly.

Threshing Floor

Boaz spent the night on the threshing floor and slept near the pile of bundles. He did this either to return to his work at the very beginning of the morning or to guard the crops so that thieves would not steal them. For threshing floors or barns appear to have been in the fields and were not fortified so that everyone could enter them. Varro, in *On Agriculture*, writes that the threshing floor ought to be in the field at a more elevated location so that the wind can blow on it, and it especially ought to be round and raised a little in the middle so that if it rains, the water does not stand still.[2]

This example teaches heads of households to care for their possessions, to guard them, and to be present with their laborers. Often on account of their negligence the things they have acquired by strenuous labor are stolen from them. In the dead of night, Boaz turned himself from side to side, or bowed himself. לפת, *laphath*, means "to bow, to grasp, to handle." Others explain it as "to turn oneself from side to side." When he turns himself and extends his feet to the lowest part of the bed, he feels that something is lying there. Terrified, he bows himself, and he discovers through touch (doubtless from the clothes) that it is a woman. So he asks who she is. It is no wonder that he was terrified. For he could have suspected that an evil spirit who had assumed a body was lying at his feet. Alessandro Alessandri, in book 2, chapter 9, writes

---

2. Varro *Rust.* 1.51.

about an apparition that had stripped off its clothes, as it seemed, and placed itself in a bed where a good man was lying. And it drew near as if it wanted to embrace him. Now the other man, when he already seemed nearly dead from fear, drew back to the bedframe and drove the apparition away when it was coming nearer.[3] See also book 4, chapter 19.[4] I can also relate other examples of this sort.

There is no doubt that Boaz, suddenly overcome by terror, entrusted himself to the Lord. For pious men have usually done this in those sudden terrors when hideous images and illusions of shadows appear to them. The ancient fathers, as we often read in their writings, protected themselves with the sign of the cross and so put demons to flight. Lactantius writes about the power of the cross in his *Divine Institutes*.[5] Now we must not think that this ceremony of the cross in itself repelled demons, but because they believed that they were delivered from the power of demons by the blessing of Christ's cross.

To Spread a Wing

Ruth modestly responds that she is his handmaid and asks that he spread the edge of his garment, or his wing, over her. כנף (*chanaph*) means "wing," "edge of a garment," and likewise, "end" and "corner." Lyra notes that a bridegroom who was contracting a marriage at that time placed his wing, or the border of his clothes, over his bride, so that the meaning is, "Betroth me to yourself, and marry me by the right of kinship," or, which is better, "Spread your wing over me," that is, "Receive me into your protection and defend me."[6] The metaphor is taken from birds, which cover their chicks with their wings and defend them.

By the way, the duty of husbands toward their wives is depicted by this metaphor, namely, that they protect, defend, and cherish them and provide what they need. Good God, how many husbands are there into whose minds these things do not even enter!

3. Alessandro Alessandri, *Genialium dierum libri sex varia ac recondita eruditione referti* (Paris: Johannes Petrus, 1532), fol. 34v.
4. Alessandro, *Genialium*, fol. 116r–117r.
5. Lactant. *Div. inst.* 4.27.
6. Lyra, *Biblia*, fol. 280r.

She adds a reason why he ought to receive her into his care: *"For thou art a near kinsman."* She says this so that he will not think that she is an immodest, audacious woman who crept into a man's bed at night. She recalls to his mind the law of God about marrying a brother's or dead relative's widow. Women, therefore, should not abuse this passage to defend filthiness. Nor should they go night or day into the bed of a man to whom they are not married, especially if he is quite drunk, or otherwise rashly expose themselves to danger. For the nature of those times was different from that of today.

Ruth 3:10–13

10 *And he said unto her, "Blessed (art) thou of the* LORD, *my daughter. Thou hast made thy latter piety more excellent than the former because thou has not walked after (hast followed not) young men, whether poor or rich.*

11 *Now, therefore, my daughter, fear not. I will do to thee all that thou sayest. For all the city (gate) of my people doth know that thou art a virtuous woman.*

12 *Now then, (I confess) it is true that I am thy kinsman; howbeit there is (another kinsman) nearer than I.*

13 *Tarry (here) this night, and when morning comes, if he will perform unto thee the right of a kinsman, it is well; let him be near. But if he will not perform it unto thee, then will I perform unto thee the right of a kinsman, as the* LORD *liveth. Sleep (therefore) until the morning."*

Ruth, a distinguished woman, asked Boaz, the kinsman of her former husband, to marry her, as was most recently said. Next follows what Boaz said in response to her. *"Blessed art (or be) thou to God (or from God) my daughter."* The Septuagint renders it, *"Blessed art thou to the* LORD *God"* (εὐλογημένη σὺ τῷ κυρίῳ θεῷ). She who modestly called herself a handmaid Boaz calls a daughter, and he prays to God, the only giver of all good things, that He will bless her with respect to body and soul. Or he says that she is adorned by God with great gifts and is favored by Him. It is a type of greeting that also appears elsewhere. In 1 Samuel 15, when Samuel comes to Saul, Saul greets him and says,

"Blessed be thou of the LORD." In the New Testament, in Luke 1, the angel Gabriel greets the Holy Virgin and says, εὐλογημένη σὺ ἐν γυναιξί, that is, "Blessed art thou among women," that is, "You are strong in grace and favor with God. It is great to be in favor with a prince, but much more with God. You are that happy and blessed woman, whom God chose for Himself out of the whole female sex, that the Messiah would be born from you." For by the word "blessing" the Hebrews understand happiness of every sort. He says that her latter חסד (chesed), "piety," is greater than the former. Her former piety or kindness was that she revered her husband while he was alive and felt affection for him, and that she did not desert her mother-in-law, even when her husband was dead. Her latter piety was that when she was free of her husband, she did not pursue lust and seek young men, whether rich or poor, but kept herself pure for the kinsman of her husband so that according to the law she would have offspring from him and preserve the name of the deceased for posterity. She could have acquired for herself a young husband either in her fatherland or in Israel, but so that she would not violate the law she preferred to marry an old man. Illustrious deeds are to be praised in men and women. Boaz certainly did not approve of the way in which she sought to obtain a husband for herself, or at any rate he could not have praised it in another who did not have a similar reason. For what she did had the appearance of evil. But he judges not according to the external appearance of this work, but according to Ruth's mind and intention. He thinks that she did what she did, not out of levity and lust, but at the command of her mother-in-law so that according to the law seed could be raised up for her former husband. He likewise thinks that up to this point she has lived honorably and behaved toward her mother-in-law in such a way that she is most worthy of the best husband.

Since Boaz judges so candidly about that deed that had the appearance of evil and interprets it positively, we certainly ought not to interpret negatively things that have the appearance of good, much less things that are good and right in their own nature. There are some who, from some depravity of nature, take the words and deeds of others in the worst way, though they are induced to do so by no probable reason. Saint Paul, in

1 Corinthians 13, says, "Charity thinketh no evil, believeth all things, hopeth all things." Ambiguous, but not shameful, words and deeds are to be interpreted positively. A man is worse to the degree that he indulges more in suspicions. They commonly say, "He who is bad, thinks bad." In this respect, they imitate the character of the devil. But those who do not want to labor under evil suspicion ought to avoid those things on account of which men come to be suspected by others. In Numbers 32, Moses suspects that the two tribes and the half-tribe, demanding the land beyond the Jordan, which was best, would abandon their brothers to dangers. Afterward, when they declared their opinion, they removed the evil suspicion from his mind and from that of the other Israelites. In 2 Samuel 10, David sends envoys to the king of the Ammonites, to comfort him concerning the death of his father. But the king, when he had listened to accusers, suspected those envoys of treachery and violated them, from which arose a very bitter war. Therefore, we must not listen to talebearers and accusers, who put evil suspicions into men's minds. In religious matters also, everything is to be set forth openly and skillfully so that grave suspicions will not be left in the minds of the simple. For there are some who, though they understand the business of religion, nevertheless speak very ambiguously about many heads of religion, lest they should incur the displeasure of great men.

The example of Ruth teaches us not to be led by our emotions and so do what satisfies the flesh, to the neglect of God's law. Ruth could have found a young husband, but she marries an old man so that she will not violate the law of the Lord. There are widows who could easily have rich men, but they either do not want idolaters, or they are unwilling to abandon their fatherless children. There are also men whom wealthy wives would marry if they would move out of places where pure doctrine is proclaimed and move to those where it has no place. They also sometimes spare their children, lest, if they marry the sorts of wives they prefer, their children will be worse off; the children ought to acknowledge this with a thankful spirit.

Boaz comforts Ruth, whom he again lovingly calls "daughter," so that she will not fear him but be of good courage. She was afraid, perhaps, that she would be regarded by him as unchaste, or that, being drunk, he would attempt to defile her, or that she would suffer rejection. He adds that he will do what she asks, that is, he indeed was prepared to take her as his wife. For it is known to the whole city, he says, that she is a woman endowed with virtue. Literally, it is, "All the gate knows," that is, the whole city, either because judgments were administered in the gate, or because "gate" is synecdochically put for the whole city.

In contracting a marriage, it especially ought to be considered that the chastity and honor of the woman whom you are going to marry is well known to everyone. But in our times the first question is about wealth, the last about morals. It is a beautiful thing if women do not labor under a bad reputation, if it is known to all the citizens that a woman has behaved rightly from her youth. On the contrary, it is an ugly thing if it is known to bleary-eyed men and barbers[1] that a woman has been filthy and unchaste.

He adds the condition on which he will marry her. "I am not saying," he says, "that I am not your kinsman (some think Boaz was Elimelech's fraternal nephew), but another is joined to you by a closer bond. I want to confer with this man about this issue, and if he wants to marry you by the right of consanguinity, fine, but if not, I will marry you by the right of kinship." He would have preferred to marry her immediately, but he was not willing to snatch his kinsman's right. If he had wanted to claim her for himself, Boaz would have wronged him, if he had married her before consulting his kinsman. The same procedure applies also in other matters. Justice is that virtue which attributes to someone what is his. We should be so far from wanting to take what belongs to another without his consent that we ought rather to defend his things from another.

He does not immediately tell her to come up to him and does not promise her marriage. This fact admonishes men who are going to get married not to hurry or act in haste and not to follow their emotions. For we must see that no impediments are lying in the way. For there are some things that prevent marriages from being contracted, and some that even dissolve marriages that have been contracted. Well known are

---

1. This classical expression, first found in Horace, means "everyone." See Hor. *Sat.* 1.7.3.

the following lines: "An error, a condition, a vow, kinship, a crime, a disparity of worship, force, orders, a prior engagement, decency, if you are related by marriage, if perhaps you will not be able to have sexual intercourse: these things prohibit marriages from being joined and cancel those that have been joined."[2] The vow of virginity under the papacy impedes marriage, as do orders, if for instance someone is a priest. There is no reason we should deal further with these things here.

Boaz settled business with his kinsman beforehand. In other contracts, we usually carefully weigh everything; in marriage, greater caution is needed. Also, in betrothals we must avoid doing anything deceitfully. After a marriage is contracted, it would be useful, on account of the many dangers that can arise from it, not to draw out the affair too long, but to confirm it publicly.

The Saints Swore Oaths

By an oath he confirms that he will marry her, if the other man refuses. We also read about other saints often using an oath in weighty matters,

---

2. The number of impediments to marriage (both diriment, which rendered a marriage null and void, and prohibitory, which rendered a marriage unlawful) varied in number (usually between twelve and sixteen) among medieval canonists. The list included here was an especially popular form and appears, for example, in Aquinas *In IV Sent.* 34.1.1. "Error" refers to a situation in which at least one of the parties to the marriage did not give his or her informed consent to what was intended. "Condition" refers to a situation in which one of the parties to the marriage did not know the legal status (i.e., slave or free) of the other party at the time of the marriage. "Vow" refers to a solemn vow of chastity. "Kinship" generally refers to the degrees of consanguinity within which marriage was forbidden as incestuous, though some other relationships are also in view. "Crime" refers to a situation in which two parties attempt to marry after one party kills, or plans to kill, the spouse of the other party, or after the other party kills, or plans to kill, his or her own spouse. "Crime" can also refer to a situation in which two parties attempt to marry after one party commits adultery with another party. "Disparity of worship" refers to a situation in which a Christian and a non-Christian attempt to marry. "Force" refers to a situation in which one party applies external force to compel the other party to enter the marriage. "Orders" refers to holy orders. "Prior engagement" refers to a situation in which one party is already married when he or she attempts to marry someone else. "Decency" refers to a situation in which two parties cannot contract a valid marriage because one party has previously had a relationship with the other party's relative, within certain degrees of consanguinity. The final impediment refers to an inability to have conjugal relations with one's spouse.

though they were not required to. This is to be noted against those who utterly reject swearing. Moreover, he swears so that he might free her from worry. Unless there was more conscientiousness in swearing in ancient times than there is today, he certainly could not have freed her from worry. For sometimes even great princes deceive others by an oath and oppress the incautious. What Boaz promised, he afterward really and fully did.

He tells her to sleep until morning. He did not want her to wander through the streets at night. It is the duty of women to stay at home at night on account of the many dangers that could befall them. It is also very beneficial for youths to be kept at home at night, for night often furnishes an opportunity for many great evils. Moreover, they will be able to while away the time at home either in reading or in other honorable exercises.

Ruth 3:14–18

14 *And so she slept at (the place of) his feet until the morning. Afterward, she rose up before one could know his neighbor. And he commanded, "Let it not be known that the woman came into the threshing floor."*

15 *Also he said (unto her), "Bring (furnish) the linen cloth that is upon thee and hold it." And (she) held it, and he measured six (measures) of barley and laid it on her. And he went into the city.*

16 *And so she came to her mother-in-law. She said, "Who are thou, my daughter? (Who are thou, or what has happened to thee?)" And she told her all that the man had done to her.*

17 *And she said, "Six (measures, sata in the Chaldean version)[1] of barley gave he me. For he said to me, 'Return not empty unto thy mother-in-law.'"*

18 *And so said she (Naomi), "Wait (be still), my daughter, until thou know how the matter will fall. For the man will not be in rest, until he have finished the thing this day."*

The sequence of the story must be carefully observed for a better understanding of this book. In the previous homily, we heard how Boaz behaved toward Ruth when she was discovered on the threshing floor. Next, we will hear about her being sent away and returning to her mother-in-law.

---

1. Tg. Ruth 3:17.

First, however, it says that she slept the whole night at his feet. After the conversation they had about entering into marriage with each other, they remained in their places. If Boaz had behaved otherwise than was proper, certainly the Holy Spirit, who did not conceal in silence Noah's drunkenness,[2] Lot's incest,[3] David's adultery,[4] Peter's denial,[5] and Magdalene's sin,[6] would not have concealed this. Boaz did not abuse the opportunity that was offered to him in order to satisfy his lust.

Example of Chastity

By his example, he teaches us continence and chastity. We read in the histories of the gentiles about great commanders who, after they had captured cities, either did not want married women and virgins who were extraordinarily beautiful to be brought before their eyes, or even if these women were brought to them and they gazed on them, nevertheless, they tempered their desires, and sending them back untouched either to their parents or to their husbands, they obtained much favor among them. When Alexander the Great was invited to see the captive daughters of King Darius of the Persians, who were astonishingly beautiful, he was unwilling to go, saying that he must not be guilty of being conquered by women when he had conquered men. But they were rather shadows of virtues than virtues among the gentiles. For what they did flowed not from true faith, but from ambition. Joseph deserves to be praised because, though he was often incited by his mistress, who was taken with his good looks, he was not willing to wrong his master and violate God's command (not yet even expressed in the Decalogue) (Gen. 39). For as it is necessary to avoid other occasions to evil, so also adultery. Even if you are alone with a woman, even at night, nevertheless, the bridles of immodesty are not to be relaxed. We must think about God's commandment, "Thou shalt not commit adultery,"[7] and about

---

2. Gen. 9:20–21
3. Gen. 19:30–38.
4. 2 Sam. 11:1–5.
5. Matt. 26:69–75; Mark 14:66–72; Luke 22:55–62; John 18:16–18, 25–27.
6. Lavater may be identifying the sinful woman in Luke 7:36–50 as Mary Magdalene.
7. Ex. 20:14.

the penalties for adultery, whoring, and lust. We must not judge wicked deeds according to the corrupt judgment of the world. How different are those young men who either under the pretext of marriage or by force violate others' daughters or wives and, likewise, some decrepit old men who (as they did to Susanna)[8] tempt others' wives to adultery? But why am I speaking about them, when monks, who vow chastity, have also often violated married women and virgins! And it is well known that they have used auricular confession and sometimes magic arts for this purpose. Yet if a woman comes into a monastery, the monks sweep the floor with brooms.[9]

Ruth got up before one could recognize another in the dark, that is, at dawn. For Boaz said (as the old translation has it), *"Beware that no one know that thou camest here."* Or, as others think, he commanded his servants not to tell anyone that she had spent the night in the barn, because it was not acceptable. What Josephus says is more probable, that he told her to leave before he woke his servants.[10] Although he had a clean conscience and had not done anything for which he deserved to be ashamed, nevertheless, he did not want to offend others and give them something to grab onto to slander him. We know from the gospel what they should expect who have offended their neighbors in words and deeds.

---

8. Sus. 20.

9. In the medieval and early modern period, a broom was a symbol of chastity; sweeping the floor symbolized the removal of moral impurity. See, e.g., Alexander Monachus Cantuariensis, "Liber ex dictis beati Anselmi," in *Memorial of St. Anselm*, ed. R. W. Southern and F. S. Schmitt, vol. 1 of *Auctores Britannici medii aevi* (London: Oxford University Press, 1969), 195. See also the Latin translation of Hom. *Od.* 22.455 in Johann Philip Pfeiffer, *Libri IV antiquitatum Graecarum gentilium* (Königsberg: Henry Boye, 1707), 369. Thus, Lavater is noting the hypocrisy of the monks. The same monks who engaged in sexually immoral behavior acted zealous for their chastity whenever a woman visited a monastery, as though they needed to remove the impurity created by the mere presence of a woman.

10. Joseph. *AJ* 5.330.

We Must Avoid Even the Appearance of Evil

He teaches (just as Saint Paul also admonishes in 1 Thessalonians 5) that we must avoid not only evil itself, but also the appearance of evil. There are many things that we could say and do with a clean conscience. But we must always have regard for our neighbor, and all our words and deeds must be directed toward the edification of others. If a woman does not want to be regarded as a prostitute, she should avoid presenting herself with the appearance, speech, gestures, clothes, and other features of a prostitute. We must take care of our reputation, according to the following very well-known lines: "If you lose everything, remember to keep your reputation, because once you lose it, you will afterward be a nobody."

A loss of wealth can easily be restored through labor and industry, but if someone's chastity is suspected, it is not so. Nevertheless, the world is not without some nefarious men who take pleasure in their wicked deeds. Isaiah, in chapter 3, says about his people that, like the Sodomites, they have boasted about their wicked deeds. He adds, "He shall reward evil unto them."[11] Jeremiah, in chapter 3, reproaches the people because they have "a whore's forehead and will not be ashamed." How many are there today who boast about lewdness and adultery, drunkenness, illicit usury, unjust murders, and other wicked deeds, which no one would know they had done if they were silent? Yet those who hide their wicked deeds will also not escape punishment. We also ought to look out for others' reputations and chastity. Boaz studiously guards against anyone suspecting that they had done anything bad.

When she is about to leave, he tells her to take the cloak or linen cloth with which she was covered and to hold it with both hands. And he measured out six barleys, that is, six bushels or measures of barley (Theodor Bibliander, my most honorable teacher, understands it to be an ephah),[12] and once the garment was tied in a knot, as it seems, he placed it on her head. Some interpret מטפחת (*mitpaach*) as "a linen cloth, cloak," others as "an outer robe, linen garment." It is not easy to say

---

11. In Lavater's text, the verb is singular. Notably, *Biblia Sacrosancta*, trans. Leo Jud, 225, which renders the verb as plural, has a marginal note explaining that the subject is "the executors, that is, of divine justice."

12. I have been unable to locate a reference to this in Bibliander's works.

how much barley there was, if it is converted to our measure. It seems there was as much as she could carry on her head. He gave her the barley so that she would take it to her mother-in-law, who was poor, and so that she also would have something to eat until she celebrated the wedding with one of the kinsmen.

The wealthy learn to use their wealth rightly and to bestow it liberally for the use of the poor. At this time, during such severe persecution of the pious and crop failure, you have a great opportunity to exercise your liberality. God will not regard as excused those who seek a defense for their greed in the fact that they did not know who was worthy or unworthy of alms.

Rabbi Solomon, according to Lyra, writes that those six measures were a sign of the six blessings of God that would come upon the Messiah, who would be born from Ruth through David, according to what it says in Isaiah 11: "There shall come forth a rod out of the root of Jesse.... And the spirit of wisdom and understanding, or prudence, shall rest upon him, the spirit of counsel and strength, the spirit of knowledge and the fear of the LORD." Lyra adds that from this saying of Rabbi Solomon two things are established: first, that the Scripture of the old law is to be expounded not only historically, but also sometimes mystically, and second, that that statement of Isaiah is asserted and understood of Christ, even by the Hebrews themselves.[13]

Boaz entered the city. He no doubt accompanied Ruth for the sake of her honor and protection. For honorable virgins and married women ought to avoid wandering in the streets at night without a lamp and honorable companions.

Ruth came to her mother-in-law, who asked, "*What has happened to thee, my daughter?*" Or, "*Who art thou?*" that is, "How is your situation? How has your business succeeded? Did your kinsman take you as his wife?" Parents ought to require an account from their children, even from their adult children, and be pleased if their neighbors or relatives do not hide the vices of their children from them.

---

13. Lyra, *Biblia*, fol. 280r–v.

Ruth did not become more insolent because of the hope of marriage, but she modestly answers her mother-in-law. She does not talk back to her but recounts in order what happened. Children, even adult children, ought to give an account to their parents about their words and deeds. Likewise, if their parents are poor, they ought to bring them provisions and support them; they ought not to steal secretly what their parents acquired through hard work. Proverbs 28:24: "Whoso robbeth the property of his father and his mother and saith, 'It is no transgression,' he is the companion of a transgressor."

The wealthy learn not to send away empty those who are truly poor. Boaz did not want a daughter-in-law to return empty to her mother-in-law, whom he knew was oppressed by poverty. He who gives bountifully to the poor lends to the Lord. We should give various contributions to them rather than to mute images.

The mother-in-law tells her daughter-in-law to stay at home until she knows how her situation will turn out. She does not want her to divulge the matter, as some talkative women would. She adds, "*Boaz will not be in rest, until he have finished the business this day.*" Good deeds are not to be procrastinated, but what is proper is to be completed immediately.

Mothers learn from these words to instruct their daughters well, to teach them good things, and to divert them away from evil. Naomi tells Ruth to sit, that is, to rest, to wait for the outcome, and then not to doubt Boaz's faithfulness and diligence. Children are to be instructed in religion and good morals, not only by words, but also by the example of one's life.

How Is Authority Acquired?

Next, we see how authority is acquired. Naomi trusts this man, that he will keep his word to Ruth, because she saw that he was endowed with other virtues. Otherwise, she would have doubted his trustworthiness, nor would she immediately have believed him when he made a promise. This is true authority, when someone's words and deeds have weight with others. For example, when a man says or promises something and men do not doubt its truth; when he does something and they consider it right; when he commands something and others obey; when he gives advice and others gladly receive it and place great stock in his judgment. But how is this reputation acquired? Not by flattering, not by pretending, but from virtue often demonstrated and from happiness. For the minds of men are kindled by their admiration of virtue and their belief that God helps the virtuous man. Many think that dignity is acquired from an external "mask," expensive clothes, magnificent titles, and pretense. Certainly, these things have no small effect on fools, but not on prudent men. This is a singular gift of God, necessary for magistrates, teachers, heads of households — no, rather, even workers and merchants. In Job 29, Job says how much he was valued among all men, because he faithfully did his duty and did not stop deserving well from everyone. Our reputation is lost if we do not do what we promise, if what we say is false, and if what we do deserves reproof. Therefore, many complain undeservedly that they have no authority, since they do not do what they ought.

Ruth 4:1–4

1 *Then went Boaz up to the gate and sat down there. And, behold, the kinsman of whom he spake passed by. And Boaz said, "You, such a one! Turn aside, sit down here." And he turned aside and sat down.*

2 *And he took ten men of the elders of the city and said, "Sit ye down here." They sat down.*

3 *And he said unto the kinsman, "Naomi, that is come again out of the country of Moab, hath decided to sell a parcel of land, which was our brother Elimelech's.*

4 *And I said, 'I will reveal in thine ear, saying, "Acquire (the field) before those sitting (in the presence of the inhabitants) and before the elders of my people."' If thou wilt redeem it, redeem it. But if thou wilt not redeem it, tell me. Now I know that there is none to redeem it beside thee, and I am after thee." Then he said, "I will redeem it."*

So far we have heard about the various evils and troubles that disturbed Naomi and Ruth. Next we will hear how their condition changed for the better. For after Boaz, a wealthy man, bound Ruth to himself in marriage, both Naomi and Ruth abounded in the things they needed to sustain their lives.

Division of This Chapter

As for the rest, the Holy Spirit observes the following order in this chapter. First, Boaz, in the presence of the judges, tries to discover the will of his kinsman, namely, whether he wants to claim for himself Naomi's estate and marry Ruth according to the law. Next, when the kinsman refuses, Boaz marries Ruth; therefore, the elders and the whole people congratulate them. Third, when he had fathered a child from Ruth, the women bless Naomi, the child's grandmother. Fourth, Boaz's genealogy is described.

This chapter is filled with numerous doctrines, just as we will hear, by God's help, in their own places. But in the first place we see that the pious can rise, by the kindness of God, out of the deepest poverty and can be raised to the highest honors. Boaz had told Ruth when she asked for marriage that he would marry her, unless the nearer kinsman were to marry her. On the following day, he sat in the gate as the principal judge, according to the Hebrews, who say that he was Ibzan, and when the kinsman about whom he had told Ruth by chance, or rather by divine ordination, passed by, he told him to come to him and to sit beside him. Then he summoned ten elders and told them to sit down, and he laid out his case.

As to the phrase, "*You, such a one! Come and sit down here,*" the Hebrew words אלמני (*almoni*) and פלני (*peloni*) mean nothing but are only put in place of a proper name, which the writer omits either because it is well known or because it is not available to him or because he does not want to mention it. The Greeks say ὁ δεῖνα ("so-and-so"). Some think his name was concealed by the providence of God because he was regarded as unworthy to be remembered by good men since he disdained to raise up a name and seed for his brother.

Gate

The ancient Hebrews administered judgments in the gates or around the gates of their cities, while everyone watched and heard what was being done, just as today also in many places public judgments, especially capital judgments, are administered in the open air. They assert the following as the reason why the senate was held in the gates: so that the location would be quickly accessible to everyone, so that farmers would not be forced to enter the cities and take on some expense, and so that once the business was finished each man might return immediately to his own home. In addition, they did this so that a multitude of witnesses could conveniently be drawn from those entering the gates. Or the gate is simply taken for the courthouse [*curia*]. The Chaldean version renders it as "*at the gate*," that is, "at the house of public judgment, at the praetorium, or courthouse [*curia*]."[1] Perhaps it is called this because houses of this sort had large gates. The Romans generally assembled the senate in temples.

Senate

He called together the elders. The Hebrews call judges זקן (*zacan*), from the word for "old age," just as the Latins also call them "elders" and "fathers." Among the Greeks, the senate is called γερουσία, from the word for "old age." The senate, by whose counsels the republic is governed, are generally chosen from among the old men, who seem especially suited for this business. For they know many things and have learned many things even from their own misfortune. Next, they are not as carried away by their emotions as the young are but administer affairs with mature judgment. In addition, since they are near death, they more often consider, or at least ought to consider, that nothing is to be done against public justice and religion, because God will shortly demand from them an account of their words and deeds. When the tyrant Peisistratus asked Solon what hope inspired him to resist Peisistratus so fiercely, Solon responded, "Old age."[2] Valerius Maximus writes about Cesselius that since he was not obeying the Triumvirs and was speaking freely and at length against Gaius Caesar, his friends warned him to beware. He said, "There are two things that give me the greatest confidence, namely, old age and childlessness."[3]

Sitting

Those elders are said to have sat down. By "sitting down," it means that judges ought to have quiet, peaceful, and tranquil minds, not disturbed by emotions, and that they ought to listen in the forum to the litigants

1. Tg. Ruth 4:1.
2. Plut. *Sol.* 31.1.
3. Val. Max. 6.2.12.

with attentive, not wandering, minds. Servius notes on book 9 of the *Aeneid* that the ancients took "to sit down" for "to consult," "to take care of," and "to consider."[4]

Afterward, he sets forth the case and says, "*Naomi hath decided to sell the field of our brother* (the Hebrews call their kinsmen "brothers") *Elimelech. Therefore, I decided to reveal in thine ear* (that is, *to indicate to thee*) *that if thou wilt redeem it by the right of kinship in the presence of the inhabitants and the elders of the people, redeem it, because there is no other who is nearer. But if it doth not please thee to redeem it, I would that thou tell me.*" He immediately answered, "*I will redeem it.*" Boaz then adds that he also must marry Ruth if he wants to acquire the field.

Law about Receiving an Inheritance

The Jews had their own particular laws about inheritance and succession. In Numbers 27 and 36, the land of Israel was divided into twelve tribes, each of which had its own possessions. God did not want them to be mixed and for the inheritances to be transferred from one to another. When a parent died, the children succeeded to the inheritance. The sons had to marry wives from their own tribes, and the daughters also were not allowed to marry outside their own tribes. If someone died without children, his brothers succeeded to his inheritance, but if he did not have brothers, his kinsmen inherited it. According to Leviticus 25, no one was allowed to sell his own possession as an inheritance, but if anyone was burdened by poverty and was forced to sell his fields, he had to offer them to his kinsman. If the kinsman failed to buy them, he had to offer them to someone from the same tribe. If in the meantime the seller had stumbled onto some money, he could always redeem his possessions from the buyer. At length, in the Jubilee the possessions returned to their original masters. Lyra notes on this passage that women indeed did not succeed to the inheritance, but that if a wife remained childless after her husband died, she had a part of the inheritance to sustain her life ("for a living" [*zŭ lybding*]) and could sell it as far as it was within

---

4. Serv. *A.* 9.4.

her right.[5] And so it says that Naomi in the same way wanted to sell the field, or part of the field, namely, that which was left by her husband and children and which she had the right to use while she was alive. But she was not allowed to sell the fields outside her husband's family, but only to his kinsmen.

To Reveal in the Ear

As for the phrase, "to reveal in someone's ear," which is frequent in sacred literature, it means, "to admonish someone," or, "to indicate something," or even, "to reveal some secret to someone." The Latins say, "to pull the ear" for "to admonish." Virgil, *Eclogue* 6: "When I sang of battles and the king, the Cynthian god pulled my ear."[6] For this is the custom, Mancinelli says, of those who encourage and admonish someone to do something or even to remember something.[7] See Erasmus's proverb, "to pull the ear."[8]

We Must Keep a Promise to Our Neighbor

"*If no one will redeem it.*"[9] The third person is put in place of the second: "*If thou wilt redeem it, let me know.*" In this passage, first, we have an excellent example of keeping a promise. He had said that he would marry Ruth unless she were married on that day by another. He does without delay what he promised he would do, though he promised privately and without witnesses, and he keeps his word. In the same way, if anyone promises marriage to another, or, likewise, other things (as when you promise someone a certain sum of money), he should do it in good faith. But before he promises, he should carefully consider whether he can do what he undertakes to do. Moreover, to do this you must diminish luxury, and you must labor day and night. In Proverbs 6, Solomon commands him who is surety for another not to rest until he has

---

5. Lyra, *Biblia*, fol. 280v.

6. Verg. *Ecl.* 6.3–4.

7. Virgil, *Opera Vergiliana*, ed. Jodocus Badius Ascensius (Lyon: Jacque Sacon, 1517), fol. 32r.

8. Erasmus, *Adagia* 1.7.40.

9. The verb in the MT is in the third person.

been freed; he does not command him to break his promise. If written assurances are added, or if there is an oath, greater responsibility falls on us. So great is the levity of men today, especially in marriages, that many refuse publicly what they promised privately to the poor and needy, as well as to strangers. No, rather, they by no means do those things to which they bound themselves by an oath.

An Example of Justice

Next, there is presented to us an example of justice. He did not defile Ruth so as to push a man out of his right and take for himself the wife and the field. The morals of men today are generally of such a sort that many men seduce virgins so that they can keep them without the consent of their parents and relatives. Justice commands that we give to each one what is his. Unjust are those who claim for themselves those things that belong to others by hereditary right or who sell or even prostitute another's children. Divine law condemns kidnappers to death. But how many are there today who, relying on their own wealth and their own power, strive to rob others under the title of "right"?

We Must Deal Cautiously with Cunning Men

In addition, we learn how cautiously we must deal with greedy, cunning, and contentious men, of which sort that kinsmen seems to have been. Boaz, who, we must suppose, knew and clearly understood the man's character, does not deal with him directly in such a way that he would say right then, "You must raise up a seed for your kinsman from his remaining wife and widow according to the law." Rather, he approaches him obliquely. First, he speaks to him about the estate, then about marrying the wife at the same time, so that all material for disputes will be cut off and he will reach his purpose by a suitable means. We ought not always disclose everything immediately, but we ought to keep some things to ourselves for a suitable time. In 1 Samuel 16, God commands Samuel, who had to anoint David as king, to take a calf and to say that he wanted to offer a sacrifice to the Lord, so that his life would not be in danger.

We Must Set Forth Matters Clearly in Judgment

In addition, we learn from Boaz's example that we must set forth controversial matters in the public square in few, suitable, and clear words. He himself set forth the case. In some republics, representatives do this, who also are not to be allowed to harm others' reputations or to babble on about many things that are in no way pertinent to the subject and so to fatigue the judges and lead their minds away from the proposed matter, as some usually do.

Lawful Contracts

Moreover, we learn that it is lawful for a pious man to sell, buy, lease, exchange, and redeem property, for this is not attributed as a fault to pious and holy men in the Scriptures. Rather, we read in Jeremiah 32 that Jeremiah the prophet, at God's command, bought Hanameel's field by the same right by which this man is commanded to buy the field. We must also take care that those contracts are made in accordance with equitable laws and in such a way that we will not be ashamed to summon many witnesses who can testify to how we have dealt with our neighbors.

Lastly, we must also note that the judges and the kinsman sit, remain silent, and do not interrupt Boaz's speech, nor do they cause a disturbance. So judges and those who appear before judges should listen attentively. When they are asked or commanded, they should respond. They should pass a just sentence in accordance with the laws.

Ruth 4:5

5 *And Boaz added, "What day thou acquierest the field of the hand of Naomi, thou shalt acquire it also of Ruth the Moabitess, the wife of the dead, to raise up the name of the dead upon his inheritance."*

Although Boaz would have gladly married Ruth because of her excellent character as soon as it was asked of him, nevertheless, he was unwilling to do this without the knowledge of the kinsman, who was closer in degree of blood. So he calls together the elders and in their presence explains the matter. To avoid digressions he first asks the kinsman whether he wants to claim for himself Elimelech's small estate according to the law. When this is acceptable to him, he tells him also to receive Ruth as his wife by the same right, which he refuses to do.

Raising Up Seed for a Brother

So that we might more fully understand this and the preceding chapter and also other passages of Sacred Scripture, I will quote the actual words of the law about raising up seed for a brother. In Deuteronomy 25, we read the following:

> *If brethren dwell together, or equally (in the same city or town, certainly at the same time, and the property of both was in one place), and one of them die without a child, the wife of the dead is not to marry without unto a strange man, but her husband's brother is to go in unto her and take her to him to wife and perform the duty of a kinsman (the Targum translates it, "She is to join with him in marriage"; Santes*

*translates it, "He is to contract a marriage with her").[1] And the first-
born which she beareth shall rise to the name (or in the name) of his
brother which is dead (or, "He is to succeed or shall succeed in the name
of his brother." Some are of the opinion that the meaning is, "He shall
be called the son of the deceased, and the inheritance of the deceased
shall belong to him."), that his name be not blotted out of Israel. And
if the man like not to take his brother's wife, let his brother's wife go up
to the gate and say unto the elders, "My husband's brother refuseth to
raise up unto his brother a name in Israel, and he will not have me by
the right of kinship." And the elders of his city are to call him and speak
with him, and if he persist and say, "I like not to take her," his brother's
wife is to come unto him in the presence of the elders and pull his shoe
from off his foot, and, spitting in his face (Rabbi Solomon interprets it
as, "before him," to brand him with disgrace),[2] is to answer and say,
"So may it be done unto that man that doth not build up his brother's
house." And his name shall be called in Israel, "The house of him that
hath his shoe removed."*

The Parts or Sections of This Law

This law, as you see, has many points. First, if a brother dies without
children, his widow ought not to marry a foreign man or an outsider,
that is, from another family, but a brother or another relative of her
former husband. And if one refuses, another who is the next closest is
to succeed him, as is clear from this book. Second, the first son who is
born from her ought to be named after the dead brother and succeed to
his inheritance. Third, if the brother of the deceased refuses to marry
his widow, she ought to indicate this to the judges so that they might
admonish him of this law and persuade him by various reasons to marry
her. Fourth, if he cannot be persuaded of this, the widow ought publicly

---

1. Tg. Onq. Deut. 25:5 and Tg. Ps.-J. Deut. 25:5 have the brother-in-law taking the
woman as his wife. It is not clear why Lavater takes וְיִבְמִנָה (in Tg. Onq.) or וְיַבֵּם יָתָהּ (in
Tg. Ps.-J.) this way. *Biblia Veteris ac Novi Testamenti*, trans. Santes Pagnino and François
Vatable (Basel: Thomas Guarinus, 1546), 138. Note that, at least in this edition, the verb
is *contrahet* ("He shall contract") rather than *contrahat* ("He is to contract" or "Let him
contract").
2. Lyra, *Biblia*, fol. 226r.

to take off his shoe and spit in his face and mark him with this public disgrace, as it were. Some think that by this ceremony it is signified that she is afterward her own master and has the power to marry whomever she wants.

Before the Law a Brother Raised Up Seed for His Brother

Even before the law was instituted there was a custom that a brother would raise up seed for his brother, as the story of Onan in Genesis 38 demonstrates.

Outside of this case, a brother was not permitted to marry his dead brother's wife. For there is a law against this incest in Leviticus 18 and 20, where it deals with the degrees forbidden by God. If children had been produced by the first marriage, it also would have been incest if the brother had married the widow. In the New Testament also, Saint John the Baptist harshly rebukes Herod because he was defiling himself by having an affair with his brother's wife while his brother was still alive.[3]

Reasons for This Law

God shows the reason why He instituted this law. He is certainly not bound to give us a reason for His laws and judgments, but so great is His mercy that He often condescends to reveal to us the reasons why He does something or gives us some command. Who among us explains to his servant the reasons why he commands him to do one thing or another? Now what reasons does He give for this law?

(1) The first reason is so that the name of the deceased will not be blotted out from Israel, so that his family will not perish and his inheritance be transferred to other families. If widows had married foreigners and transferred part of their property to foreign families, their inheritances would have been dissipated and diffused and their families would have perished from want. For we often see that good families are scattered because of poverty. God wanted the distinction of tribes and families in Israel to be preserved on account of the promises concerning the

---

3. Matt. 14:3–4; Mark 6:17–18; Luke 3:19–20.

Messiah, who had to be born according to the flesh from the tribe or family of Judah. It is also very useful to republics if they have ancient and illustrious families. For those who are descended from them can be employed in great affairs and especially in governing the republic, For we gladly submit ourselves to those to whom the splendor and dignity of their family imparts authority. Also, those who have had illustrious ancestors generally wish not to do anything unworthy of their virtue or to stain them indelibly. "New men"[4] either insolently use their power or are pressed down by others' envy. The ancient histories of the Romans, Greeks, and other nations demonstrate this, as does experience. Therefore, God wanted to bestow this good also on the Israelite republic, that it would always have capable men who could usefully manage the republic. Certainly, the sons of heroes are often harmful. Nevertheless, if a spark of their fathers' virtues shines in some of them, their ancestors' worthiness and faithfulness to the republic procures for them great authority.

(2) In addition, it was also to take care of widows, for unless this law had defended them, many immediately would have been thrown out of their homes that they had managed well. But because of this law it was permissible for them to keep their husbands' possessions if they had married the brother or kinsman of the deceased.

(3) Likewise, God wanted to prevent divisions among brothers. Some often desire the death of others' brothers so that they might seize their inheritance, but this could not happen if the brother had died without children.

(4) It also admonished others of their duty toward the dead, so that they would not allow their memory to be erased.

---

4. The term *novus homo*, originating in the Roman republic, referred either to a man who was the first in his family to become a Roman senator, the first in his senatorial family to become a consul, or most often, to a man who rose to the consulship from a nonsenatorial family. Later, the term began to refer more broadly, as here, to a man who attained political power but whose family was not socially or politically prominent.

(5) Africanus also assigns another reason for this law. According to Eusebius, when Africanus writes about the different genealogies that are related by Matthew and Luke, he says, among other things, "Those are indeed considered natural successions that descend from true seed or blood, but they are considered legal successions when someone is substituted as a son for someone who did not father him. For when the hope of resurrection had not yet been received among them, by this means they portrayed an image of resurrection so that the name would not be abolished through the fault of barrenness."[5]

(6) Augustine in *Against Faustus the Manichaean* exposits this law spiritually: "A brother was commanded to marry his brother's wife for this reason," he says, "so that he might raise up a progeny not for himself, but for his brother and call him by his brother's name, though he was born from him. What else does this prefigure except that every preacher of the gospel ought to labor in the church so as to raise up a seed for his dead brother, that is, Christ, who died for us, and that the seed that is raised up should take His name?"[6]

(7) Some think that it also signifies that those who once have been received into the number of the citizens of spiritual Israel will never perish. In the gospel, Christ says, "Rejoice, because your names are written in heaven."[7] But if someone should object, "Could not families also have been preserved in some other way, and could not those dangers be avoided?" I respond that we must simply obey the command of God, who knows best why and how He does everything.

This law, whether ceremonial or judicial, endured for a long time. Certainly, the possessions were so confused by the Assyrians and Babylonians that there could appear no distinction among them, and so this law temporarily had no use. But afterward when the Jews were led back

5. Euseb. *Hist. eccl.* 1.7.2.
6. August. *Faust.* 32.10.
7. Luke 10:20.

to their fatherland and the possessions again began to be distinguished, this law again was observed. We gather this from the case that the Sadducees propose to the Lord about the woman who married seven brothers in order, from which they erroneously want to conclude that there will be no resurrection of the dead (Matt. 22; Mark 12; Luke 20).

This Law Has Been Abrogated
But after Christ suffered the death of the cross for us, as other ceremonial and political laws of the Jews, so also this one was abolished. And when the whole polity of the Jews was destroyed and they were dispersed throughout the whole world, although they especially wanted to keep this law, nevertheless, they could not. Therefore, no one may use it as a pretext for his own nefarious lusts or incestuous marriage, because this law no longer has a place since the reason for it was removed. Although the ceremonial and judicial laws are said to be abrogated, nevertheless, their marrow and kernel is to be observed, as in this law, that we should have regard for the dead, that we should not transfer inheritances (which adulterers, as well as others, do, who often fraudulently substitute another's child as heir), and likewise, that brothers should be concerned about preserving the progeny of their brothers and kinsmen.

From all these reasons we now can understand why Boaz was unwilling to marry Ruth before the other kinsman renounced his right. Since the kinsman wanted to redeem the field, Boaz adds that he cannot claim the field for himself unless at the same time he also marries Ruth and preserves the name and lineage of his kinsman.

Whether the Law in Leviticus Should Be Taken
of the Wife of a Living Brother
Before I move on from here, it seems that I must not omit that some reconcile the law that appears in Leviticus 18, about not uncovering the nakedness of your brother's wife, with the other law in Deuteronomy 25, about raising up a seed by a brother, in such a way that they say that the former law is to be understood only of the wife of a living brother. This, however, is inconsistent, because the same thing would also have to be said about the other persons with whom it is not lawful to be joined

sexually. Besides, more remote persons are prohibited. On this view, Saint Augustine writes as follows in question 61 on Leviticus:

> "*Thou shalt not uncover the nakedness of thy brother's wife; it is thy brother's*[8] *nakedness.*" *We ask whether this is prohibited while the brother is alive, or dead. And it is no small question. For if we say that the Scripture speaks about the wife of a living brother, this prohibition also is surely included under the one general precept by which a man is prohibited from approaching another man's wife. Why then is it that the text so carefully distinguishes these persons, whom it calls "family members," from the rest with particular prohibitions? Surely what it prohibits concerning a father's wife, that is, a stepmother, would also have to be construed as though the father is still alive and not rather dead, wouldn't it? You see, if the father is alive, who does not understand that it is much more prohibited, if it is prohibited to stain any other man's wife with adultery? Therefore, it seems to be speaking about those persons who, not having husbands, could enter into marriage, unless they were prohibited by law, as is reported to be the custom of the Persians. But again, if we understand it to be prohibited to marry a brother's wife when the brother is dead, we run into what Scripture commands must be done for the sake of raising up a seed if the brother died without children. And, therefore, when we compare this prohibition with that command, so that they will not contradict each other, we must understand there to be an exception, that is, that it is not lawful for anyone to marry his dead brother's wife if the dead brother left behind descendants. Or also that it is prohibited so that it would not be lawful to marry a brother's wife even if she had separated from a living brother through divorce. For at that time, as the Lord says, because of the hardness of the Jews Moses had permitted a certificate of divorce to be given, and by this dismissal one could have thought that anyone might lawfully marry his brother's wife, where he would not fear adultery, since she had separated through divorce.*[9]

---

8. The text has *fratris patris tui*, "of thy father's brother," apparently citing accidentally from verse 14.

9. August. *Quaest. Lev.* 61.

Whether It Should Be Taken Simply

But others take the law in Leviticus about not marrying a brother's wife simply, without any exception, as the laws against murder, adultery, theft, and so on, so that incest will not appear to be commanded and the laws will not appear to contradict each other. For they say that we must not think that God, for some external advantages, permitted marriages that He previously called incestuous. They say that by the term "brothers" in the other law about raising up a seed it does not mean actual brothers, but relatives, according to the Hebrews' usage, and indeed, those whose marriages were not forbidden. For a father's brother's sons [*patrueles*], a father's sister's sons [*amitini*], and a mother's sister's sons [*consobrini*] are called "brothers." Now, we may note in passing, the sons of two men who are brothers are *patrueles*. The sons of two siblings, one male and the other female, are *amitini*. The sons of two sisters are *consobrini*. In this very chapter, Elimelech is called the "brother" of both Boaz and his kinsman. Saint Augustine, in *Against Faustus the Manichaean*, writes as follows: "Scripture testifies that among the ancients male and female blood relations were usually called by the general term 'brothers' or 'sisters.' Lot is called Abraham's 'brother,' although Abraham was his paternal uncle. From this usage of the word, those called the Lord's 'brothers' in the gospel are by no means those whom the Virgin Mary bore, but all his kinsmen by blood."[10]

Ibn Ezra, in *On Leviticus*, testifies that the ancient Hebrews held this view, but that the Cabalists, after better weighing the matter, abandoned it.[11] In our time also, a pious and learned man who deserved the best from the church of God embraced this view. And thus he expounds the passage in Matthew 22 concerning the seven brothers who married one widow; he says that they were related to each other and, indeed, within the degrees in which it was lawful to marry one and the same woman.[12] But it can be demonstrated by two arguments from the book of Ruth that this law about raising up a brother's seed must be taken of

---

10. August. *Faust.* 22.35.
11. I have been unable to locate this reference.
12. I have been unable to determine the identity of this "pious and learned man."

actual brothers. For first, Naomi, to whom this law could not have been
unknown, tries to persuade her daughters-in-law to return home,
because even if she were to have a husband and hope of offspring, nevertheless, it would not be advisable for them to wait until they had grown
up. Next, Boaz says that the other kinsman by his right may buy the
field and marry Ruth, since Boaz is not a nearer kinsman than he is.
Hence the second closest relation on the father's side would not have
been admitted unless the former had refused. Onan was punished
because he was unwilling to raise up seed for his brother Er (Gen. 38).
In addition, we must not depart from the proper sense of the words in
laws, especially if they do not occur elsewhere. The Hebrew word יבם
(iabam) in the whole of Scripture means nothing other than a *levir*, a
husband's brother, and יבמה (iafamah) means nothing other than the
woman who is to be married by right of affinity or kinship in this case.
And so this law first should be understood of actual brothers and next
should be applied to other near kinsmen also. And so the other judicial
or municipal law in Deuteronomy is an exception to that general and
moral law in Leviticus, which exception, as we said, was removed by
God for special reasons. Nor is there any reason why today it should be
adopted as an example.

Ruth 4:6–8

6 *The kinsman answered, "I cannot redeem it for myself, lest perhaps I erase (lose, squander) mine own inheritance. Redeem thou the right of my kinship to thyself, for I cannot redeem it."*

7 *Now this was the manner in former time in Israel concerning redeeming and changing, for to confirm any business. A man plucked off his shoe and gave it to his neighbor. And this was a testimony of surrendering a right in Israel.*

8 *Therefore the kinsman said unto Boaz, "Acquire it for thee (Possess thou it)." And at the same time he drew off his shoe.*

When the kinsman heard that Naomi had decided to sell her field, he immediately says that he will buy it according to the law. But afterward when he hears that by the same right he is also to marry Ruth, he renounces his right. He adds that the reason is so that he will not perhaps lose or squander his inheritance. But how would he have lost it? Perhaps because Ruth was young he feared that he would father more children by her. It is not evident whether he previously had a wife and children. Likewise, the law about marrying a brother's wife does not express whether a brother ought to have married his brother's wife if he previously had a wife. Certainly, if he had a wife and children, it would have been very inconvenient to take a new wife and to produce more children. For rarely do children fathered from different mothers get along with each other. In addition, he saw that not only poor Ruth, but also elderly Naomi needed to be supported. He did not fear that if he had more fields he would not be able to cultivate them more (which often happens, and therefore it is better to cultivate a few fields well than many fields badly), for he would have been willing to have this field too, but not the wife. Lyra comments that some of the Hebrews expound it of the posterity that would come from Ruth if he were to take her, because it was written in Deuteronomy 23, "Moabites and Ammonites shall not enter into the congregation of God forever." "But if he alleged this," he says, "he spoke falsely because that penalty falls neither on women nor, consequently, on their progeny from an Israelite man. Therefore, it is explained of the progeny that he already had from another wife. For if he had taken Ruth, he would have had to attend to raising and providing for the progeny that he already had from another woman. He calls this an 'erasure' according to the common way of speaking, by which it is said of someone that he is destroyed or erased if he suffers some notable loss."[1]

Care for Household Property Should Not Be Disparaged

He does not sin because he cares for his household property and because he prefers to increase his inheritance than to lose it. For as long as we can preserve and increase our wealth without a loss of piety, we should do it. First Timothy 5: "But if any provide not for his own, and especially for those of his own house, he hath denied the faith, and is worse than an infidel." But care for household property ought not to drag us into usury and other illicit means of acquiring wealth. But this kinsman, whoever he was, sinned in that he was inconstant. At one moment, he wanted the field. The next moment, he refused, saying that he could not take it along with the widow. He says contrary things about one and the same matter. Next, the law is acceptable to him where it is convenient for him; where it is not, there he rejects it.

And what insolence or audacity was it that he says that he will lose his inheritance if he does what God had commanded His people to do so that their inheritances would be preserved? Does he want to seem wiser than God? Does not God preserve households and promise

---

1. Lyra, *Biblia*, fol. 280v.

and bestow His blessing on those who obey His commandments? Can someone's household be safe and unharmed if God is unwilling? If he was going to suffer some loss of wealth, would not God have been able to restore it? Or was he not to consider that this would result in his brother's honor?

This man has many imitators in our times. There are many who indeed speak grandly of the doctrine of the gospel and extol it with wonderful praises for the reason that they hope that by it they will obtain wealth and honors. But afterward they either are unable to obtain what they sought or now they have obtained wealth and fear danger lest they lose their wealth, and they hate the gospel and revile it. Many only approve of some things in the doctrine of the gospel, such as that in Christ it reveals to us all salvation, but reject those parts that it teaches about restraining the flesh. They hate auricular confession, excommunication, and papist fasts. But they do not give up bacchanalian and lupercalian feasts, or other feasts of this sort. Subordinates gladly listen when others speak about the duty of superiors, but they refuse to do their own duty. When it is convenient, they temporarily approve of laws and rights. When it is inconvenient, they are displeased with and completely despise them. Some, on the contrary, disparage and revile many errors, such as false worship and superstitions. Then, captivated by the foods of false teachers and corrupted by their gifts, they turn their sails and praise and defend this worship and these superstitions. The author of *A Bundle of Times*, a historian who is not to be despised, writes about a master who argued strongly against a plurality of benefices, as they call them, and against the riches and arrogance of prelates. When this was reported to the pope, he responded, "Let us give him a good provostship, as well as these and other favors, and he will be placated." When this was done, the master immediately changed his view, saying, "I never understood this matter before now." For he had suddenly gone from being poor to being rich.[2]

---

2. Werner Rolevinck, *Fasculus temporum* (Rougemont: Henricus Wirtzburg, 1481), n.p.

Now how many are there and have been in every age who, no differently from that kinsman, regard it as quite settled that they are going to perish if they order their lives according to the law of God? For example, they think they are going to perish if they rest on the Lord's Days and also grant rest to their servants and, likewise, supply enough food for their servants and hirelings and give liberally to the poor, while in other respects they are obligated to care for their household property and to conserve it. It is common for men to want to ward off dangers and increase their possessions by transgressing the law of God.

The kinsman, after he said that he would not marry Ruth and take her field, now urges Boaz to enjoy that privilege himself. He renounces his right with words and with a sign or external symbol. The law orders the brother's wife to take off the shoe from her relative by marriage, if he is unwilling to marry her, and to spit in his face, adding, "So may it be done unto that man that will not raise up seed for his brother." And this man's house is to be called, infamously, the house of him who has his shoe removed.[3]

Taking Off a Shoe

The Jews have many superstitions about this shoe, of what leather it ought to be made and how it ought to be sewn, and many other foolish things, by which it can be perceived how eventually they slipped and fell in the interpretation of sacred literature and rejected Christ, the true light. In this passage, the man himself takes off his shoe, not his kinswoman, so that she might disgrace him. Nor does she spit in his face, perhaps because Boaz voluntarily succeeded to his place, accepting the small estate and the widow at the same time. It does not expressly say that Ruth was in the gate, no doubt because the near kinsman was addressed about discharging the right of protector (as Borrhaus notes) not by Ruth, but by Boaz.[4]

---

3. Deut. 25:9–10.
4. Borrhaus, *Commentarius*, 293.

The Shoe Was Taken Off in Every Surrender of a Right,
Not Only Concerning Marriage

It does not seem to me that this passage is to be explained, as is commonly done, by that law in Deuteronomy 25 about the shoe being taken off by the brother's wife. But I simply think that it indicates that it was a solemn rite among the Hebrews in buying and selling fields, that if anyone should wish to cede his right and hand over his possession to another, he would take off his shoe and give it to the other, for he himself takes off the shoe.

I think this is signified by a shoe [*calceamentum*] so that they might show that the buyer thereafter has the right to tread [*calcandi*] on this field, or to go through it, or through the estate that was handed over to him by the seller. Some are of the opinion that during Absalom's sedition, David walked with bare feet, since taking off one's shoe is a sign of yielding (2 Sam. 15). Our men profess that they are ceding their right by giving their hand, *globend an die hand*. Some are of the opinion that the prophet alludes to this when he says in Psalm 60:8, "Over Edom will I cast out נעלי (*naeli*, my shoe)." Others expound it as "my fetter." These same words are repeated in Psalm 108. Santes Pagnino cites Rabbi Immanuel, who expounds it as both "fetter" and also "glove," no doubt because it encloses and protects the hand.[5] For the word נעל (*naal*) means "to shoe" and "to enclose" or "to fasten." The same rabbi adds that it was the custom of kings when they besieged a fortified city to throw down the glove, signifying that he would not withdraw from it before it was captured. Santes applies to this what Cicero writes about Antony in his *Eleventh Philippic*: "For he is accustomed to take manacles," that is, gloves, "and not to endure the fear of a siege for long."[6] This passage of Cicero, however, can be explained differently. For manacles bind the hands; fetters bind the feet. In the second book of Virgil's *Aeneid*, we read, "Priam himself first orders the manacles and the tight bonds to be removed from the man."[7] Having compassion on Sinon, he removes his

---

5. Santes Pagnino, *Thesaurus linguae sanctae* (Lyon: Sebastian Gryphius, 1529), 1436–37.

6. Pagnino, *Thesaurus*, 1437. For the Cicero reference, see Cic. *Phil.* 11.26.

7. Verg. *Aen.* 2.146–47.

manacles, which are epexegetically called "tight bonds." Plautus, in *Asinaria*, writes, "The manacles have scarcely embraced your hands."[8] The sense of the passage in Cicero, then, is, "Usually, he immediately gives himself up and surrenders to the enemy." There are also gloves made of iron that protect the hands. Juvenal: "What splendor if there is an auction of the wife's possessions, the swordbelt and manacles, crests, and the half-covering for the shin of the left leg!"[9] If you take it in this sense, the meaning will be, "Usually, he immediately takes his manacles off his hands, that is, he removes them, lays down his arms, and surrenders himself to the enemy; he is unwilling to fight." But if you understand it to refer to the long sleeves [*manicis*] of his clothes, the meaning will be the same, namely, that he immediately lays down his arms and puts on his long-sleeved [*manicatas*] clothes. In Virgil, Numa, reproaching the besieged Trojans for their effeminacy, says, "And your tunics have long sleeves [*manicas*], and your turbans have ribbons."[10]

But these comments are in passing. Relevant here is that the Chaldean paraphrase renders this passage in the same way, according to Cinqarbres's translation.[11]

> Now this was the ancient and usual custom among the Israelites when they received, or gave, or redeemed, or exchanged with each other. To confirm the whole business, he (who was ceding his right) would remove the glove from his right hand and through it would relinquish his possession to his near kinsman. In this way indeed the Israelites were accustomed to give up their possession to their near kinsman in the presence of witnesses. Then the redeemer said to Boaz, "Receive the possession, and possess it for thyself." Then Boaz took the glove from his right hand and received the possession.

In connection with this passage, there occurs to me a story about Conrad, the last Duke of Swabia, grandson of Emperor Frederick II. As Aventinus writes in the *Bavarian Annals*, Conrad made many complaints

---

8. Plaut. *Asin.* 304.

9. Juv. 6.255–57.

10. Verg. *Aen.* 9.616.

11. Tg. Ruth 4:7–8. I have not been able to locate Cinqarbres's translation of Tg. Ruth.

about the injustices of the Roman pontiff. Just as he was about to offer his neck to the executioner to be cut off, he threw his manacles or gloves into the air and said that by his right he was bequeathing his kingdoms of Aragon to the king, his kinsman.[12] This happened in 1258.

It is evident that in many matters the ancients used rites and symbols of this sort. For example, in weddings among the Romans, the bridegroom would give the bride an iron ring. Pliny writes that afterward golden rings began to be given.[13] Likewise, in contracting marriages they used water and fire, signs of married life together. Keys were given to a wife who was brought into the home, but they were taken away from her again in a divorce. Among us, bridegrooms and brides join hands, which is a sign of entering into marriage. Today, to offer keys to a victor is to hand over to him the right to govern the city. In manumitting slaves, the masters would slap them, turn them around, and put a cap on their heads. Moreover, they touched them with a rod. It was also common in nearly all nations to use some rite in the elections of the orders. The following were the insignia of the ancient emperors: an ivory throne, a laurel wreath, an ivory scepter, a purple garment, lictors with axes and fasces, and fire carried before them. As for the German emperor, according to Trithemius, a sword is first girded on him. Next, bracelets are put on his arms. Afterward, a scepter is handed to him. Lastly, a crown is placed on his head.[14] In the other kingdoms, sometimes only a spear is used, sometimes a sword, often both. If someone wants to know more about this, he should read chapters 22 and 23 in the *Feudisticis* by the very brilliant lawyer, and the greatest student of all antiquity, François Hotman, in which he compiled many things of this sort that he diligently observed and collected from various authors.[15]

12. Johannes Aventinus, *Annalium Boiorum libri VII* (Leipzig: Johann Friedrich Braun, 1710), 672.

13. Plin. *HN* 33.4.

14. Johannes Trithemius, *Annalium Hirsaugiensium…complectens historiam Franciae et Germaniae, gesta imperatorum, regum, principum, episcoporum, abbatum, et illustrium virorum* (St. Gallen: Johannes Georgius Schlegel, 1690), 73–74.

15. François Hotman, *De feudis commentatio tripertita* (Lyons: Jean Lertout, 1573), 68–76.

The kinsman resigns the whole right that he has. He does not ask for the field to be given to him, but for Ruth to be given to Boaz, as those do who leave an inconvenience to others and pursue their own personal convenience and who, though they have no right over others or their goods, nevertheless, against laws human and divine, want to claim those things for themselves. The impudence of these people should be severely restrained by princes.

Ruth 4:9–10

9 *And Boaz said unto the elders and unto all the people, "Ye are witnesses this day, that I have acquired (taken possession of) all that was Chilion's and Mahlon's of the hand of Naomi that handed it over.*

10 *Moreover Ruth the Moabitess, the wife of Mahlong, have I acquired to be my wife, to raise up the name of the dead upon his inheritance, that the name of the dead be not cut off (perish) from among his brethren and from the gate of his place. Ye (I say) are witnesses this day."*

This passage explains what Boaz did after the kinsman, whose name the Holy Spirit for some reason kept silent, ceded his right. First, he clearly testified that he was acquiring the possessions of Elimelech and his sons. Next, that he was marrying Ruth the Moabitess, not for the sake of pleasure, but so that the name of the deceased Mahlon would not be blotted out from among his brothers, that is, his kinsmen, and from the gate of his place, that is, from Bethlehem. With these words he shows the excellence of Mahlon's stock, that many from it have sat in the gate, that is, have discharged the office of judges. It would have been lamentable for such a distinguished family to perish, which also in later times could supply rulers.

Whether Boaz Was Right to Marry a Foreigner
The question is raised in the passage whether Boaz violated the laws about not marrying foreigners. Although the Lord, in these laws, includes those peoples whom He had devoted to destruction, nevertheless, the laws must also be extended to other unbelievers because of the danger

of idolatry, as we have shown above in the third homily on chapter one. Where there was no danger of defection, marriage was not completely illicit. Ruth had already converted to the faith and worship of the one God, and she had given evidence of her faith by illustrious works. So Salmon, Boaz's father and David's great-great-grandfather, married Rahab the Canaanite, who had saved the spies and had eminently proved her faith.[1] We must always have greater regard for the worship of the true God than for wealth and kinship. In Genesis 24, Abraham binds his servant by an oath not to turn aside to the Canaanites but to go to Abraham's kinsmen to seek a wife for his master's servant Isaac. Isaac, or rather Rebekah, sends her son Jacob to Laban so that he will not intermingle with idolaters (Gen. 28). It behooves parents to imitate this example. When they are about to enter marriages, idolaters make many promises that they do not afterward keep. "He who loves danger," as it is said, "will perish in it."[2] Daughters who are given to superstitious men are exposed to greater danger than young men to whom are joined superstitious or idolatrous women. Children should also remember their duty and not seek such marriages against the will of their parents. Esau is given to vice because he offended against his parents by marrying idolaters (Gen. 27). A marriage lawfully contracted between pious people has many troubles. What good, then, will you expect from such an unequal marriage? In other circumstances it is dangerous and distressing to live with idolaters. What if you are completely bound to them? Do not deceive yourself with the vain hope that you can win your wife, or a wife her husband, for we see that the opposite generally happens. And it is commonly known what happened to Solomon, the wisest of mortals, when he married idolaters.[3]

Boaz publicly dealt with both these points in the court, first with the possessions and then with marriage to Ruth. Moreover, he dealt with nothing secretly, admonishing us by this fact that we should so make contracts in buying, selling, exchanging, and redeeming as if we are doing

---

1. Josh. 2:1–21; Matt. 1:5.
2. Sir. 3:26.
3. 1 Kings 11:1–8.

this publicly in the court before many witnesses, or even in the sight of all men. How many are there who make contracts with their neighbors in such a way that they dare not say, without shame, how they did this and what the conditions of their contract are? They name a sum of money that they should have given to their neighbor. They say that they dealt with him lawfully and without evil deceit when they know that they are lying. In addition, they wish to fortify their false account books with the seals of good men. They should have considered that we must give an account and that we will have two witnesses against us, namely, our conscience and God, the one who knows and punishes our crimes.

Clandestine Weddings

In addition, marriages are not to be contracted in secret, but in the presence of witnesses. No one is to be tricked into marriage, but everything is to be carried out in good faith. Rarely do clandestine weddings (which are commonly brought about by madams, vain promises, drunkenness, and other things of this sort) have a good and happy outcome. Virgins should not listen to young men who promise them marriage if they will first give them access to their bodies. For if the young men are honorable, they will prefer to begin a marriage with you by offering prayers in the sacred assembly than by sleeping with you.

Marriages Are Consecrated in the Sacred Assembly

It was also rightly and prudently established by the ancients that the betrothed are to be joined together by a minister of the church publicly in the sacred assemblies. For in this way we testify that marriage is a holy matter, not a work of darkness of which we ought to be ashamed. Those who do evil fear the light and seek hiding places and shadows. Other benefits are also added. For we see those who are lawfully married and those who are not. It also encourages couples to keep conjugal faith with each other, because in the sacred assembly, with the minister of the church leading them in the recitation, they promised to do this both verbally and by giving their hands. If someone promises in the presence of three or four people that he will do something, he altogether does it if he is a good man and can do it with a good conscience. How much more ought spouses to perform those things that they promise each other in the sight of God, His angels, and the whole church? In addition, the whole church prays that the marriage will be happy and prosperous, about which we will say more later.

How Witnesses Ought to Behave

Boaz says to the elders and all the people, "*Ye are witnesses* (he afterward repeats this) *that I have done*" such and such. They respond, "*We are witnesses*," as if they should say, "If it is necessary, we will testify that this is what happened." Witnesses should tell what they have heard, seen, or found out by some sure method; they should not be unreliable or dishonest. They sin grievously who are unwilling to say anything, lest they offend someone, or who do not speak accurately what they do speak, or express another man's words with a different sense, or add or omit some things that are pertinent to the matter. They are false witnesses whom Solomon in Proverbs 6 numbers among those six or seven things that the Lord abhors. In chapter 19, he twice says, "A false witness shall not be unpunished, and he that speaketh lies shall perish." A false witness sins very grievously. For he deceives the judge, who trusts witnesses who have taken an oath, according to that saying, "In the mouth of two or three witnesses shall every matter be established or fall."[4] Next, he severely harms his neighbor in his fortune, reputation, body, and life. In addition, he horribly wrongs God, whom the false witness makes a patron of his treachery. For these reasons there are weighty laws, divine and civil, against false witnesses. Accordingly, everyone should act in good faith when giving testimony.

Nor should we only use witnesses in matters of great importance, which perhaps was sufficient at that time, but we should also take care that our purchases, acquisitions, and other things of this sort are recorded in account books or otherwise attested carefully and without ambiguity, lest disputes arise in the future. It is well known that long ago there were short account books of purchases and agreements. Now men can scarcely be compelled to do their duty by long, extensive books.

---

4. Deut. 19:15; Matt. 18:16; 2 Cor. 13:1.

Ruth 4:11–12

11 *And all the people that were in the gate and the elders said, "We are witnesses. God make the woman that is come into thine house like Rachel and like Leah, which two did build the house of Israel. And do thou virtue (act thou boldly) in Ephratah, and get a name (for thyself) in Bethlehem.*

12 *And let thy house be like the house of Pharez (whom Tamar bare unto Judah) of the seed which the* LORD *shall give thee of this young woman."*

After Boaz publicly testified that he was not only accepting the kinsman's fields, but was also taking the widow as his wife, the elders and all those who had come together in the gate first say that they are witnesses that Boaz joined Ruth to himself in marriage.

Next, they pray that God will condescend to bless their marriage. And they especially desire numerous children for them, which they make clear with two examples.

Leah and Rachel

"God make Ruth," they say, "like Rachel and Leah." The patriarch Jacob, who was also called Israel, had four wives, of whom these two were primary. Leah, whom he married first, was older, but here she is mentioned second, and Rachel is put before her, perhaps because he loved Rachel more because of her beauty and her other excellent qualities. For her sake he served Laban and would have married her first, if he had not been deceived by his father-in-law (Gen. 29). Perhaps for this reason she is principally called Jacob's wife (Gen. 46), not because Leah was not also his wife. From these two he fathered eight sons, from whom the same number of the tribes of Israel arose and for whom they were named.[1] And this is what they mean when they say that they built the house of Israel, because through them his family and posterity were increased and preserved and were propagated until Christ. Afterward, they say, *"Let thy house become like the house of Pharez, whom Tamar bare unto Judah."* Judah, Jacob's son, in a quite similar case, married Tamar, a foreigner, his daughter-in-law, from whom he fathered twins, Pharez and Zerah, and so the race and family of Judah was perpetuated.[2] For from them descended many distinguished families. From Pharez was born this Boaz, through whom descended the line of our Lord Jesus Christ.[3] For from him was He born into this world according to the flesh. If you review the whole story from the book of Genesis, you will understand this prayer more plainly.

A Multitude of Children

In the Old Testament it was a remarkable blessing if someone had numerous offspring. Barrenness was regarded as a disgrace. This is obvious from the example of Rachel, who is mentioned in this passage and who was initially barren, and from the examples of other ladies, as we will say later. In Genesis 24, when Rebekah is leaving, her parents bless her as follows: "Become thou a thousand thousands, and let thy seed possess the gate of thine enemies."[4] In Psalm 128, the prophet

---

1. Leah had six sons, each of whom fathered a tribe of Israel: Reuben, Simeon, Levi, Judah, Issachar, and Zebulun. Rachel had two sons: Joseph and Benjamin. Benjamin fathered a tribe, and Joseph's sons, Manasseh and Ephraim, who received the double blessing from Jacob, each became a half-tribe. Each of these half-tribes can be referred to as the "tribe of Joseph" (Num. 13:11; Rev. 7:8), and together they can be referred to as "Joseph" (Ezek. 47:13). Thus, Leah and Rachel produced eight sons who fathered eight tribes of Israel. The fathers of the four remaining tribes (Gad, Asher, Dan, and Naphtali) were the sons of Zilpah and Bilhah.

2. Gen. 38. It is not clear why Lavater considers the relationship between Judah and Tamar to be a marriage.

3. Ruth 4:18–21; Matt. 1:3–16.

4. In the text, Rebekah's brother Laban and her mother bless her; Lavater presumably considers Laban to be Rebekah's "parent" because he is her guardian.

sings, "May thy wife be as a fruitful vine by the sides of thine house, thy children like olive shoots round about thy table." The fruitfulness of marriages is also mentioned among the blessings of the Lord in the law. But what is said about a multitude of children should be understood of those who are compliant, pious, and have good character. For degenerate children are rather a curse. Holy children are the seedbed of the church and the republic; through them the true worship of God is propagated. Moreover, just as a multitude of children, so also a multitude of men in general ought to be counted among the blessings of God. "But many regions are so cramped," you say, "that men cannot comfortably live in them." I answer, "This is rather caused by the vice of men than the narrowness of the land, when there is no place among them for frugality." So much concerning the first blessing or petition.

Second, they desire for them an abundance of wealth and property, saying, "*And that thou create*," obtain, or increase, "*wealth (chail) in Ephratah*," that God will bless their labors, so that they can honestly obtain the wealth that they need, so that they will not be forced to beg for food or suffer want. Property is necessary for preserving one's family. And the diligence of men in collecting those things by which they care for their families is not illicit. On this issue there are many maxims and precepts in the Proverbs of Solomon. But we must avoid attributing an abundance of possessions to our industry and diligence rather than to the Lord's blessing. For his "blessing" or favor "maketh rich" (Prov. 10). All our labors are useless unless the Lord gives success. In Luke 5, although the apostles labored all night, they caught nothing, but when they cast their net at Christ's command they enclosed such a large multitude of fish that the net was breaking. We are not to long for wealth with insatiable desire, as the greedy do. Psalm 62: "If riches abound, set not your heart upon them." Some accumulate wealth by any means, right or wrong, but they do so unhappily, because this wealth does not profit their home, but rather overturns it.

If you have no wealth, or only moderate wealth, let what Solomon says in Proverbs 15 enter your mind: "Better is little with the fear of the LORD than great treasure and grief therewith." Proverbs 17: "Better is a dry morsel and peace therewith than an house of strife full of sacrifices."

Proverbs 16: "Better is a little with righteousness than a multitude of revenues without right."

Chail

Others render these words as "*and do thou virtue, act thou boldly.*" For חיל (*chail*) in the Scriptures means many things: "bodily strength," "mental strength," "riches and opulence," and likewise, "an army and multitude of people." Chapter 3 above called our Ruth "a woman of *chail* (of virtue)," that is, a woman endowed with extraordinary virtues. Chapter 2 called Boaz "a man of *chail*," that is, a brave man. In Exodus 18, about ruling the republic, Jethro says that men of *chail* should be chosen, that is, men of fortitude, brave men. Others translate it as "wise men," "robust men," "vigorous men," and likewise, "wealthy men," who in judgment cannot be led away from their duty either by threats or by bribes or promises. There are many passages all over the place where *chail* means "wealth." Job 20:18 says about the impious, "He shall restore his labor, and shall not swallow it down, according to *chail* (the strength, the wealth) of his restitution, and he shall not rejoice." The sense is he will not rejoice about the wealth that he took and that he will restore it to its place. Job 31:25: "If I rejoiced because my wealth was multiplied and because mine hand had found much," understand, "I would perish," or something similar.

Or they desire that in their numerous offspring they will equal a great army, although they previously spoke about children. Or it means, "*Act thou boldly and bravely,*" from which flows the second wish, the discussion of which now follows.

Fame

The third thing for which they pray is that he will be famous and illustrious in Bethlehem, which is also called Ephrathah and the city of David, about which see chapter 1 above. Literally, it says, "*Call the name,*" that is, "May you have a great name." They pray that they will behave in such a way that they will obtain fame and praise. Fame and authority are produced by zeal for virtue. Agesilaus was asked how a man could obtain for himself a good reputation (what the Greeks call εὐδοξίαν) among men. He responded, "If he speaks what is best and does what is most honorable."[5] Isocrates said that we must be more zealous to leave an honorable reputation for our children than a great accumulation of riches.[6] For wealth can be obtained through reputation, but reputation is never redeemed by money. Proverbs 10: "The name of the just remaineth, but the name of the wicked rotteth." Proverbs 22: "A good name is rather to be chosen than great riches, and good favor rather than silver and gold." In Ecclesiastes 7, it says, "than precious ointment." By wicked deeds and a shameful life a good reputation is lost.

It is evident that this prayer was not vain and useless. For Boaz and Ruth had children and grandchildren. They increased in riches and obtained great fame. For they are included among the grandfathers and grandmothers of Jesus our Savior. Many powerful kings descended from them.

We learn to pray for blessings for newlyweds, for ourselves, and for others, and to do so publicly and privately. We gather from this prayer what are the most important goods we are to wish for. Philosophers divide goods into goods of the soul, goods of the body, and the goods of fortune, all of which are contained in this brief prayer. For they pray that they will have holy offspring, wealth or zeal for virtue, and fame. Moreover, these goods are to be sought from the inexhaustible fountain of every good, that is, God. There are various afflictions and dangers in marriage with which God exercises us; therefore, we need His grace and blessing to endure all troubles patiently. Hence we must beseech God publicly and privately, that He will either mitigate or remove those troubles that happen through the fault of the spouses, as well as other troubles.

Most in our time do not worry at all about praying when they hear about newlyweds. They apply themselves entirely to criticizing the vices of the bridegroom, the bride, and their parents or their kin. In the sanctuary, many think about feasting, dancing, and other things rather than pray for blessings on the married couple. No, rather, the spouses

---

5. Plut. Mor. 213C, Apophth. Laconica, Agesilaus 65.
6. Isoc. Nic. 32.

themselves are rarely devoted to prayer when they are led to the sanctuary to receive the blessing, nor are they devoted to prayer when they return home. Their last care is about the Word of God and prayers. So no one should be amazed that many marriages are unhappy. Our prayers would not be ineffectual if we would inaugurate our marriages with them and also afterward persist in them. For God has given us many extraordinary promises that He will mercifully condescend to hear our prayers that proceed from an ardent faith.

Twenty-Fifth Homily

Ruth 4:13

13 *So Boaz took Ruth, and she was his wife. And he went in unto her, and the LORD gave her conception. And she bare a son.*

The Holy Spirit finally comes to the point for which this book was especially written, namely, that Boaz married Ruth and fathered by her his son Obed, David's grandfather.

The Scope of This Book
For the scope of this book is to indicate what patriarchs from Judah, to whom Shiloh had been promised,[1] lived up to the time of David, to whom the promise was renewed. In these few words, the Holy Spirit, as is His custom, includes many things. Boaz, He says, took Ruth, and she was his wife. We say, "He held a marriage feast with her and guided her to the church and street" (*Er hatt hochzyt mit iren gehalten und sy zur kirchen und straaß gefürt*). When the other kinsman had given him permission to marry her, he did not put off the wedding. For once they are betrothed, it is not useful to put off the wedding for long. For in the meantime Satan can sow tares and turn agreements into disagreements. We must also praise Boaz because he enjoys the marital right only after a lawfully contracted and approved marriage.

---

1. Gen. 49:10.

God Approves of Marriage

From the fact that it does not grieve the Holy Spirit to report about Boaz in this passage, and elsewhere about other holy men, that they took wives; about Ruth, and elsewhere about other holy ladies, that they married husbands; and likewise, about conception, birth, midwives, wet nurses, and raising children, we conclude that married life does not displease God. There are also other things that commend marriage to us, such as that it was not invented by men, but established by God Himself in Paradise before the sin of Adam and Eve, our first parents, and that God joined them in marriage and blessed them.[2] Likewise, there are many passages in the Sacred Scriptures showing that God approves of marriages, which passages must be carefully noted and collected by the pious. Marriages are protected by the law of God, "Thou shalt not commit adultery."[3] Christ our Savior was born from a married woman on purpose.[4] He adorned a wedding in Cana of Galilee with His presence and by making wine from water.[5] He also prescribes through His apostles the proper duty of those who are married. And He sets forth to us and expresses in marriage an image of the love between Himself and His bride.[6] These and other things of this sort must be set in opposition to the perverse judgment of those men who condemn or prohibit marriage. For in all ages Satan plots against marriage. Before the apostles departed from this life, he stirred up the Nicolaitans, who used women promiscuously and who are mentioned in Revelation.[7] Afterward arose the Tatians and Encratites, who, affirming that prostitution differs in no way from marriage, received no one into their sect who was married. Eventually, the monks, nuns, and priests, who vowed perpetual celibacy, emerged and pretended that celibacy deserves remission of sins. They extolled virginity with wonderful praises, as if these praises pertained

---

2. Gen. 2:21–24.
3. Ex. 20:14.
4. By calling Mary *coniugata*, Lavater is referring to her status as betrothed to Joseph in Matt. 1:18.
5. John 2:1–11.
6. Eph. 5:25–32.
7. Rev. 2:6, 15.

to those impure men. They spoke about marriage in such a way that many, repudiating their vocation and marriage at the end of their lives, assumed the habit of monks and nuns. How many marriage-haters are there today who pursue their wandering lusts? Therefore, those things that the Scriptures note about the dignity of marriage must be carefully observed. And in all the hardships of marriage, our minds are to be encouraged by the knowledge that God clearly approves of marriage.

Next, we must observe that Scripture says, "*He went in unto her*," for, "He had relations with her." It modestly notes in these words that which is done decently in marriage. So Genesis 16 says that Abraham "went in unto Hagar." Chapter 29 says that Jacob "went in unto" his wives.

Holy Language

Münster, drawing from the commentaries of the Hebrews, comments on Deuteronomy 23 that the Hebrew language is called holy because no proper names are found in it that signify the private parts of both sexes, sexual intercourse, excrement, and other things of this sort, but shameful and obscene matters are expressed by circumlocution in a decent and modest periphrasis.[8] In place of the word for "lying together," it also uses the word for "knowing," "sleeping," and so on. In 1 Samuel 24, Saul, while in the cave, is said to have "covered his feet," that is, to have emptied his bowels.

Against Obscenity in Speech

These phrases teach that we must avoid αἰσχρολογίαν, or obscenity in speech, if our conversation touches on sexual matters or other obscene matters. Paul teaches the same thing in Ephesians 4 and 6 and Colossians 3. People usually call men who have profane mouths "witty." But even among the gentiles the Cynics, who spoke obscenely and shamefully, had a bad reputation. In the introduction to the laws of Charondas of Catania, we read, among other things, the following words, as reported by Stobaeus: "No one should speak what is shameful, lest he defile his soul with obscene deeds and fill his mind with impudence and wickedness. For things that are honorable and dear to us we call by fitting

---

8. Münster, *Hebraica Biblia*, fol. 188r.

names that are written in the law, but things that we hate, we abhor even naming them because of their shamefulness. Therefore, it should be shameful even to say something shameful."[9] In Sirach 23 there is also a warning that we should not habituate ourselves to shameful and obscene speech. For from it arise evil thoughts. The apostle testifies that delicate minds are gravely offended by speech of this sort. He says, "Evil communications corrupt good manners" (1 Cor. 15). Saint Chrysostom calls obscene speech a vehicle for whoring, because it leads men into it.[10] What is said about speech must also be applied to shameful poems and songs. We ought always to keep in mind that we must render to God an account for an idle word, and so much more for a dirty and obscene word. Scripture indeed sometimes uses filthy words, as in Ezekiel 23, where it describes the treachery of both kingdoms, that is, Judah and Israel, who are compared to two women. But it does so for a good end, like the physicians, who sometimes prescribe remedies against filthy diseases with obscene words.

Children Are a Gift of God
It does not simply say that Ruth conceived and bore a son for him, but that the Lord gave this son to him. For children are a gift of God and, therefore, must be raised with religion so that they will be made acceptable. In Genesis 33, when his brother Esau asked about his children, Jacob responded, "They are the children which God hath given thy servant." When his father Jacob asked who those two young men were who were standing by his bed, Joseph responded, "They are my sons, whom God hath given me, that is, in this place." He does not say, "whom I begat," or, "whom my wife bore for me."

Barrenness
The women of Bethlehem prayed above that God would make Boaz's wife fruitful. For among other works of God, Psalm 113 also celebrates the fact that God makes the barren fruitful. In 1 Samuel 2, Hannah, in her hymn, sings that the barren woman, surely by the kindness of God,

---

9. Stob. *Flor.* 4.2.24.
10. Chrysost. *Hom. Eph.* 17.

has given birth to seven children. This must not be understood only of those who are utterly beyond childbearing age, such as Sarah was when she conceived Isaac from Abraham (Gen. 17). Likewise, Elizabeth was aged and hopelessly barren (Luke 1). Nor is it to be otherwise understood of barren women, such as Rebekah, Isaac's wife, was at the beginning (Gen. 25), and Rachel, Jacob's wife (Gen. 30), and Hanna, the mother of the prophet Samuel, and likewise, Elisha's hostess, who through the prayers of the prophet obtained a son whom, though he was dead, he brought back to life (2 Kings 4). But it is also to be understood of those who are fruitful by nature. For God is the author of all things. He has His reasons why He makes some fruitful and others barren.

It says that she gave birth to a son. If she had given birth to a daughter, her parents no doubt would have greatly rejoiced. But they took greater joy from the fact that to them was born a son, who was the pillar of the family. Since the Messiah had been promised to the tribe of Judah, the parents no doubt hoped that from their son the Messiah at some time would arise, just as it in fact happened.

She did not immediately give birth, but as it is added elsewhere, when the time for her to give birth was complete. Aristotle, in his *History of Animals*, writes that to the human being alone has there been given various times for giving birth.[11] For she can give birth even in the seventh, eighth, and ninth months, and most commonly in the tenth.

It said above that the women of Bethlehem prayed for the prosperity of the newlyweds. It is shown that their prayers were not in vain. For Boaz and Ruth obtain what the women prayed for them. Today, too, God grants our wishes and prayers. If you say that the future would have been the same had they done otherwise, we respond that although all things happen in the order of providence and most things happen by the course of nature, nevertheless, prayers are not offered in vain, nor are prayers to be separated from the order of God's providence. Often the order and series of affairs is overturned by them. The women about whom we spoke a little before, being eager for children, by their prayers obtained fruitfulness from God.

11. Arist. *Hist. an.* 7.4, 584a36–584b1.

Ruth 4:14–15

14 *And the women said unto Naomi, "Blessed be the LORD, which hath not let thee this day be without a kinsman, and his name shall be declared in Israel.*

15 *He also shall restore thy life (become a restorer of thy spirit) and nourish thine old age. For thy daughter-in-law, which loveth thee, which is better to thee than seven sons, hath born him (unto him)."*

Boaz fathered a son by Ruth, which was considered among the Hebrews to be the greatest blessing, especially in the tribe of Judah, from which the Messiah was to be born according to His human nature. According to His divine nature, He is eternally begotten of the substance of the Father in an ineffable way.

Next, the women of Bethlehem congratulated the child's grandmother. *"Blessed be,"* or, *"Praise be to God,"* they say, *"because He was* unwilling to leave you without a protector and kinsman." Unless a son had been born to her by Ruth, she would have been destitute of all relatives. For though that other relative was still alive, nevertheless, she could have expected no help from him.

Friends

There is no one so wealthy and powerful who does not sometimes need the help of friends. There is a proverb that says, "A friend is more necessary than fire and water."[1] For this reason the Latins also call their

---

1. Plut. *Mor.* 51B, *Quomodo adulat.*

friends "necessaries." Poor men who are surrounded by wealthy kinsmen and relatives are not so subject to injuries from others as those who do not have them. But even if we are destitute of friends, nevertheless, we should not despair. For we will have God not only as a friend, but also as a Father, if we trust in Him and rightly order our lives.

Next, they show what sort of child the newborn will be and what he will do. First, they say, "*His name shall be declared in Israel*," that is, he will be famous and will have a great name. They conclude this from the fact that he had pious and distinguished parents. Likewise, they hope that he is to be rightly taught and that he will be great on account of his parents' fame and his own virtues. Those children whose parents were famous easily obtain for themselves a great name, if they behave rightly.

Children Gladden Their Parents

Second, they say, "*He shall be unto thee a restorer of thy life.*" In chapter 1, she said that she was bitter because the Lord had afflicted her. Now they say, "*He shall restore thee.*" While he was little, he could cheer up his grieving grandmother with his jokes and games. Later, when he was older, she could infer from his pursuits that he would become a distinguished man. Proverbs 20 says, "Even a child maketh himself known by his pursuits, whether his work will be pure and right." And so she is cheered up more. There are many maxims by Solomon that show that children for whom there are high hopes, who have a good character, and who are endowed with virtue bring their parents joy. Proverbs 10 and 15: "A wise son maketh a glad father, but a foolish son is the sorrow of his mother." Proverbs 23: "The father of the righteous shall greatly rejoice, and he that begetteth a wise child shall have joy of him. Cause thy father and thy mother to be glad, and she that bare thee to rejoice."

Third, they say, "*He shall nourish thine old age,*" that is, "He will not allow you to lack the things necessary for sustaining life." It appends the reason: "*For thy daughter-in-law, which is better to thee than if thou hadst seven* (that is, *many*) *children hath born unto him* (or *hath born him*)." The number seven is the number of a multitude in the Scriptures. In 1 Samuel 1, Elkanah says to Hannah, "Am I not better to thee than if thou hadst ten sons?" They hoped that Ruth would not change her mind with her fortune in such a way that, after getting a rich husband, she would disregard her poor little mother-in-law, which often happens. Next, they hoped that Ruth would instill in her son love for her mother-in-law, so that he would support her since she was weakened by old age. For it matters much that mothers rightly inform their children about their own relatives and others. They gravely sin who incite children, sometimes against their parents, sometimes against their grandmothers, and sometimes against their relatives. A similar example of congratulations appears in the New Testament. In Luke 1, when Elizabeth had given birth to her son John and her neighbors and relatives had heard that the Lord had generously shown His mercy toward her, συνέχαιρον, that is, "They congratulated her." From the congratulations of these women some things are to be inferred for our instruction.

We Must Rejoice with Those Who Rejoice
First, we learn that we must give thanks to God and rejoice with those who increase in children, wealth, and other goods. Saint Paul commands us to rejoice with those who rejoice and to weep with those who weep.[2] We should not rejoice in the evils that befall others, laboring under hatred and envy. For God does not allow this perverted joy to go unavenged. But if we ought to congratulate others and thank God for those blessings that He bestows on them, how much more if He heaps on us His blessings, and especially for that general and memorable blessing, that He willed for His Son, our Lord Jesus Christ, to be born a man from the Virgin Mary to deliver us from eternal death? In our times, if anyone has increased in children, rank, or another good, banquets are held, and God is rarely mentioned.

Next, since they praise and thank God because Naomi has gained a blood relative, they confess that this is a singular gift of God. We do not thank someone for something that we have not received from him. All blessings flow from God, the perennial fountain of blessings. He still preserves families and raises up friends for us. We often have people close to us who despise us, but God can easily cause them to love us, care

2. Rom. 12:15.

for us, and honor us with reciprocal duties. Strangers sometimes love us and advance our interests. This too we ought to enter as a receipt from God. But God wants to make even their enemies be at peace with those whose ways, that is, whose endeavors, He approves, as it says in the Proverbs of Solomon 16. Do not think that it happens at random that men hate you or love you, are your enemies or your friends.

The Piety of Children toward Their Parents
In addition, we perceive from the words of these women what the duty of children is toward their parents, namely, to refresh their spirits and to support them in their old age. Those who do not gladden their own parents but throw them into weighty cares and sorrow by their shameful life are all but parricides. Nature itself teaches that we must support our parents when they are weakened by old age. For it is just that we support those by whom we were supported and who did for us innumerable other favors. How many mothers must abstain from certain types of foods that delight them so that they will not harm their unborn child? How many fathers and mothers must go without food so that their children will not suffer famine? How many children interrupt their parents' sleep with their crying? How many parents are alarmed because of the various unexpected falls of their children? Therefore, do not say that they are overly critical and complaining. Consider rather what you have been and what you will be through the corruption of age, if the Lord prolongs your life for many years. There are noble examples in the gentiles' writings of filial piety toward parents. An example of this sort is that of the daughter who nourished her mother with her own milk in prison, which is mentioned by Valerius Maximus.[3] Pausanias, writing about those who were called pious Catanians, says,

> When the fire boiled up from Etna into Catania (a Sicilian city at the foot of this mountain), they gave no regard to gold and silver, but during the flight, one man carried his mother on his shoulders, another carried his father. But since they did not hasten quickly, the fire enclosed them in a rapidly moving blaze. But not even

---

3. Val. Max. 5.4.7.

under these circumstances did they put their parents down. And so they say that the flames leapt apart on two sides and both young men and their parents passed by without suffering any harm.[4]

He says that even in his own time these men were held in honor by the Catanians. Storks also show their gratitude to their parents when they are weakened by old age. Hence ἀντιπελαργεῖν is taken to mean "to recompense."[5] Among Christians, you may find children who, though they abound in wealth, nevertheless push their parents away from them and all but allow them to waste away through famine. Often daughters would gladly do their duty, but the sons-in-law are not willing. Sons would often do likewise, but the daughters-in-law prove themselves difficult. Of them it can never be said what those women proclaim about Ruth, that she was better to her mother-in-law than many sons. Children often plead poverty as an excuse but, meanwhile, indulge in drinking, dress lavishly against all decorum, and make many worthless expenses. If parents have several children, the parents are sent back from one child to another, especially if the children previously squeezed them for money. Therefore, those act prudently who keep their wealth to themselves and do not confer it on their children (Sirach 33).

From the fact that it says that Ruth was more beneficial to her than seven children, we draw comfort that though we may be destitute of our children's help, God can easily raise up other men who are more beneficial to us than our own children, to whom we ought especially to be of concern.

Daughters-in-law also learn again from this example how they ought to behave toward their mothers-in-law.

Lastly, women learn what conversations and what kinds of conversations they ought to have if they bring children for baptism and visit women who are in labor. Namely, they should thank God for His blessings which He bestows on us and beseech Him that the children will be raised with religion and will serve God; they should not talk about trivial and scurrilous things.

---

4. Paus. 10.28.4.
5. In Greek, πελαργός is the word for "stork."

Ruth 4:16–17

16 *And so Naomi took the child, and placed it in her bosom, and became nurse unto it.*

17 *Further, her female neighbors gave it a name. They said, "A son is born to Naomi." That is to say, they gave him the name Obed. He is father of Isai, the father of David.*

Three things are contained in these words. First, Naomi was the child's nurse. Next, the women named the child Obed. Third, he was King David's grandfather. We read that Naomi took the child and placed him in her bosom. She embraced him with great joy. For in this way we see that it is established that grandfathers and grandmothers often love their grandsons and granddaughters more than they love their own children. She performed the duty of nursing the child. She did not actually suckle him, but she gave him food and drink and bathed him. As it concerns the word מינקת (*meiaenkaeth*), "wet nurse," it is derived from ינק (*ianak*), "to suck," in the *hiphil*, "to give suck," and means a woman who suckles a child. In Genesis 22, we read about Rebekah's wet nurse. In Genesis 35, we read about Deborah's wet nurse. In 2 Kings 11, we read about a nurse (*ein saugam*). Now אמנת (*omaeneth*) is also a wet nurse. Second Samuel 4 says, "His nurse took him up." The term is from אמן, "to nurse," "to raise," and means "an attendant" (*ein warterin*). מילדת (*meialaedeth*), "midwife," is from ילד (*ialad*), "to give birth," because she helps the one who is giving birth, *ein hebamm*, which they elsewhere call *ein weemüter*.

Although her body was now worn out, and therefore she was not suited for labor, nevertheless, she did not want to live an idle life. She did what she could. Old women should imitate this example, care for children, instill piety in them, and divert them from vices. First Timothy 5: "If any widow have children or grandchildren, let them learn," or rather, as Calvin renders it, "teach (for μανθάνειν means both "to teach" and "to learn") her children or grandchildren to exercise piety toward their family, and to requite their elders in return. For that is acceptable before God."[1]

From the fact that God fills Ruth with great joy, in part by joining her in marriage to a distinguished husband, in part by giving her a male child, we are taught that God sometimes, even in this life, blesses children who honor their parents. Ruth was faithful to her mother-in-law, and so a happy and peaceful marriage, great wealth, and fame were granted to her by God. Therefore, children, do good to your parents and give them what they need, and do not provoke them to wrath.

Changing Fortune

Next, we conclude that God, without any trouble, can restore men to their former condition, however afflicted they are. He usually all but burdens down His people with tribulation and afterward allows them to rise up again. For a long time these widows were burdened by poverty. But now God raises up both of them. He gives Naomi a son-in-law, and from him a grandson to support her. As fair weather follows great storms and a pleasant, delightful spring follows a rough winter, so happiness follows misery. God, however, tempers it with some evils, so that we will not stray from the way of salvation. Sacred history is filled with public and private examples. Therefore, we should not be impatient in adverse circumstances, but encourage ourselves by thinking frequently on similar examples.

The neighborhood women said that a son was born to Naomi. But Naomi was not his mother; Ruth, her daughter-in-law, was. They

---

1. John Calvin, *In omnes Pauli Apostoli epistolas, atque etiam in epistolam ad Hebraeos, Io. Calvini commentarii* (Geneva: Jean Crespin, 1557), 492.

speak in this way because grandmothers are also mothers of their grand-children. Children are also said to be born to those who have adopted them. Or it is the sort of expression that appears in Isaiah 9: "Unto us a son is given." Likewise, in Luke 2: "Unto you is born this day in the city of David a Savior, which is Christ the Lord," that is, "for your good."

Obed

They gave him the name Obed. Obed means "farmer, servant, husband-man." It does not express why they called him by this name. Perhaps it was because Ruth, who previously had served Naomi faithfully, had this child by a distinguished man. Or because Ruth, by laboring strenuously among Boaz's servants, became known to him and was brought into his family. Or (this view is more satisfying to me) so that he would serve God. All pious worshipers of deity are called servants of God.

Names Given to Children

The ancient fathers did not give their children names at random, but they named them after some event so that they and their children would be perpetually reminded of God's blessings and their duty and so would be stirred up to faith and thanksgiving. Sometimes they pre-served the memory of past events by naming their children after them. Israel named nearly all his children after an event. Moses, in Exodus 18, names his son Gershom, because he was a foreigner when he was born. The other he names Eliezer, since the Lord helped him. Samuel is so named because Hannah prayed to God that she would bear him.[2] Next, because they wanted to preserve or revive the memory of their parents or relatives, they named their children after them. In Luke 1, the neigh-bors and relatives dispute about the name of John. They wanted him to be named Zachariah, but his mother says that he is to be named John. And when they say that no one in their family has this name, they refer the matter to the father, and he writes on tablets that he is to be named John. For an angel had commanded this to be done. This name is derived from "grace," partly because he obtained great grace from God,

---

2. 1 Sam. 1:20.

partly because he was obligated to proclaim to the world the grace of God offered in His revealed Son. For God Himself, through His angels, sometimes named men to signify past or future events, sometimes even before they were born. He named Adam for the earth from which he was made,[3] Eve because she would be the mother of the living,[4] Ishmael because God had heard Hagar (Gen. 16), Solomon because there would be long-lasting peace under his reign,[5] and Jesus because He would save His people.[6] Sometimes He changed names, as He called Abram "Abraham" because he would be the father of many nations (Gen. 17), and Sarai because many princes would come from her.[7] Christ our Savior named Simon "Peter" because he needed great faith and steadfastness.[8] The Roman pontiffs have imitated this, who, when they are chosen, adopt other names for themselves. They write that this custom has continued from the time of Sergius, the second pope, who was previously called "Pig's Face" and who, on account of the shamefulness of the name, assumed the name "Sergius," to our own times. Although it makes no difference to salvation by what name anyone is called, nevertheless, it is fitting for Christians to avoid superstition in giving names. In several previous ages, they consecrated their children to the worship of that saint by whose name they were called. There are those who out of some vain ostentation name their children after gentiles, such as Hannibal, Scipio, and Catiline. There are many noble names that remind children of their duty. There are Hebrew names, such as Abraham, Jacob, and Isaiah; Greek names, such as Chrysostom, Christopher, and Theophilus; and Latin names, such as Benedictus and Fortunatus. There are also many noble German names that have an elegant meaning. It is beautiful for pious parents to give their children names, the remembrance of which rouses them to virtue. As often as we hear our name, so often ought we to consider that in sacred baptism we have been adopted into

3. Gen. 2:7.
4. Gen. 3:20.
5. 1 Kings 4:24–25.
6. Matt. 1:21.
7. Gen. 17:15–16.
8. John 1:42.

the family of Christ. And if we are named after holy men, we should endeavor by faith and integrity of life to walk in the footsteps of those whose names we bear. Other names taken from duties occur, about which it would be needless to write in this place.

Why Obed Did Not Receive Mahlon's Name
Why Obed is called the son, not of Mahlon, but of his natural father Boaz, Saint Augustine shows in question 46 on Deuteronomy. He says:

> *The law about marrying a brother's wife to raise up a seed for one's brother, who died without children, says, "He shall be established on the name of the deceased, and his name shall not be blotted out of Israel," that is, the name of the deceased. It seems that we can conclude from this that he who is born is called by the name by which the deceased was called, for whom he is in some sense propagated. Unless perhaps it says this, not so that he will take his name, but so that he will be established as the heir on the name, that is, as the son, not of him by whose seed he was fathered, but of the deceased, for whom he was raised up as a seed. For the added statement, "And his name shall not be blotted out of Israel," can be understood thus, not that the boy will consequently take his name, but that he will not seem to die without a posterity. And so his name, that is, his memory endures. For even if he had fathered a son, he would not have bestowed his name on him, so that his name would not be blotted out of Israel, since he would not have departed this life without children. And his brother is commanded to fulfill this role toward his wife which he could not. For even if he had no brother, his near kinsman would marry the wife of the man who had died without children to raise up a seed for his brother, just as Boaz did by marrying Ruth to raise up a seed for his near kinsman, whose wife she was and by whom she had not given birth to a child. And yet the child born from her was indeed established on the name of the deceased, since he was called his son. And so the name of the deceased was not blotted out of Israel, though he was not called by his name.*[9]

---

9. August. *Quaest. Deut.* 46.

Others say that sons produced from such a union were indeed to be called by the name of the dead brother but that sometimes, it seems, this was neglected, because there were no brothers, or because some preferred to father sons for themselves than for their brother.

The last thing in these words is who Obed was, namely, Isai's father and King David's grandfather, the discussion of whose genealogy follows next.

Ruth 4:18–22

18 *These are the generations of Pharez: Pharez begat Hezron.*

19 *And Hezron begat Ram, and Ram begat Amminadab.*

20 *And Amminadab begat Nahshon, and Nahshon begat Salmon.*

21 *And Salmon begat Boaz, and Boaz begat Obed.*

22 *And Obed begat Isai, and Isai begat David.*

All Passages of Sacred Scripture Are Useful

There are some passages in the sacred books that seem to be of little use. But we must recognize that nothing is put in them rashly and in vain. For if a serious man says nothing without a reason, and much less writes anything that will come into the hands of many people without a reason, who thinks that God, who is wisdom itself, dictated something to His writers that would be of no use to the readers? Indeed, one passage is more fruitful than another, as one field is more fertile than another, as one river is fuller of fish than another. But absolutely nothing exists in the Scriptures that does not have its own use, although it may seem completely unprofitable at first glance. Metals lie hidden in hard rocks. Health-giving herbs are found in squalid places. Gold chips sometimes appear in barren deserts, and precious stones lie hidden there. Aristotle, in *On the Parts of Animals*, writes that nothing in the nature of things is so insignificant, vile, and abject that it does not impart to men some admiration.[1] For the works of nature were not made rashly, but all

---

1. Arist. *Part. an.* 1.5, 645a5–20.

things were made for the sake of their own end. In this passage, Heracleides of Tarentum comes to my mind. We read that when he lodged in some shepherd's cabin, he shouted, "Enter! There are gods here too."[2] The same thing can and should be said about those passages of Sacred Scripture which seem completely barren, for they nevertheless have a splendid usefulness. This list of fathers perhaps seems unpleasant and useless to many, as though it contains only a dull series of names. But this whole book was written for this purpose, namely, that we would know the genealogy of David and, consequently, of Christ, who was specifically promised to him. Indeed, this list is so important that Matthew and Luke translated it verbatim into Christ's genealogy.[3]

The Sum of Apostolic Doctrine

For the scope of the evangelists and the apostles is that Jesus is the Christ, that is, the King and High Priest of those who truly believe. And so they needed to show that He descended from those to whom He was promised. For with singular diligence the Holy Spirit steadily showed from the beginning of the world from which fathers Christ was to be begotten. When our first parents, Adam and Eve, were about to be thrown out of Paradise, God promised them that the seed of the woman, that is, the Messiah or Christ, would crush the serpent's head.[4]

Christ's Lineage

The lineage of Christ descends to Noah, not through Cain, but through Seth. Noah had three sons, but the lineage is drawn to Abraham through Shem. From Abraham the lineage descends not through Ishmael, but through his promised son Isaac and, afterward, not through Esau, Isaac's firstborn son, but through Jacob, who is also called Israel.

---

2. Arist. *Part. an.* 1.5, 645a20–24.

3. For the parallels in these genealogies, see Matt. 1:3–6 and Luke 3:31–33. For the full genealogies, see Matt. 1:1–17 and Luke 3:23–38. Lavater repeatedly refers to the content of these texts in the remainder of the commentary, so I will not cite these passages or verses from them again.

4. Gen. 3:15.

The Prophecy of Jacob the Patriarch about the Messiah

Although Jacob had twelve sons, when he was about to die he prophesied to Judah by the inspiration of the Holy Spirit, that he would possess
the kingdom, that the scepter or rod—that is, royal power—would not
depart from his tribe, and that the scribe or legislator (the Chaldean
translator interprets it as "prince" and the LXX interprets it as "leader,"
with the same sense)[5]—that is, the judges of secondary power—would
not depart from his feet, namely, from the tribe of Judah.[6] This is to say,
they would not be abolished (we also say, *Einem ufz den füssen gan* [give
to one upon one's feet]) until Shiloh, that is, the Savior, the Messiah,
should come. The ancient Hebrews explained the word in this way. But
more recent Hebrews extraordinarily twist this passage and contrive the
most absurd meanings so they will not be forced to confess that the
Messiah has come into the world. The patriarch adds that the gentiles
would gather to Judah, that is, gentiles too would come to the Messiah
and would believe in Him. Although this prophecy seems to speak only
about the duration of the kingdom of Judah and does not seem to say
clearly and plainly that Shiloh would come from the tribe of Judah, nevertheless, afterward this was expressly predicted by other prophets. For
although there were many distinguished families in the tribe of Judah,
as that of Caleb and others, the prophets prophesied that the Messiah
would come from the family of Jesse, and of David. From David were
descended the most powerful kings, and although his family seemed to
be all but extinguished and crushed, nevertheless, God preserved for
him a lamp and predicted that the Messiah would be descended from
Jeconiah, David's descendant, from the son of Jehoiachim. He fathered
Shealtiel, from whom the two evangelists draw the lineage of Christ
to Joseph, to whom the Holy Virgin had been betrothed, from whom
was born Jesus Christ, the King of Kings. In this passage, the series of
fathers is drawn from Judah, the son of Jacob, to David.

---

5. Tg. Neof. Gen. 49:10 and Tg. Ps.-J. Gen. 49:10 have ספרין. Tg. Onq. Gen. 49:10
has ספרא. It is not clear why Lavater reads any of these as "prince." The LXX has
ἡγούμενος.

6. Gen. 49:10.

Pharez

Pharez and Zerah were twin sons of Judah by Tamar, his daughter-in-law and wife (Gen. 38). By them are prefigured two peoples, Jews and gentiles. They went down into Egypt with their father, and there Pharez fathered Hezron.

Hezron

Hezron was Pharez's son (Gen. 46). He went down into Egypt with his father and grandfather, as also Hamul his brother did (Gen. 46). Concerning Hamul's posterity, nothing is extant, except that the family of the Hamulites took its name from him (Num. 26).

Ram

Ram, who in the books of Chronicles and by the evangelists is called Aram,[7] was Hezron's son, born in Egypt after Jacob's death.

Amminadab

Amminadab was Ram's son, David's great-great-great-great-grandfather, born in Egypt.

Nahshon

Nahshon was Amminadab's son and David's great-great-great-grandfather. He went with his father out of Egypt, and after him was the prince of the tribe of Judah through the desert, where he fathered Salmon (Num. 1, 2, 7; 1 Chron. 2). It is doubtful whether he was hanged together with the other princes in the plains of Moab for whoring and worshiping Baalpeor.[8] His sister was Elisheba, Aaron's wife (Ex. 6). Some write that Elimelech the Bethlehemite, Naomi's husband and Ruth's father-in-law, and Nahshon were brothers. But Lyra commented on chapter 3 of this book that Elimelech and Boaz's father, that is, Salmon, were brothers and so Nahshon preceded Elimelech by one degree.[9] According to this view,

---

7. Ram is not called Aram in the MT of 1 Chron. 2:9–10. But 1 Chron. 2:9 in the LXX lists four sons of Hezron, not three. One of these is called Ram (Ῥὰμ) and another is called Aram (Ἀράμ), who is then called Arran (Ἀρρὰν) in verse 10.

8. Num. 25:1–4.

9. Lyra, *Biblia*, fol. 280r.

Boaz and Mahlon were cousins, which does not seem likely. For no one would have been more closely related than Boaz, with the exception of his brother, if he had one, for these two sons were childless.

Salmon
Salmon, who in this book and in 1 Chronicles 2 is called by another name, Salma, Nahshon's son, David's great-great-grandfather, was a prince in the tribe of Judah when Joshua entered the promised land.[10] He married Rahab the Canaanite.

Boaz
Boaz, David's great-grandfather, who was born from his father, Salmon, and his mother, Rahab, married Ruth. The Hebrews think that he was Abesa the judge. The Chaldean translator calls him "just" and writes that because of his equity the land of Israel was saved from enemy oppression and that by his prayers he lifted a famine from it.[11] But it is not evident to me from where he gets this.

Obed
Obed was the son of Boaz and Ruth the Moabitess, and he was David's grandfather.

Jesse
Isai, who is called Jesse by the evangelists, was Obed's son. He is mentioned in Isaiah 11. Christians are sometimes called Jesseites after this man. He is also called Nahash, that is, "Serpent" (2 Sam. 17). The Chaldean translator, on this chapter, says that he was named "Serpent" because he was adorned with great prudence, by which he avoided the snares of the devil.[12] Reinerius Reineccius, a very learned and diligent man, in his book on the illustrious families of the Israelite kings and priests, comments that Nahash seems to him to have been a different person than Jesse.[13] For it is possible that Abigail was David's sister from the same

---

10. 1 Chron. 2:11.
11. Tg. Ruth 4:21.
12. Tg. Ruth 4:22.
13. I have been unable to locate the reference.

mother (ὁμομήτριος). We read that this Isai had eight sons (1 Sam. 16 and 17:12). Isai made seven of his sons to pass before Samuel. Samuel afterward asked whether he still had one more. In Chronicles, David is called the seventh of the sons of Isai, whose names are as follows: Eliab, the firstborn; Abinadab; Shimeah, who is also called Shammah; Nethaneel; Raddai; Ozem; and David.[14] The name of the eighth son is not extant. Some think that he died prematurely and left no children. Others think that Jonadab, Shimeah's son, or another grandson was included among his sons.[15] He had two daughters, Zeruiah and Abigail. Zeruiah's three sons were Joab, Abishai, and Asahel, who are known from sacred history.[16] David calls them the sons of Zeruiah, after their mother, perhaps because they had an obscure father.[17] Abigail's son was Amasa.[18] From David descend nineteen kings (Solomon, Rehoboam, and the rest).

Question: How Was Boaz Salmon's Son?

The question raised in this passage is, How are Salmon, Rahab's husband, and Boaz, Ruth's husband, joined in two generations when the sequence of history evinces that from the first year of Joshua (in which many think that Jericho was captured and Rahab was saved) to the time of Abesa (whom some think was Boaz, Rahab's son) and, likewise, to the times of Eli (in which, Josephus writes, Ruth came with Naomi to Bethlehem)[19] many years intervened? I simply respond that it is not sufficiently evident from sacred literature in what year after Jericho was captured Salmon married Rahab, and when he fathered Boaz by her, or when Boaz married Ruth. Likewise, it is not evident whether Boaz and Abesa the judge are one and the same person, and therefore it is not necessary for us, with some Hebrews and Lyra, to suppose that there were three Boazes, one of whom succeeded another as grandfather, son, and grandson, which three would be included under one name.[20] Moreover, it is not absurd if we say

14. 1 Chron. 2:13–15.
15. 2 Sam. 13:3.
16. 1 Chron. 2:16.
17. 2 Sam. 3:39; 16:10; 19:22.
18. 1 Chron. 2:17.
19. Joseph. *AJ* 5.318.
20. Lyra, *Biblia*, fol. 281r.

that God prolonged the lives of Salmon and Boaz for many years, as He also prolonged the lives of other fathers after the flood.

Sinners in Christ's Genealogy

In addition, we must observe that great sinners are included in Christ's genealogy. Judah, the father of Pharez, committed many serious sins. Some think that Nahshon was defiled by whoring and the abominable worship of Baalpeor.[21] Boaz's mother, Rahab, is expressly called a prostitute by Paul and James.[22] But by the providence and will of God Christ was descended from such people so that no one would think that this happened because of the merits of the patriarchs. Likewise, it happened to comfort sinners so that they will not fall into despair but know that He came because of sinners, according to 1 Timothy 1: "This is a faithful saying…" God will be gracious to them on account of His Son, if they repent.

Pharez's mother and, likewise, Boaz's mother and wife were gentile women who were converted to the worship of God. The Son of God desired to be descended from them so that not only the Jews, but also the gentiles would be encouraged to hope to obtain salvation through Christ, who was born from gentiles also, and for their salvation. Jews and gentiles are joined together in Christ the cornerstone. Initially, the Jews could scarcely and, indeed, not even scarcely, be persuaded of this. Even believers among the Jews, no, even the apostles themselves initially were horrified at having fellowship with gentiles. Therefore, God first strengthened Peter, whom He was about to send to Cornelius the centurion, with a heavenly vision, so that he would not be horrified at having social intercourse with him.[23]

Moreover, the fact that God exalted David to such majesty, though he was descended from humble parents (for although the family itself was famous, nevertheless, his father was a peasant), causes us to recognize God's mercy and power. David himself in Psalm 113 sang that God brings up the needy out of the dung, that He may set them in the seat

---

21. Num. 25:1–4.
22. Heb. 11:31; James 2:25.
23. Acts 10:9–18.

204 Ruth Explained in Twenty-Eight Homilies

of the princes of His people. Josephus, concluding this history, says, "I related the story about Ruth out of necessity, because I wanted to show the power of God, that it is easy for Him to bring even ordinary people to an illustrious rank, to which He also raised David, though he came from such people."[24]

We Must Know the Books of the Old Testament

We also see from these words that those Anabaptists are entirely mistaken who deny that Christians must read the Old Testament since those things that pertain to our salvation are fully contained in the New. But who, for instance, could understand these words in Matthew, "Boaz begat Obed of Ruth," unless he has carefully read this book? Certainly, in his statement "of Ruth, which was a Moabitess" a weighty mystery is contained. For the evangelist shows that Christ desired to be born from gentiles and for them. But this position of the Anabaptists is an intolerable error, which we should refute at length.

Some make Boaz a type of the Messiah and Ruth a type of the church, the Messiah's bride. I do not deny that the Messiah, together with His bride, is represented figuratively in various ways in the Scriptures, but I have preferred to follow the simple and literal sense. Those who delight in allegories should seek them elsewhere.

To this point I have explained to you the book of Ruth, from which we have gathered various lessons. It is not enough, however, daily to hear and read these and other texts unless we endeavor to listen fruitfully and order our actions according to the rule of the Word of God. For a servant who knows his Lord's will and does not do it will receive a more severe flogging.[25] And so let us earnestly pray to God the Best and Greatest that He will condescend to open our minds so that we will not only correctly understand His oracles but will also use them to strengthen our faith and emend our lives.

---

24. τὰ μὲν περὶ ῥούθην ἀναγκαίως διηγησάμην ἐπιδεῖξαι βουλόμενος τὴν τοῦ θεοῦ δύναμιν, ὅτι τούτῳ παράγειν ἐφικτόν ἐστιν εἰς ἀξίωμα λαμπρὸν καὶ τοὺς ἐπιτυχόντας, εἰς οἷον ἀνήγαγε καὶ δαβίδην ἐκ τοιούτων γινόμενον. Joseph. AJ 5.337.

25. Luke 12:47.

Appendix
Exposition of the Book of Ruth

Konrad Pellikan

First Chapter

1. *In the days of one judge*: The end and scope of the Law and the Prophets is Christ the Lord, born from the seed of David according to the flesh. For this reason His genealogy is so carefully constructed, from the beginning of the human race, from Adam himself, through Noah and Abraham, to David, and also from David, through the kings of Judah, until it comes to Christ. So the book of Ruth, which is an appendix to the book of Judges, was written to demonstrate David's lineage. It shows that by God's providence Christ is descended from foreign women, and so, as the ruler over the whole Israelite nation, He kept the promise to the gentiles and was the certain expectation concerning the salvation of the whole world. And therefore, it shows that He will be the King, Messiah, Savior, and Teacher not only of the Jews, but also of the gentiles, as the whole world meanwhile seems to be filled with the latter, with only the blind Jews protesting. By their obstinate and ambitious longing for a carnal kingdom, they suffer the damage of a disturbed conscience and also very deservedly suffer penalties for their unbelief. The Jews also do not know under what judge this famine and the story of Ruth, the noblest woman, happened, although the Syrian translator, whom the Jews follow, says that Boaz was the distinguished man who in the book of Judges is called Abesa.[1] But our people put him in the times of Eli the priest. The shortness of the time, however, does not allow this. In the end, whoever

---

1. Tg. Ruth 1:1, 6; 4:21. "The Syrian translator" is Pellikan's designation for the author of the Targum.

this judge was, it contributes nothing to the matter of the Davidic gene-alogy, which is the aim of this book. Therefore, the writer preferred to indicate the days of one, or any, judge from among those who temporarily ruled the people rather than to define what is uncertain and unnecessary to know. The famine oppressed the land of Judah for no other reason than that they neglected to observe the law of God. Otherwise, if the Israelites had faithfully worshiped God, they would not have had to fear such a severe chastisement as starvation from famine in their own very excellent land. But since they violated the covenant and worshiped idols instead of their God, it was necessary that they should experience every misfortune, since curses were repeatedly pronounced on them in the law itself and promised by Moses and Joshua and all the prophets. On this passage, the Jews list ten times of famine from Adam to the Messiah, saying that the last famine for them will be not a lack of bread and water, but a lack of hearing the Word of the Lord by the prophets.[2] They can-not deny that they have suffered this famine since the times of Christ our Lord. At the same time, however, the grace and knowledge of God is propagated throughout the world and the religion of the one true God is sown by the Holy Spirit in the hearts of believers, who acknowledge and worship the Lord of Hosts, the God of Abraham, Isaac, and Jacob, and the Son of David, the Messiah, as much as this is done by various rites, while the enemy sows tares in the good field. Elimelech, a wealthy man from Bethlehem-Judah, with his wife and children, in violation of the law, deserted his paternal inheritance that God had given to him and thought he could evade the famine, either because he was ignorant of the law or because he despised it. No doubt the famine would have ceased for him if out of love for and observance of the law of God he had returned home to his very distinguished family. But out of treachery toward God, or motivated by some other reason, in violation of the law he moved to a people with whom the Israelites were forbidden to associate, even to the tenth generation, that is, to the field of Moab.

---

2. Amos 8:11.

2. *He was called*: The wife and two sons are named. They are called Eph-rathites, and according to the Hebrews, they were nobles in the tribe of Judah, famous for their reputation and wealth. They also say that Elimel-ech was a magistrate during the reign of Eglon, the king of Moab, who gave his daughter Ruth as a wife to Elimelech's son. The Jews usually tell such fables for their own glory, which they always strive for and either do not obtain it or do not know how to keep it once they have it.[3]

3. *And he died*: Day by day Elimelech was protected by his wealth in Moab, since he had arrived wealthy. Eventually, he also died and left his sons in a foreign and hostile nation. For the change in his location, in violation of the commandment of the Lord, had turned out unhappily for him. He instead should have hoped in the Lord and entrusted the troubles from the famine to the Lord. He should have helped the poor of his nation. He should have avoided vice. He should have been roused to observe the law.

4. *They took*: In violation of the law, they married Moabite women. Then they died with their father. In their fatherland they escaped poverty, but they fell into it, along with death, elsewhere. We do not escape the hand of the Lord even if we try to flee. But by the mercy of God their guilt was ordained for the glory of God and the fulfillment of the divine oracles. The lives of the surviving women accumulated miseries. The three were alike widows, and in addition Naomi was destitute of the comfort of her sons in a foreign and hostile land. At the same time, they were poor.

6. *And she arose*: Roused and comforted by a pleasing rumor about fer-tility having been restored to her fatherland, she sets out on her way as an elderly mother with the young widows who had survived her sons. The latter were going to travel from Moab to Judah, for they had learned from their husbands and father-in-law about the wonderful works done by the God of Israel. They had imbibed the faith of the one, true God and now had become proselytes in the house of believers. The Jews were

3. Pellikan, like Lavater, held the view, common among European Christians of the medieval and early modern periods, that Jews were characteristically dishonest.

commonly more zealous for the law of God when they were sojourning outside their inheritance than when they were living peacefully within it.

8. *She said unto them, "Go!"*: Naomi, feeling compassion for her daughters-in-law, who were planning to desert their fatherland and who were going to be weighed down by such severe poverty, advised them to return home so that they would live more comfortably among their own mothers and relatives than as exiles from their fatherland. She commends their obedience, charity, and patience, rare virtues of daughters-in-law toward their mothers-in-law. And on the other hand, she prays that the Lord will bless them, that is, that they will be provided with happier marriages. She does not urge the young women to perpetual widowhood, but she desires for both of them more delightful and more fortunate husbands. In return, with tears they kiss their mother-in-law. They are prepared to experience the fortune common to those who live among foreigners.

10. *"We will go with thee"*: They seem to have desired a seed and posterity from the nation of Judah, since the Spirit of God was more personally urging them to this. For so they accommodate themselves to affairs that are preordained by the providence of God to happen. But Naomi tries to persuade them to return and says that new husbands cannot be born for them from her womb. The holy women of that time and nation desired the blessing of propagating holy offspring, not the pleasures of lust. It is proper for pious ladies and honorable young women to be such. They ought to marry, become housewives, give birth to offspring to be raised in a holy manner, and be ruled under the power of their husbands. This way of living was approved long ago by the holy fathers and mothers. Yet the dangers that threaten evangelical preachers, in their own time, advise against marriage. Likewise, the moderate temperature of the flame of their sexual desire, not going as far as impatient sexual desire, as well as their ardent love for helping and establishing the churches and for expending themselves for the churches, can be considered. These considerations, that is, the unique circumstances of evangelical preachers, preserve and promote the chastity of a pure celibacy that is worthy in the sight of God, serenity of mind, and a fuller peace in business of this

sort. But leisure and chastity of mind and body are incompatible in both sexes. And if the opportunities provided by incautious friendship and an abundance of provisions are added, as well as impunity in wrongdoing, no condition in the world will appear more scandalous.

14. *Then they lifted up their voice*: The reason why Orpah departed but Ruth clung to her mother-in-law is not to be sought in anything else except divine election and the eternal order of providence by which Ruth belonged to the holy genealogy. She would be one of the mothers from whom the salvation of the world would come forth. It will be pointless for us to discuss whether Orpah returned to the vomit of idolatry and was condemned, since questions of this sort do not at all edify, and the truth of such things is not known without proof.

16. *"Be not against me"*: Ruth responds to her mother-in-law,

> I will accompany you forever, wherever you go. Day and night I will not forsake you. I will also devote myself to your religion. In the same way, I will love you and your people with every good wish. I will insist on observing its trappings in every way as you do. The Lord your God, the Creator of the world, the Almighty, and the only true God will also be my God besides whom I will hereafter acknowledge and worship no other. I will be enclosed in the same tomb with you. I also will not regard it as a burden to risk my life for you.

In these words is revealed a fitting and pious character in the young woman, which also progressed with age, so that she also will be celebrated among the best women as noble and worthy to be inserted into the sacred list of illustrious women among the people of God.

18. *So when Naomi saw*: She was no longer to be pushed away, since with such an obstinate soul she was offering herself as a follower of true piety and a disciple of true religion. She was carried by such great affection for the Israelite church, from which she could not have been excluded save for the cause of impiety. For even the laws of God are not without exceptions, but rather holy men of God, imbued with the Holy Spirit,

are ordained by the Lord, beyond their intention, for the glory of God, whom all things serve and no one can resist.

19. *They went together*: The women of Bethlehem marveled at Naomi's unexpectedly changed condition when she returned, which was far different from that in which she had left. For she had gone away rich and honored with a husband, sons, and wealth. Now she returns a widow, bereaved, and poor. Women also commonly gossip in such a way that with their customary idle scoffing they mock and marvel at one who is unhappy.

20. *She said unto them, "Call me not"*: Naomi's name can be translated as "pleasant" and "elegant," which she certainly was, and very happy. But now she confesses and laments that she has been reduced to bitterness and calamity, with which the Almighty has filled her. She indeed had lost all her fortunes, but she had not lost a prudent and honorable spirit. She credited to the Lord what she had suffered. She did not blaspheme. She did not impatiently bear adversities. But she more strongly depended on the goodness of the Lord. She confesses that His judgment concerning her is just, that everything is moderated by His providence. He led her out rich and brought her back empty. He is able again to fill her with greater goods, because He is God, the Almighty, and the All-Sufficient.

22. *So Naomi came*: The time of her return is noted, so that the reasoning of the following story will be made clear. For they came at the time when the barley in those regions rather quickly ripens and is harvested. The Hebrews designate the time of Passover for this business, in which the poor begin more conveniently to support themselves by the first harvest and the crops that are beginning to ripen.

Second Chapter

1. *Now the man had*: There is an extraordinary virtue in the woman, zeal for labor, so that she will not idly eat her bread. She does not neglect the time of harvest. She plans on collecting the crop of poverty, the stalks left behind the reapers, that is, of the master whose regard she found favorable and whose permission she found willing. She does not want

to trouble anyone. She is not willing to enter the field unless the head of the household assents. Naomi calls her "daughter" since she clung to her mother-in-law with filial affection.

3. *So she went*: By chance, that is, by divine providence, she happened to begin gathering in the field of Boaz, who, since he was wealthier and a more religious observer of the law of God than others, did not drive away any of the poor who were gathering the stalks left behind the reapers. There she, a prudent and charming foreign woman, joined herself to a man who was a kinsman of Elimelech, Ruth's father-in-law, and from his family.

4. *And, behold, he*: The wealthy head of the household visits the reapers in his field. He does not sit lazily at home, but prudently turns his attention to his household property. He speaks kindly to the laborers. He prays that God's favor and help would be on them. They in turn give a friendly response to his greeting and pray for God's blessing on the beloved man's affairs. So it is proper to speak honorably to everyone and always and especially for the presence and kindness of God to enter our minds. In this way the laborers serve their master, honor him, and commend themselves to him.

5. *And Boaz said*: The servant boy presided over the reapers, prudently ordering all things in his master's absence. He either had to drive away or admit the gatherers. Boaz interrogates this assistant to the reapers about the unknown young Moabitess. He hears that she had returned with Naomi, a lover of her religion and nation, that she had asked for the opportunity to be given her to gather along with the young men, and that she had diligently devoted herself to her work for the whole day. Even now she had scarcely been idle for a moment in the house or cottage because of the summer heat. Her perseverance in her work is shown under the open sky, in the sun, and for the whole day, with no regard for her beauty and fatigue.

8. *"Hear thou, daughter"*: Because of her age he calls her "daughter." Delighted by her work, he comforts her and commands her not to enter

another field, but to remain in his and, to the best of her ability, to gather without anxiety and shame along with the rest of the young women. It is proper for believers to deal in an especially friendly manner with those who are novices in the faith so that they will not be scandalized by hardness and intractability. Foreigners should be embraced as friends and not be doubly burdened, that is, by poverty and contempt. The ornament of true religion is charity and beneficence, without which piety does not exist. Finally, he tells her to look around as carefully as possible, to pass over nothing, to gather eagerly, and that no one is to trouble her, but rather when she is thirsty, she should drink without hesitation along with his domestic servants. Boaz is a noble example of humanity to poor foreigners, and especially young women who are modest and taught discipline.

10. *She fell*: Ruth herself also presents a model of gratitude and modesty by behaving humbly and acknowledging a kindness that is broadly shown. Fear, modesty, and prudence and economy in words is the extraordinary glory of young women.

11. *He answered her*: A weighty commendation given to a young woman by so noble, good, and prudent a man reveals in Ruth, even after the death of her husband, a perfect friendship that daughters-in-law rarely have with their mothers-in-law, so that we may understand with what kind of reverence, honor, and love she clung to her living mother-in-law, since she followed her mother-in-law with such great reverence after the death of her husband. She shows herself worthy to be joined in marriage to the best man, whoever it might be, and the kind of woman the Lord God will reward with a distinguished portion among His people and a place among illustrious women.

13. *She said*: Ruth first commends the man's mercy, with which he not only did not scornfully reject her, but favorably comforted her and took away her fear with friendly conversation, which is for the Hebrews "speaking to the heart." She presents herself as an obedient girl and acknowledges herself as lowly compared with others.

14. *And he said unto her*: In the first place, he had permitted her to gather and drink with the rest. Now, delighted by the girl's prudent modesty and considering the noble character of the foreign woman, he promises her greater things, namely, food and a morsel dipped in vinegar, according to the custom of the region, for relief against the heat. Therefore, she immediately takes courage, sets aside her bashfulness for a little while, and sits more confidently with the reapers as they eat. To free her from her shyness, Boaz first reached out and offered her parched barley, of which she either ate so sparingly or he had given her so abundantly that there was some left over after she was satisfied. Discipline is preserved among the pious, and there is no poverty among the faithful. The saints give plentifully to the poor. The poor learn to abound and to suffer want.

15. *And then*: The woman's earnestness in labor is commended and the wealthy, upright man's liberal generosity goes so far as to take away all the shy girl's embarrassment so that she returns to her mother-in-law more satisfied and more cheerful. So we learn to give alms so that, if it can be done, we may prevent them the trouble of asking for alms and liberally give to the one who receives alms so that he will not at all be put to shame.

17. *So she gleaned*: Perseverance in good work is commended. The poor should not neglect an opportunity to scrape together honestly what they need. The less they lazily beg out of weariness with labor, the more they deserve more abundant alms. She immediately beat out the gathered ears of grain in accordance with the custom of the nation, and found the fruit of her labor to be by far the most abundant, since the blessing of God increased it. And she brought home a measure, that is, of barley, containing ten homers.

18. *In addition, she brought forth*: She pulled out the remaining parched barley and kindly gave to her mother-in-law what she had left over. Piety and faithfulness to the Word of God is generous.

19. *And her mother-in-law said unto her*: So careful an inquiry by the elderly woman was not useless when her daughter-in-law, a girl who was

dear to her, had gathered so much grain in a short time. But the marvel of God's goodness had also intervened, and the most fruitful diligence arising from her zeal was to be commended by her mother-in-law. For praise is the reward for good work, especially for younger people, whose virtue increases when it is praised.[4] She also rejoiced for the provision of sustenance so sufficiently procured in one day.

20. *Naomi answered her*: Because Naomi is grateful to the Lord for a rather small kindness, she deserves greater favor and the grace of God that is to be praised in all ages. The fact that grace and kindness were shown both to the dead and to the living can be credited to Boaz, who, as he had loved Elimelech and his sons when they were alive, so now also helps the dead in helping their widows. So this also can be credited to God, who does not desert those who hope in Him either when they are dead or when they are alive. Boaz says that he is a close relative and kinsman to the point that he can be brought forward as a protector and redeemer of the inheritance, and the redeemer's duty can be performed according to the law.

21. *And Ruth (said), "This also"*: She boasts that she was invited to gather ears of grain on other days, whereby she commends to her mother-in-law the man's greater grace. The favors done by the rich for the poor are rather inconsiderable, yet the poor are often helped and comforted very much by them. So riches are aids to virtue for the pious. So the riches of the patriarchs were used for the relief of the needy, and the more willingly they were disbursed, the more they increased.

22. *Her mother-in-law said unto her*: Seeing that she had acquired such a gentle patron with whom both could be supported, she ought not to have sought a more uncertain patron. Otherwise, generous friends are not to be burdened in seeking favors from them. Finally, it was safer for such a charming girl to be exposed to danger among relatives than among strangers and people she did not know.

---

4. I have emended *laudanda* to *laudata*, conforming the text to the related passage in Konrad Pellikan, *Commentaria Bibliorum* (Zürich: Froschauer, 1533), vol. 2, fol. 58v.

23. *She joined*: When the barley harvest was finished and she was invited to come and gather wheat, she was not sluggish or negligent. She had learned to labor eagerly and so could not have been in need of anything.

Third Chapter

1. *Now afterward*: Naomi formed a plan from the Lord both to look out for the posterity of her sons, which holy women especially always seek, and for the promise of her daughter-in-law. For it was not suitable that a young woman who was refined in manners and faith, in prudence and earnestness, should be destitute of a worthy husband, but she was perceived by everyone to be fit to bear children and become a housewife. So at last God had provided, at whose pleasure and by whose gift she was advised by an honorable lady. This happened not so much by feminine foresight as by the eternal wisdom of God. For there are no honorable plans except from God, who governs even depraved plans for good. Moreover, Naomi seeks for her daughter-in-law a quiet and happy condition, that is, that she might become rich without such heavy labor and might end up as the wife of a nobleman. But really a mystery is pressed forth by the eternal plan of God, that from the gentiles noble King David and the one who was going to sit on David's throne forever, David's son, the Messiah, did not despise to have this woman as a mother and that the sonship of the gentiles in the faith was preordained.

2. *"This Boaz, whose"*: It is probable that the elderly woman had in mind something merely human, that she wanted to look out for her dear daughter-in-law. But God brought her womanly thoughts back to the business of His wisdom. She advised Ruth to join herself, with more refined clothing, to Boaz's girls, and with an honorable disposition to entice the husband owed to her by nature and by law to honorable love and lawful affection. Honorable girls in Israel did not pursue lusts, but the glory and blessing of children. The better and more numerous the children they had, the happier they were considered to be. It is honorable for girls to be dressed for honorable marriages. A harlot's attire reveals impudence and prostitutes her reputation along with her modesty.

3. *"Wash thyself therefore"*: The outcome shows that the woman's plan came from the Lord. To wash and be anointed, in accordance with the nation's custom, was honorable. She was told to carry out her business in secret so that the girl would not be branded with slander and so that such a noble man also would not be branded with slander, if everything did not turn out like he wanted. Otherwise, men should pursue their wives, not the other way around, except for a special reason. She is told to conceal everything until supper is finished in the evening. At the opportune time she is to seek to capture the heart of the most honorable man, whose uprightness was so conspicuous that Naomi did not hesitate to instruct her daughter-in-law to yield to the man in everything and to acquiesce to his plans.

7. *And when he had eaten*: The farmers finished the threshing on the threshing floor with shouts of joy and feasting, no less grateful for the kindnesses of God, to whose kindness they attributed the abundance of the annual produce. Boaz, being such a distinguished head of the household, did not refuse to spend the night in a part of the threshing floor, sleeping by the heap. He was present with his workmen and looked out for his business. He did not effeminately choose to sleep at home while his servants were working. Ruth, obeying her mother-in-law, secretly placed herself at the feet of the old man. They both were in imminent danger from the feasting, if the fear of the Lord had been emptied out by the wine and immoderate rejoicing.

8. *And, behold, at night*: To spread a garment for the Hebrews is to get engaged or to support someone's right. So that she would not appear to be seeking this dishonorably, she immediately mentions the law of God as the reason, by which she is commanded to raise up the seed and name of her husband by a kinsman.[5] No one here should have in mind anything filthy regarding holy women.

10. *And he (said), "Blessed"*: His response is worthy of a brave and pious man. Not thinking at all about lust, but nevertheless wishing to declare

---

5. Deut. 25:5–10.

his right, he defers the business by praising the girl's faith and zeal, that she has not sought to get any other's wealth or lusts, but though a foreigner, she has put obedience to the law of God before every lust. Without doubt the Moabitess deserved to be included in the list of holy women. Already her faith and uprightness were famous throughout the whole city, that is, since she loved the Israelite nation more than anyone and had forsaken her fatherland and her household gods because of her love for God, whom she, as holy and chosen for this purpose, very religiously worshiped. Meanwhile, other Israelite women were superstitiously bowing down to foreign gods and goddesses. That her later compassion surpassed her first compassion means that she not only loved and dealt worthily with her former husband when he was alive, along with her mother-in-law, but that she also wanted to propagate his name and glory for posterity, which was a sign of great uprightness in a foreign woman.

12. *I do not deny*: "Indeed, I am truly your near kinsman, but there is a kinsman nearer to that right than I. If he cedes it, I will not neglect it." The justice of the ancients and the sanctity of the law are noted; for this reason, the Jews say that Boaz himself was a judge in the nation of Israel.

13. *"Rest this night"*: He very carefully admonishes her to remain there that night and not to brand them both with slander by leaving, if she should be seen by someone. As much as possible, we (especially girls and magistrates) must look out for the reputation of our chastity. He wants to refer to the other man the choice of pursuing his right, that is, of purchasing the inheritance, which belonged to Elimelech and his sons and which the mother-in-law intended to sell to him who wanted to marry Ruth. If the other kinsman had chosen this, it was certainly fine, but if not, Boaz, a righteous man, makes himself readily available and swears to accomplish what she is seeking. The remarkable continence of both of them is taught here, and a chastity far more chaste than of those who regard it as the most religious thing not to look at or touch a woman and yet who, when they are away from her, do not stop lusting, burning, and playing with their desires with an adulterous heart, no matter how much they promise themselves an unclean cleanliness in their bodies.

14. *And so she slept:* She sleeps quietly and leaves before light, so that his reputation will not be ruined by a sinister eye gazing at her as she leaves in the morning or arrives at night. And so he loads her up with six measures of barley rolled up in a garment to carry home to the city from the threshing floor. Those six measures, according to the Targum and Rabbi Abraham, represent the six righteous men who are going to be descended from Ruth: David, Daniel with his three companions, and the Messiah.[6] According to Rabbi Solomon, they represent the six gifts of the Holy Spirit with which the Son of David, the Messiah, who was going to descend from her, was to be blessed, about which see Isaiah 11.[7] But their assertions militate more against the Jews than they support us.

17. *And she said, "Behold, six":* He resolved to alleviate the poverty of both Ruth and Naomi and at the same time enticed her with the hope of future marriage. Honorable people who are truly poor are not to be sent away empty by wealthy believers. Through kindnesses of this sort the wealthy lend to the Lord on interest.

Fourth Chapter

1. *Then went Boaz up:* Boaz did not put off claiming the right from the nearest kinsman according to the law, because he was a righteous and truthful man. He retired to the gate, where according to custom the things to be done by the senate were done publicly so that the poor and the rich could equally come and a multitude of witnesses could conveniently be assembled from those entering and exiting. It happened by divine ordination that the man who possessed the right of kinship, whose name Scripture does not indicate, was passing by. For the character of that man does not deserve to be remembered by the good, since he has disdained to raise up a name and a seed for his brother, and it deserves the disgrace of those who have their shoes removed and eternal oblivion. Therefore, Boaz says, "Turn aside, that is, to me, and sit down by me, whoever you are, with a name so obscure that I cannot call you by your

---

6. Tg. Ruth 3:15. I have been unable to find this reference in Abraham ibn Ezra's commentary on Ruth, but see also Rab. Ruth 7:2.

7. Lyra, *Biblia*, fol. 280r–v.

own name." So the Hebrews read it in this sense. "Yet he turned aside and sat down."

2. *And Boaz took*: Boaz appears to have been a man of great authority from the way of speaking, that is, since it is written that he took ten men of the elders of the city to sit as judges and witnesses of the judgment.

3. *A parcel of land*: The case is expressed more clearly here, which was not previously mentioned, except in one discourse, according to the usage of the language and nation. That is, it is expressed in a forensic style that a man spreads his garment over his brother's widow, that is, he buys the inheritance of his dead brother and from his brother's surviving wife and widow raises up a seed according to the law. For he sets forth the case in these terms: "Naomi will sell a parcel of Elimelech's land (that is, one part, since the other part belonged to the other brother), which I did not want to be hidden from you. If you want to buy it, there are contract managers now present here, so that you may buy it with their consent and decision, as you can by right. But if not, I will buy it." He immediately responds that he will redeem the possessions of his dead brother. It is easy here to succeed his brother through the convenience of receiving the inheritance when the annexed burden is not considered.

5. *"When thou buyest"*: Boaz prudently and suitably revealed the greed of the lazy man. Being a prudent man, he likewise exposed his treachery in the forum so that for it the man would receive a double accusation. Boaz did so by annexing the burden, annexed to the inheritance by divine right, of marrying the dead brother's wife and of supporting the mother-in-law, a poor old widow.

6. *"I cede the right"*: He fears that he will be weighed down with the care of supporting a wife and any child that would be born. He has no concern for raising up seed for his brother when he was already weighed down by raising his own children. He complains that he cannot do this without losing his own inheritance, and he cedes his right to Boaz.

7. *Now this was the manner*: The author here describes the ceremonies performed in the forum, when someone ceded the right of kinship to

another by removing his shoe and giving it to the other, according to the law, although not entirely. For customs were added to words, just as we drink wine together when a contract is accepted by both parties.

9. *Therefore the kinsman said:*[8] He calls them to witness that he has bought whatever belonged to Elimelech, as he is now the closest kinsman, since he who was truly the closest kinsman ceded his right, and since Naomi, whom he received as his own along with Ruth, was selling it. He will raise up a posterity for his dead kinsman, if it should please the Lord, from a Moabite wife, who is now a believer and most highly praised. Moreover, a proper reason is cited, that the name of his brother (that is, his nearest kinsman according to the flesh, for Boaz appears to have been his father's brother's son) will not be cut off and erased. In Hebrew, it adds, "from the gate of his place" to indicate the reputation of his family, from which were chosen judges in the gate and the nobler and better elders of the people. And so it would have been wrong for such a distinguished family to have been neglected and to have gone extinct entirely. Although the best parents commonly produce destructive offspring, nevertheless, this judgment should not be made too soon. But rather, with great care we, and even, in special cases, the magistrate, must make an effort that the children of the best citizens, if they have lost their parents, be very diligently educated, provided that sparks of their fathers' virtue are perceived to shine in them, and provided that their ancestors' worthiness, perceived for a long time, and faithfulness and readiness to serve the republic merit public compassion on their posterity. This caution should not be called partiality, but a just and necessary recognition of merit.

11. *All the people answered:* The favorable prayer and public acclamation of the whole people could have been regarded as a sign of a very happy marriage. Marriages should be begun with prayers of this sort. That is, that the wife, like Leah and Rachel, will be blessed with an abundance of holy children, from whom will grow up a mighty multitude of saints,

---

8. Although the verse number is 9, the quoted material is from verse 8. Yet the commentary addresses the material in verse 9. I have preserved the originally cited material here.

whose Lord will be their God and through whom the worship of the true God will be propagated in the world through every age. Finally, they desire that the town of Bethlehem will be blessed by the very holy offspring born from this woman, by which the family of the Ephrathites will be remarkably ennobled and made illustrious, though it had otherwise always formerly been honorable and distinguished.

12. *"And let thy house be"*: Marriages contracted in the tribe of Judah were blessed in this way. So it is probable that individual tribes were honored for the individual merits of their ancestors as an example to their posterity and that blessings were composed with profit and praise. Therefore, they likewise pray that just as Tamar, who was by no means born from the nation of Israel, but was, so it seems, a Canaanite, and yet became a very famous example of chastity and religion and was very devoted to the Jewish nation, bore, by the very well-known grace of God, for the patriarch Judah very blessed sons, Pharez and Zerah, from whom came a countless multitude of saints.[9] "So also," they pray, "may holy Jewish offspring be born, by the will and favor of God, from the remarkable girl standing here." Therefore, blessings and the most devout prayers of this sort are not to be omitted in the church. In this passage, Scripture teaches that they turned out very happily and that by God's providence there arose far greater goods than they had hoped.

13. *So Boaz took*: After all these deeds and words, and not before, Boaz took Ruth as his lawful wife, who conceived by the gift of God and bore not a daughter but a son. The neighborhood women, full of congratulations, returned thanks to the Lord for the child, as is fitting, because the Lord comforted Naomi, who had been miserable a short time before, bereft of sons and destitute of wealth, and made the grandmother happy with a new son from a holy daughter-in-law, indeed, a very faithful daughter. Hence the child acquired an immortal name, and throughout the whole world it is sung that Boaz fathered a blessed son by Ruth.

---

9. Gen. 38.

15. *"And you shall have one to comfort (you)"*: The talkative women continue by the Holy Spirit to pray for Naomi that she will be joyful from her heart for as long as possible because of the blessed new family of Boaz, from whom she and her daughter-in-law will have enough of all the things they need, and that she will have a happy relationship with Ruth and her grandson Obed, who will be dearer to her than seven, that is, many sons.

16. *And Naomi took up*: With a pious simplicity it describes the grandmother Naomi's applause for her grandson, that is, since she reclined the little infant on her own breast. For the love of the elderly for their grandchildren is commonly sweeter than for their children. So here Naomi is described as discharging the duty of a nurse, not because she suckled the child, but because she stayed very busy taking care of her grandson and enjoyed her old age because of the son whom she had regained, whose memory the noble and illustrious girl Ruth had brought back.

17. *Further, (her) female neighbors*: It is not new for women to name children. Here, for their mutual rejoicing, the ladies of the neighborhood name the little child Obed, though the reason for this name is not expressed. This Obed fathered Isai, David's father. This touches the scope of the book. For this whole narrative is included in the sacred books so that the genealogy of David, the very holy king and prophet, will be regarded as most certain.

18. *These are the generations*: Lest anyone should accuse David for having been born from a Moabitess, the writer carefully goes through the list all the way back to Judah, the distinguished patriarch. And now here, in the second and last place, is completely written out in six letters תולדות, "generations," where the Syrian translator seems to assign a reason for the genealogy. According to him, in David's generation, the obligation of original guilt, which Eve imposed on all her children through the sin of disobedience, was abolished. So the generation of all men was imperfect and flawed until David, who for us is none other than Christ the Lord, the Son of David according to the flesh. Christ was not only born without original guilt, but through His merit wiped away and destroyed, for

God's elect, all the natural wickedness of human nature by His innocence and obedience to death on the cross.[10] And so Judah fathered Pharez from Tamar, and Pharez fathered Hezron. Hezron fathered Ram, who is called Aram in Matthew.[11] Aram fathered Amminadab. Amminadab fathered Nahshon. (Amminadab was a prince of the tribe of Judah.) Nahshon fathered Salmon. Salmon fathered Boaz from Rahab, according to Matthew.[12] This Boaz was the first of his name; his grandson Boaz fathered Obed from Ruth. Obed fathered Isai, who fathered David, chosen by the Lord to be the king and prophet of all Israel. His generation and posterity would endure forever, not, indeed, according to the multitude of carnal propagation, but in the Lord Christ, the King of all the saints and the Savior of the faithful, whose kingdom will have no end,[13] through whom, as He received all pvower in heaven and on earth according to His humanity,[14] so according to His divinity all things were created by the Father,[15] with whom, together with the Holy Spirit, He is consubstantial and rules for endless ages.

The End of the Book of Ruth

10. Tg. Ruth 4:22.
11. Matt. 1:3–4.
12. Matt. 1:5.
13. Luke 1:33.
14. Matt. 28:18.
15. Col. 1:16.

Bibliography of Early Modern and Modern Sources

Alessandri, Alessandro. *Genialium dierum libri sex varia ac recondita eruditione referti.* Paris: Johannes Petrus, 1532.

Aventinus, Johannes. *Annalium Boiorum libri VII.* Leipzig: Johann Friedrich Braun, 1710.

Biblia Sacra utriusque testamenti, et vetus quidem post omnes omnium hactenus aeditiones, opera D. Sebast. Munsteri evulgatum, & ad Hebraicam veritatem quoad fieri potuit redditum, collatis ubique vetustissimis & probatissimis eius linguae scriptoribus. Novum vero non solum ad Graecam veritatem, verumetiam ad multorum utriusque linguae & interpretum & codicum fidem, opera D. Eras. Rot. ultimo recognitum & aeditum. Translated by Sebastian Münster and Desiderius Erasmus. Zürich: Froschauer, 1539.

Biblia Sacrosancta testamenti veteris & novi, e sacra Hebraeorum lingua Graecorumque fontibus, consultis simul orthodoxis interpretibus, religiosissime translata in sermonem Latinum. Translated by Leo Jud, Theodor Bibliander, Konrad Pellikan, Petrus Cholinus, and Rudolf Gwalther. Zürich: Froschauer, 1543.

Biblia Veteris ac Novi Testamenti, summa fide ac studio singulari, cum aliorum doctissimorum interpretum, tum vero in primis S. Pagnini ac Fr. Vatabli opera ita ex Hebraeis Graecisque fontibus expressa, & latinitate donata, veterum insuper codicum aliquot collatione emendata, ut nihil relictum sit quod a pio & Sacrae lectionis studioso desiderari posse videatur. Translated by Santes Pagnino and François Vatable. Basel: Thomas Guarinus, 1546.

Borrhaus, Martin. *In sacram Iosuae, Iudicum, Ruthae, Samuelis & Regum Historiam, mystica Messiae servatoris mundi adumbratione refertam, Martini Borrhai commentarius.* Basel: Johannes Oporinus, 1557.

Calvin, John. *In omnes Pauli Apostoli epistolas, atque etiam in epistolam ad Hebraeos, Io. Calvini commentarii.* Geneva: Jean Crespin, 1557.

Erasmus, Desiderius. *De civilitate morum puerilium.* Leipzig: Nicolaus Faber, 1534.

———. *Desiderii Roterodami Erasmi opera omnia emendatiora et auctiora, ad optimas editiones praecipue quas ipse Erasmus postremo curavit summa fide exacta, doctorumque virorum notis illustrate.* Vol. 2. Edited by Johannes Clericus. Leiden: Petrus Vander Aa, 1703.

Fabellae Aesopicae quaedam notiores, et in scolis usitatae. Edited by Joachim Camerarius. Leipzig: Valentin Bapst, 1552.

Giraldi, Giglio Gregorio. *De deis gentium varia & multiplex historia, libris sive syntagmatibus XVII comprehensa.* Basel: Johannes Oporinus, 1548.

Gordon, Bruce. "Remembering Jerome and Forgetting Zwingli: The Zurich Latin Bible of 1543 and the Establishment of Heinrich Bullinger's Church." *Zwingliana* 41 (2014): 1–33.

Heidegger, Johann Heinrich. *Enchiridion Biblicum IEPOMNHMONI-KON.* 2nd ed. Amsterdam: Boom, 1688.

Hotman, François. *De feudis commentatio tripertita.* Lyons: Jean Lertout, 1573.

Jerome. *Explanatio Sancti Hieronymi Presbyteri in Jeremiam Prophetam.* Vol. 4 of *Sancti Eusebii Hieronymi Stridonensis Presbyteri Operum.* Edited by Dominic Vallarsi. 2nd ed. 11 vols. Venice: Zerletti, 1767. Typically, Jerome's *Commentarii in Jeremiam* would appear in the ancient sources index. But this modern edition seemed so accessible that I have included it here.

———. *Opera.* Edited by Desiderius Erasmus. 9 vols. Basel: Froben, 1516. Typically, Jerome's *Opera* would appear in the ancient sources index. But this early modern edition is so accessible that I have included it here.

Laetus, Pomponius. *Romanae historiae compendium ab interitu Gordiani Iunioris usque ad Iustinum III.* In *Opera Pomponii Laeti varia.* Mainz: Schoeffer, 1521.

Lavater, Ludwig. *The book of Ruth expounded in twenty eight sermons, by Levves Lauaterus of Tygurine, and by hym published in Latine, and now translated into Englishe by Ephraim Pagitt, a childe of eleven yeares of age.* London: Robert Waldegrave, 1586.

————. *In Libros Paralipomenon sive Chronicorum, Ludovici Lavateri Tigurini commentarius*. Zürich: Froschauer, 1573.

————. *Liber Ruth per Ludovicum Lavaterum Tigurinum, homiliis XXVIII expositus*. Zürich: Froschauer, 1578.

Münster, Sebastian. *Hebraica Biblia: Latina Planeque Nova Sebast. Munsteri tralatione, post omneis omnium hactenus ubivis gentium aeditiones evulgata, & quoad fieri potuit, hebraicae veritati conformata: adiectis insuper e Rabinorum commentariis annotationibus haud poenitendis, pulchre & voces ambiguas, & obscuriora quaeque elucidantibus*. Vol. 1. Basel: n.p., 1534.

Nicholas of Lyra. *Biblia mit Glossa ordinaria, Postilla litteralis von Nicolaus de Lyra und Expositiones prologorum von Guilelmus Brito*. Venedig: Paganinus de Paganinis, 1495.

Ogle, Marbury B. "The Way of All Flesh." *Harvard Theological Review* 31, no. 1 (January 1938): 41–51.

Pagnino, Santes. *Thesaurus linguae sanctae*. Lyon: Sebastian Gryphius, 1529.

Pellikan, Konrad. *Commentaria Bibliorum et illa brevia quidem ac catholica, eruditissimi simul & piissimi viri Chonradi Pellicani Rubeaquensis, qui & Vulgatam commentariis inservit aeditionem, sed ad Hebraicam lectionem accurate emendatam*. Zürich: Froschauer, 1533.

————. *Explicatio brevis, simplex et catholica libelli Ruth, ea forma, qua totius veteris testament Canonici libri expositi sunt, & aedentur, si meliora propediem alius non anteverterit, quod ut fiat optatur*. Zürich: Froschauer, 1531.

Rodríguez, Felix. "Concilio I de Zaragoza: Texto crítico." In *Primero Concilio Caesaraugustano: MDC aniversario*, edited by Guillermo Fatás Cabeza, 9–25. Zaragoza: Institución Fernando el Católico, 1981.

Rolevinck, Werner. *Fasculus temporum*. Rougemont: Henricus Wirtzburg, 1481.

Trithemius, Johannes. *Annalium Hirsaugiensium…complectens historiam Franciae et Germaniae, gesta imperatorum, regum, principum, episcoporum, abbatum, et illustrium virorum*. St. Gallen: Johannes Georgius Schlegel, 1690.

Vega, Cristóbal de. *Liber de arte medendi*. Lyon: Guillaume Rouillé, 1564.

Vermigli, Peter Martyr. *Loci communes*. London: John Kingston, 1576.

Virgil. *Opera Vergiliana docte et familiariter exposita: docte quidem Bucolica: & Georgica a Servio Donato: Mancinello: & Probo nuper addito: cum* adnotationibus Beroaldinis. *Aeneis vero ab iisdem praeter Mancinellum & Probo & ab Augustino datho in eius principio: Opusculorum praeterea quaedam ab Domitio Calderino. Familiariter vero omnia tam opera quam opuscula ab Iodoco Badio Ascensio.* Edited by Jodocus Badius Ascensius. Lyon: Jacque Sacon, 1517.

Voetius, Gisbertus. *Exercitia et bibliotheca, studiosi theologiae.* 3rd ed. Frankfurt: Wohlfart, 1685.

Ancient Sources Index

Scripture Index

Subject Index

"drunk," in what sense the fathers
became, 124–25
drunkenness, impels to evil, 117

ear, to reveal in the, 147
elderly, duty of the, 40
elderly women, duty of, 112–13
ephah, what it is, 102
Ephrathah, 16–17
Ephrathite, 17
Esther, book of, from where it gets
its name, 7
examples
household especially move us,
52
various kinds of, 118–20

faith
from where it comes, 89
Ruth was endowed with, 87–88
faithfulness, to mother-in-law,
103–4
falls, of the saints, 118–19
fame, 176–77
famine, a scourge of God, 15–16
favor, to find, 92–93
favors, ours do not come to
nothing, 110
feast, of the scythe, 117
fertility, from God, 33–34
fetters, what they are, 165
food, we ought to supply enough
for laborers, 96–97
foreigners, to be received with hospitality, 21–22
friends
true and steadfast, 108–9
we need, 185–86

gate
for the courthouse, 145
judgment administered in,
144–45
is taken for the city, 132
gentile wives, who married them,
169–70
gleaning, 66–67
go, in unto someone, 181
gods
of Moabites, 49–50
of Philistines, 50–51
good works
use of, 91
what they are, 89–90
grateful, we should be to
benefactors, 109–10
gratitude, example of, 84, 116
greeting, 74–75

heads of households, should care
for their possessions, 75–76
heart, to speak to, 93
hospitality, 21–22
house, mother's, 35
household property, care for is not
disparaged, 162
humanity, toward the afflicted,
82–83
humility, example of, 93

idolatry, is compared to fornication, 24–25

justice, example of, 148

kissing, 46–48
know, someone, 84